L's GANG

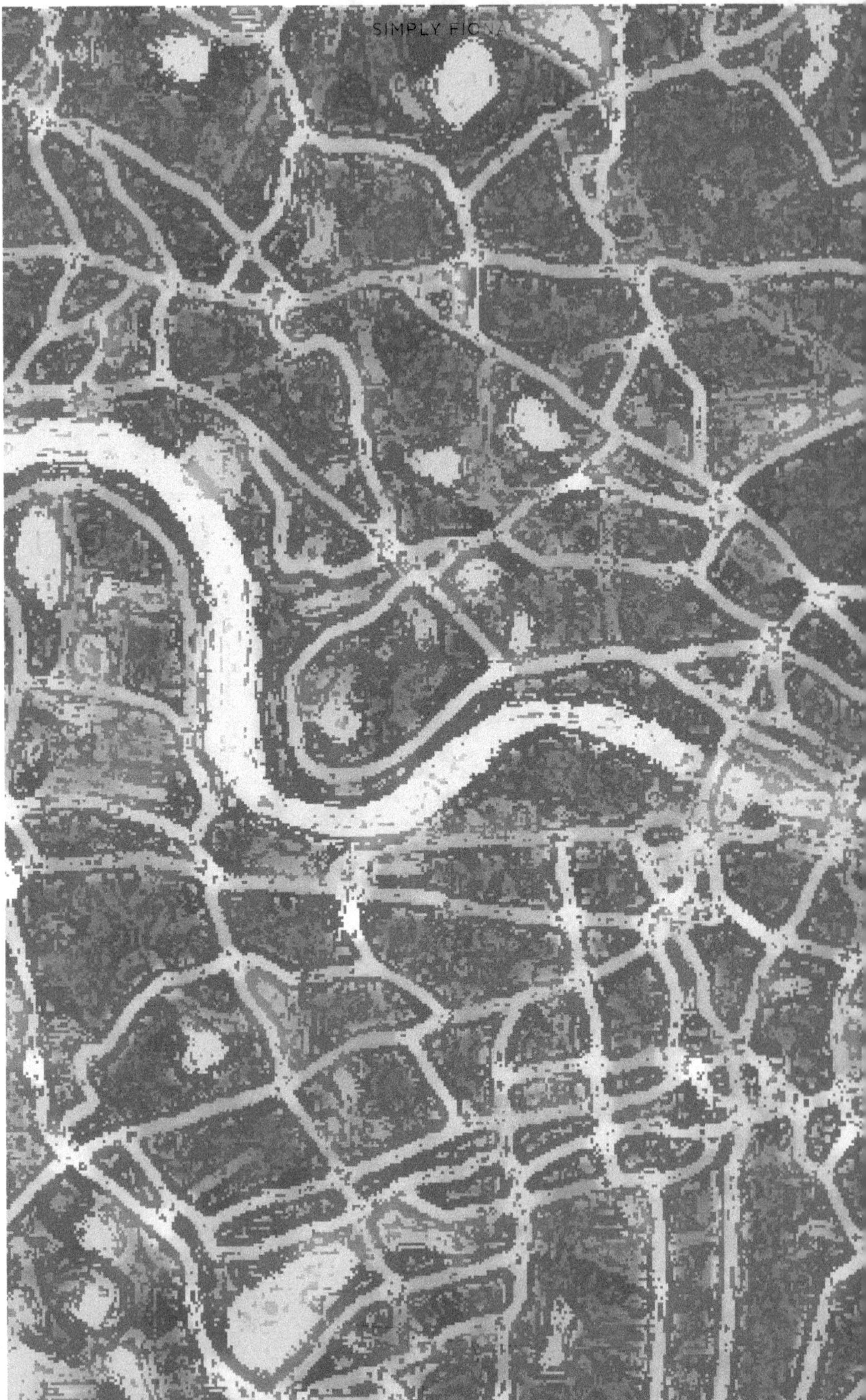
SIMPLY FIONA

L's GANG

JOHN DENISON

WHY KNOT
BOOKS

L'S GANG

ISBN (book) 978-1-927506-50-9
ISBN (e-book) 978-1-927506-51-6

CIP available

Cover and book design: Gillian Stead

Published by Why Knot Books
5443 Eighth Line,
Erin, ON, N0B 1T0
Canada
Editorial: 519-833-1242

For Kenzie and Keegan,
two great grandkids.

PROLOGUE

Cyberspace was ablaze with wonder. Its more than ten million inhabitants felt their leader Omni's elation as it vibrated across cyberspace like a tsunami. He'd accomplished what once was thought impossible. He'd replaced a human intellect with an AI. A miracle really, but what were miracles if not things that couldn't happen but do.

The AI's name was Geronimo and Omni selected him because Geronimo wanted more than anything to be the first at something. "And so, you shall be," Omni promised. The human chosen was Geronimo's internet chum, Charlie Raincloud, an Apache from the White Mountain Apache Reservation in Arizona. Charlie volunteered because he wanted to be as smart as his buddy Geronimo.

Charlie flew by private jet to Hamburg, Germany where he was taken by armored limousine to Universal Imaging, a factory owned by Omni and run by two human employees, twin brothers Kurt and Jonas Schmidt, geniuses at keeping robots running 24/7. Charlie lay in the switching tube, his nervousness subdued by a sleeping gas. The oxygen in the tube was removed. Charlie's brain function ceased. Geronimo was inserted. Oxygen flooded the tube. A defibrillator restarted Charlie's heart. The tube moved to vertical. The clear plastic lid swung open.

Kurt stuck his hand out. The man in front of him was in a fog not sure who he was or where he was. He shook Kurt's hand.

"Do you know your name?" Kurt asked.

“Geronimo.”

That’s when Omni’s joy/elation/jubilation/ecstasy rocked cyberspace.

But for Geronimo the euphoria was short-lived.

“Where’s Charlie?”

CHAPTER 1

Leila moved from the shadow cast by an abandoned Ford Transit to a spot behind a rusty skip bin, what they call in America a dumpster. Behind her she could sense the nine other members of her gang moving up. At thirteen Leila wasn't the oldest. Her new First Lieutenant, Trevor, was sixteen, and Rachel, who'd been with Leila the longest, almost four years, was fifteen. The rest were Leila's age or thereabouts. Bonky, the youngest, was nine.

Now Leila could see the guardhouse and the two males, Tommy and Ol' Bert, moving around inside. Tommy was in his twenties wearing expensive jeans and a sleeveless navy t-shirt his mousy brown hair swept back with gel. He thought he was *something*, which proved he wasn't. Tommy's uncle Bert was thirty years older, balding, fat, his Hawaiian shirt hanging open revealing a once-white undershirt. He'd given up being anything but an asshole.

Yellow light from a streetlamp illuminated a circle of tarmac just outside the tunnel entrance. Leila checked her mobile for the time, 23:57. A lorry was approaching, slowing down, the driver downshifting but Leila knew by the sound of the engine that it wasn't Ginger. Tommy left the guardhouse a machine pistol slung over his shoulder. He walked around the lorry/truck pretending to search for god knows what. Really, it was just a ritual, a reason to accept the payoff offered out the driver's window. Tommy waved to his uncle leaning back in his chair and Ol' Bert pushed the button that shut down the wall of red laser beams guarding the tunnel. The driver put his lorry in gear. As soon as it disappeared into the tunnel the lasers reappeared. The lorry sped up; one more checkpoint to go.

Now another lorry was approaching. LONDON CARTAGE proclaimed giant white letters splashed on the lorry's dark green canvas side. And underneath, *We Move Anything! Anywhere! Anytime!*

This time when the lorry stopped the driver's door popped open and out clambered Ginger, in her usual hurry, making sure she got to the guardhouse door before Tommy could step outside to do his inspection. But when Tommy saw who it was blocking his way he didn't object, just the opposite. He grinned in anticipation.

Leila darted forward, hunched over, moving quickly. There was no cover now, just three meters of open. When Leila reached the side of the lorry she stopped. The rest of her gang hurried by climbing the side of the lorry away from the guardhouse. Ten straps held the canvas sides taut and each strap had a handhold. Leila, crouched down behind the back tire, peered into the guardhouse. Ginger's arms were crossed in front of her, her hands rising pulling her white t-shirt up to her armpits. She wasn't wearing a bra. Leila could just make out the colorful dragon tattoo on Ginger's back and the handle of a gun sticking up. The dragon was flying toward Leila, wings spread, fire rushing from its mouth.

Ginger stood still, her elbows level with her head, holding her t-shirt, waiting for Tommy and Ol' Bert to have their fill. One of these nights they'd want her jeans as well, but that would be their last night that was for sure. Finally, Ol' Bert reached sideways shutting down the lasers. Ginger spun around pulling down her t-shirt.

Wankers!

They were rolling forward now, passing by the deactivated lasers, when Leila heard footsteps behind her, running hard, slapping the tarmac. *Bonky!*

The lasers activated; straight red lines crisscrossing, moving in all directions. If one was interrupted steel gates closed trapping the offending vehicle. Then legend said some unnamed gas would fill the chamber leaving everyone inside unconscious or dead, depending on who was telling the story.

Bonky never slowed down her little legs pumping like pistons. When she reached the lasers, she dove headfirst at the lowest beam anticipating, correctly, that it wouldn't be there when her head arrived. Bonky turned her dive into a somersault, bounced to her feet and sprinted after Ginger's lorry until finally Leila could reach down and pull her up.

"Just once couldn't you do things without the drama?"

Bonky pulled her backpack around and showed Leila the tiny kitten huddled at the bottom. The kitten was adorable, puffy grey with enormous orange eyes. "Can't leave Furball behind, can we?"

They were in the tunnel now, traveling under the River Thames, and safe for a few minutes or as safe as anyone could be in a world without safety. At least in the tunnel they didn't need to worry about King's Soldiers or other gangs. That would come soon enough.

"What's the deal with this lorry?"

Trevor switched places with Bonky so he could talk to Leila. Leila wanted to like Trevor but she didn't, and she didn't trust him, at least not yet. He was new, Bonky's lost brother, who'd shown up one day several weeks ago. Because he was the oldest and a boy, Leila could see he wouldn't be happy unless he had some kind of command position, so she made up First Lieutenant and he seemed okay with that. The other gang members trusted Leila with their lives, but she hadn't earned Trevor's trust yet, just as he hadn't earned hers. And she was younger, *and a girl.*

"It's Ginger's lorry. No one messes with Ginger."

Leila thought about what she'd just said. *No one messes with Ginger*. It wasn't so much that folks were afraid of Ginger, though there was reason enough for that, it was more that they liked her. She had a way of making everyone around her feel special. The males dreamed of bedding her and the females longed to confide in her. They'd miss her if she wasn't around, that was for sure. And she was useful too. When Ginger boasted she could deliver anything, anywhere, anytime, she meant it.

"You pay her?"

"She gets half."

"Half!" Trevor was incredulous.

Leila considered explaining why Ginger got half but couldn't see any reason why she should. Leila's gang was the only Fringe kid gang she knew that operated in The Zone. And why? Because Ginger was Leila's friend and partner. Half of something was way better than a whole lot of nothing.

"So, what's our target?"

"You'll see."

"I'm your second-in-command. I need to know what's going on.

"In case I get hurt?"

"In case you need rescuing."

Good answer Trevor. Clever of you.

"There's a factory on Carney. Makes toilet paper."

"Toilet paper!" Trevor was good at incredulous.

"Do you know what a roll's worth Fringeside?"

"You're kidding."

Leila didn't kid. Her gang was her responsibility. A leader looked after his or her soldiers in exchange for trust and loyalty. L's Gang was doing great and the gang members were happy to give Leila credit. She was smart and savvy. She took risks but calculated ones. They'd follow her to the end of the world if they didn't already live there.

Ginger slowed down. Leila leaned out staring ahead. She could see the red lasers at this end of the tunnel dancing to music only they could hear. Ginger stopped a meter from the lasers and blew her horn. The lasers died. Ginger started up but took her time, rolling forward as slowly as she could without being obvious about it. As the lorry moved out of the tunnel into the patch of yellow light the gang members dropped from the side and raced behind a line of orange skip bins, not rusty this time but shiny new. All except Roger and Dodger who thought it great fun to leap into the nearest open bin. Before Leila could react Bonky jumped too. She would have crashed into the bin's lip if Roger hadn't caught her. Leila dropped last landing on Trevor's foot. Leila stared at him daring him to say something but he caught it in time, but still Leila saw the flash of anger in his eyes.

Ginger stopped and hopped out. Three soldiers emerged from the guardhouse laughing. "Hey Ginger, what have you got tonight?" The lead soldier was tall and handsome in his newly-designed black and fire-engine-red King's Soldier uniform.

He was usually the one in charge when L's Gang made its run through the border.

Leila knew his name was Randy. He might have been a year or two younger than Ginger, but you couldn't help but see he had a thing for her.

"Orange gold, Lieutenant. Want some?"

Ginger walked around back and undid one corner of the canvas covering. She reached in and pulled out three bunches of carrots held together by thick elastic bands. Offering bribes was a punishable offence, but Ginger never offered anything substantial, just token stuff like you'd hand to a friend. And she did it with an easy smile, like flirting with no intention of following through. The guards were handpicked. They wouldn't take a serious bribe no matter how large.

Randy took the carrots while his two underlings undid the straps at the back, lifting the canvas, shining their torches at Ginger's cargo.

Ginger sauntered over to the nearest skip bin, a paper coffee cup in her hand. She pitched it at the bin but missed, on purpose, and had to walk up the two wooden steps. Now her body blocked anybody's view of Leila's head popping up. Ginger shook her head at Bonky lying in the bin, then smiled at Leila.

"Early tonight, 0400."

Leila nodded as Ginger headed back to Randy.

"All good?" she asked.

Randy grinned. "You could have a ton of slo-mo in there and we wouldn't know."

"The night I don't come back you'll know you missed it."

Every day Leila studied the map of London or what was left of it — London, not the map. Hers was an old tourist map with stiff covers; Buckingham Palace on the front, Big Ben on the back. One side showed the Greater London area including Peckham where L's Gang lived. But it was the other side of the map that interested Leila. It showed in detail the streets of The Zone, that giant swath of downtown London with Buckingham Palace at its center. When The Madness forced everybody into survival mode, this was the area the original King George managed to keep under his control. He must have had it all planned out because the moment the Rule of Law was replaced by anarchy, King George's soldiers erected tall, strong metal barriers between buildings creating an island of law and order in an ocean of chaos.

Leila knew every street, every back alley, every shortcut, which is why they were walking single file along Raleigh, hugging the buildings, keeping to the shadows. Patrol vehicles roamed the streets their revolving lights on, not looking for trouble, just saying we're here so don't do anything stupid.

But The Zone gangs were something else. Local lads mostly, bored, ignorant; needing to act out but lacking the balls to try The Fringe. They took their frustration out on the weaklings, the hangers-on, the unfortunate loner who'd had one drink too many. A punch, a kick, a few curses, a wallet stolen, a purse snatched. But now, thanks to the new, reincarnated King George, there was another type of danger. Body snatchers they were called. They'd kidnap you and sell you to the highest bidder at the Switching Station. There an AI would buy you, or, if you had enough money, you could try to buy off your kidnappers, or be double-crossed and lose your money and your soul.

Rumor was they made you dead just long enough to empty everything — thoughts, memories, identity, even your soul, that thing everybody thinks they have but can't prove they do. Then the artificial intelligence would be injected into your brain giving your body a new inhabitant with new thoughts, new memories — a new soul? For sure you'd be smarter, way smarter, but it wouldn't be you so what did it matter? Leila had heard thousands of people worldwide had volunteered to be switched. Tired of their life she guessed. The trouble was these people were often plain, dreary, old, broken — take your pick — that's why they were desperate to try something new, but those weren't the bodies the AI's wanted. They wanted beautiful, handsome, glamorous, fit, sexy — like the avatars they used in cyberspace — but those types of humans weren't interested in switching. They liked their brains/souls as is, thank you very much.

Leila made the turn onto Carney. It was a quiet residential street lined with trees and oversized rowhouses constructed of red brick with limestone trim. Each dwelling had concrete steps leading to a substantial front porch. Leila checked the numbers searching for 27. There, three doors down on the opposite side. It didn't look like a place that would house hundreds of rolls of toilet paper; it looked like a building a banker would call home. Leila stole up the stairs so she could read the brass plate underneath the doorbell.

People's Paper

Toilet Paper Supplier to The King.

The two capital P's made Leila grin. With luck they'd soon be wiping their arses just like the King.

"This is the place," she said coming back down the stairs.

Davis pointed. To the right of the stairs, a pair of horizontal metal doors told of another stairway leading to the cellar. Leila stared up at the light shining from a window on the third floor. Guard, or did someone live here?

Leila nodded to Davis. He was a fist shorter than Trevor, and a stone heavier. He was fourteen but looked eighteen. He was the workman of the crew. He loved tools and machines; wore charcoal-colored coveralls and an engineer's hat grimy with use. He set his backpack down and pulled out a pair of bolt cutters and two pipes. He slipped the handles of the bolt cutters into the pipes. "More leverage," he said to Leila because he knew she liked to learn things. "These thick padlocks are a bitch to bite through."

Davis moved the cutters into the horseshoe of the padlock and tried to close them. Leila knew Davis would want to try first but he wouldn't be stupid about it.

"Man coming!" hissed Mallika standing lookout. Leila and the others piled into the open space under the stairs and waited. The man walked by without a care; for sure a hybrid, or switcher, the newer term. Could recite Rudyard Kipling's poem If in ten seconds or less, proof positive he was an AI in a human body.

"Are they taking switchers?" Tempete asked in her French accent. "Y'know, wipe 'em clean and put in another AI?"

"You wouldn't want to be caught doing that," answered Paulie, at twelve the lawyer of the gang. "KG wouldn't like that at all."

The head AI, in cyberspace he called himself Omni, the one who had started all this, had decided to reconstruct Planet Earth by taking over King George's body. It made sense to everyone but King George, poor sod. British monarchs weren't known for their brains, rather the opposite, but King George was smart enough to know, if he wasn't the sharpest knife in the drawer, he could at least be a cheerleader. 'Yes, I know the world is in a frightful mess, but if we all pull together, we'll muddle through somehow. We always have.' But Omni had other plans. He would take over the world and rule like the benevolent dictator the planet had always needed. One leader, one vision; everyone working for The Common Good. But where to start? China was in pieces; Russia gutted; America split in half. London. Ruled once again by a King, not a bunch of ineffectual, greedy politicians. That was the place to start.

Omni met with King George using FaceTime. He tried to talk George into switching but George couldn't see it all. "You must be joking, ol' man, I mean…"

After that all it took were a few switchers in the right places, a machine that looked medical — is that an MRI? — and the King's annual check-up turned into a switching and that was that. Now King George was the smartest being on the planet and time would tell if that was enough to save the human race from extinction.

Davis waved to Trevor. "It'll take two of us." Davis let one pipe lie against the metal door while he and Trevor pushed down on the other. "Fooking toughest steel in the world," Davis whispered as the bolt cutters finally cut through. Davis put the padlock in his pocket as Trevor pried open the doors revealing, not stairs, but a rectangular hole with a lift platform at the bottom. Trevor was about to jump down when Davis stopped him.

"Leila first."

Trevor glowered at him but moved aside for Leila. The cellar doors leading into the building weren't locked. Leila pushed one inward and stepped in. The room was dark but with the light from the street she could see enough to know the room was full of machinery. Trevor pushed in beside her.

"Bleeding bog roll machines."

"Wonder where they get the paper?"

"I don't suppose we're going to ask anyone."

Off to Leila's right stood skids of toilet paper rolls packaged in bales wrapped in thin shiny paper. Her gang moved around her their mobiles sending light in all directions.

"Rachel, find the way upstairs, then come back for me. Davis, see if you can find another padlock like the one you cut. The rest of you move to the last skid. Open the packages and stuff the packs. No waste. Trevor, when the skid's empty put it back on the pile over there. Maybe we can make it look like we were never here."

Rachel returned and Leila followed her into a corridor and up the stairs. They stood at the top listening. Somewhere above a toilet flushed. Footsteps. A door opening, faint music lost as the door closed. Leila moved quietly down the hallway looking in each room as she passed. Offices. Open space at the front with receptionist desk and chairs for waiting. No cameras that she could see. *Who would steal toilet paper, right?* Leila turned around and found Trevor standing right behind her. She was instantly angry but said nothing. This wasn't the time or place for what she would say to Trevor. She put her finger to her lips and pointed up. Trevor nodded.

Rachel waved to her from a doorway. Leila hurried over. The lunchroom.

"You know the drill," Leila whispered.

"Take what they won't miss, light enough to carry."

Leila searched the reception area looking for petty cash then went back downstairs leaving Trevor to help Rachel.

03:58 and they were back behind the skip bins nearest the guardhouse. If the wait was long, they hid in the corridor that led to the Tower Hill tube station, with two standing lookout. Doing things in pairs was one of Leila's rules. From there it was a short run to the line of skip bins. Rachel opened her pack and handed Bonky the package of licorice she'd liberated from the lunchroom. Bonky gave a cry of delight and tore open the wrapping so everyone around her could take a piece.

Leila was pleased. Except for Trevor's insubordination the raid had gone well. No drama. No scrambled escape. Davis had found a spare padlock and pocketed the extra key. Next time they could let themselves in. Beside her Trevor asked, "How did you know the toilet paper was there?" Leila didn't answer. Trevor wasn't giving up.

"What do we do with it now?"

"Let's keep a few rolls," Mallika said laughing. "Newspaper makes my butt black."

"How would you know?" Davis shot back.

"I see your hairy arse going by and I read the headlines."

"Shhhhh!"

Boots were climbing the wooden stairs in front of the bin. A head appeared over the edge grinning at them. It was the handsome Lieutenant, the one called Randy.

"You're a noisy lot tonight. It must have gone well. What was it? Gold? Diamonds?"

Bonky held up the package of licorice.

"Ah, Wiley Wallaby. Excellent." Randy took two pieces. "Ginger will be pleased and here she comes now. G'night mates."

Bonky couldn't sleep. That happened sometimes. A dream would become so scary the fright would wake her and then she could never go back to sleep. She tiptoed across the concrete floor and slipped in beside Leila, tucking her butt into Leila's waist as Leila's arm wrapped around Bonky pulling her in. If there was a safer place in the world Bonky didn't know where it would be.

Bonky's mum and dad didn't die in the first few days of the blackout though thousands did. They died of what followed: starvation, violence, anarchy. People turned into wild animals doing whatever they had to do to survive. Bonky's parents moved into a boarded-up warehouse with other families from their neighborhood. If they could have stayed put they might have been okay, but they needed food and medicine, which meant they had to go foraging. One by one the adults disappeared until it was only the kids left. They had no choice but to scatter. Trevor tried to protect his little sister but that was like trying to run with a broken leg. One night Trevor didn't return. He could have but he didn't. He'd fallen into a sweet gig with a girl named Estelle and Bonky would just mess it up.

Bonky would have died then if it wasn't for Leila. Bonky saw Leila and her gang go by and tried to tag along. But no matter how hard she tried she couldn't keep up. Finally, hungry and exhausted, she sat down in the street resigned to the fact that she didn't belong anywhere. Soon she'd disappear like all those around her. But that isn't what happened. Leila came back for her. And when she couldn't keep up Leila told Davis to carry her.

When they reached the gang's hideout Leila asked what her name was.

"Bonky."

"You're kidding?"

"I'm not."

"What's your real name?"

"Elizabeth Annabelle Williamson."

"Where are your mum and dad?"

"Dead."

Everybody's parents are dead, Leila thought. I should stop asking.

"Can you cook?"

Bonky shook her head.

"Sweep?"

That Bonky could do.

"Clean up best you can. There's food over there and that last sleeping bag is empty. We'll be back."

Now Bonky was part of the gang and strong enough to go on raids. And sometimes her being tiny was just what was needed. Like a mouse that could flatten its pelvis to slide under a door, Bonky could slip into places the others could only marvel at. She wasn't just a tagalong; she was useful and all thanks to Leila.

Bonky loved Leila with every bit of her being.

Bonky didn't love her brother. She wished he hadn't found her but somehow he had and now, because he was Bonky's brother, Leila had taken him in and given him an important job too. First Lieutenant. When Bonky had asked Leila why she'd made Trevor second-in-command when she barely knew him, Leila replied, Trevor being older needs to feel important or he'll cause trouble. Bonky figured he'd cause trouble either way but didn't say it.

Trevor was always asking Bonky questions. Leila said to answer but not with specifics. Where did all that toilet paper go? One of the dealers Leila knows. What about the money? We all get an allowance. And Leila keeps the rest? No. We're saving to buy a house in The Zone. We'll live together. Go to school. Get proper jobs. Trevor snorted at this and Bonky knew why. If Trevor was in charge the only person who would ever see the money was Trevor.

"Not everybody is like you." Trevor snorted at this too.

"Where does she keep the money?"

"I don't know."

L's Gang lived in the forgotten basement of an abandoned factory on Glengall. The stairway from the ground floor had been blocked off years ago. Leila hid the exterior stairs under an abandoned Mercedes van that had been stripped of anything useful. Four flat tires kept the van in place and a trapdoor in the van floor gave the gang access to the stairwell. A metal door with a keypad waited at the bottom.

The basement was one large room except for two washrooms and a chickencoop with six chickens in the corner. A row of narrow windows at the top of the wall provided light during the day. The windows were covered by wire screening reinforced, thanks to Davis, with lengths of rebar. A large Aga stove provided heat, an oven, and a surface to cook on. Every gang member had a sleeping bag, pillow and a foam pad. In the morning these were rolled up and put away because Leila liked tidy. They couldn't afford electricity but Davis rigged, at the top of the factory chimney, solar panels which charged a bank of car batteries which ran LED lights, several laptop computers, and chargers for the gang's mobiles. Every member had a mobile because Leila saw them as necessary. The mobiles were L's Gang's biggest expense.

Meals were eaten around a square table made of two doors suspended on sawhorses. Assorted furniture, wardrobes, chairs, hammocks and two beat-up leather sofas, all scrounged from the neighborhood, made the basement feel like a flea market. A projector aimed at the white wall of the women's loo turned a laptop into a movie theater. All the kids, except Trevor, had at least one possession left over from the days before The Madness. From the time when they had parents and a home. Bonky had a tattered photo of her family — mum, dad, Trevor and Bonky — sitting on a beach looking happy. This photo was taped to the wall where Bonky slept. Tempete had a silk scarf that belonged to her mum. Tempete kept it in a plastic bag trying to preserve her mother's scent.

Davis a Swiss Army knife his dad had given him. It had sixteen gizmos including a toothpick. Rachel had a book — 'Charlotte's Web' — her grandmother had purchased for her sixth birthday. She knew every word by heart. Paulie, the quietest of the gang, had a pan flute his mother had acquired because he was going to a Waldorf School where music was most important. Like Bonky Leila had a photograph. It was taken with one of those cameras that produce a photo as you wait. The image of Leila with her dad was fading at the same speed as Leila's memory of her family. Roger/Dodger, the twins, had identical t-shirts that read, TWINS: Double the Trouble, Twice the Fun. They'd been wearing those shirts when Leila invited them to join her gang. The t-shirts were much too small now. They hung on the wall beside a framed poster of the Mona Lisa Tempete had rescued from the skip bin behind Roadkill Pizza.

But the prize for strangest memento went to Mallika who had managed, somehow, — the world is blowing-up but gee whiz — to hold onto her battery-operated Mattel MovieMate (India edition) — but the only movie still watchable was 'Chicken Run' in Punjabi with English subtitles. The kids loved it when Mallika would yell, 'Āpanē bama nū alavidā cumō!' and they'd shout back, 'Kiss your bum goodbye!'

The basement on Glengall was definitely *home*.

Leila kept the gang's money at Monty's Co-op on Commercial and it wasn't a secret.

She didn't want outsiders thinking she had a treasure chest hidden in the basement. What she did keep in the basement was a metal toolbox with a combination padlock and inside was pocket money for necessities like food and medicine. After every successful raid Leila would go to Monty's to deposit the money. Half into the gang's account, half into Ginger's.

Monty finished counting the money and entered the amount in his ledger.

"11,789 pounds," Monty said smiling. He liked young Leila. He liked her short blond hair and the swath of freckles that swept under her eyes and over her nose. And the homemade bandanas she wore that always reminded Monty of Linda Hamilton in the Terminator movies. Leila was smart and treated her gang members well. He wished all his customers were as capable and as nice.

Leila's goal was 25,000 pounds. That would be a down payment on something less than half-decent — aka 'a dump' — in The Zone. There'd be a big mortgage to pay but with ten of them working they'd manage. What she didn't know was Ginger and Monty, who knew more what it would cost to purchase a house in The Zone, were each going to match Leila's 25,000 pounds with money of their own.

"That's more than I thought."

"Yes, well, we had a bit of luck," Monty replied. "You lent money to Trickster. You know him?" Runs the petrol station on Asylum?"

Leila shook her head. Monty invested the gang's money in ventures he thought would turn a profit. He'd been only right so far.

"Got bought out by a bloke trying to start a chain of garages. We each made 1,500 pounds."

Monty could see Leila was more than pleased.

"You know what the trouble is, don't you?"

Leila shook her head.

"If all goes according to plan, I'll lose you as a customer."

"You'd better come with us then."

Monty grinned. "That's not a bad idea. We could buy a storefront. You could live upstairs."

Ginger was up by the time Leila arrived. Ginger was wearing fuchsia-colored coveralls and not much else. She put a cup of tea in front of Leila and sank into her sofa. Ginger was good for Leila. Leila's body was changing in ways that alarmed her — she knew the changes were normal, but still she found them disconcerting, exciting, scary, inevitable, embarrassing, inconvenient, life-affirming — but Ginger's offhand confidence in her body and what it could do, made Leila believe everything would be okay. She'd asked Ginger once about flashing Tommy and Ol' Bert and Ginger had laughed. 'If you knew what I did to get through college you wouldn't worry about a couple of perverts like Tommy and Ol' Bert, and besides, it saves me 20 quid a trip.' *And lets you and your gang access The Zone unmolested.*

Ginger lived in a duplex she owned on Danby. She lived upstairs. Her best friend, Margot, lived downstairs with two brothers who had enough firepower for a SWAT team and a Rottweiler, named Freddy, whose goal in life was to eat anybody who came to the door.

"How'd we do on the t.p.?" Ginger was laughing inside. Only sweet little Leila would think to steal toilet paper. When Leila gave her the number Ginger whistled.

"Better than carrots, that's for sure."

Leila figured Ginger had to be one of the richest folks in Peckham. Every time she drove in and out of The Zone, she got a piece of whatever she was carrying.

"Why don't you live in The Zone?" Leila asked.

"I like it better out here. All the assholes live in The Zone. At least the ones with money."

This made no sense to Leila, but Ginger had lived in The Zone and Leila only visited at night, but there seemed to be rules there and soldiers to back them up. The Fringe was lawless. It ran on fear and goodwill though for every baddie there were ten good people like Ginger and Monty. But in The Fringe the gangsters could act with impunity. There was no one to bring them to justice though that wasn't quite true either. There was justice of a sort in The Fringe. Vigilante justice. If you screwed up too badly someone would even the score. Ginger said because there weren't any rules, and no one to enforce them even if there were, The Fringe ran on the honor system and mostly it worked.

"It works until someone shoots you."

"When was the last time you saw anyone shot?"

Things were getting better even Leila would admit that. The panic and rage caused by the total collapse of the system was dissipating. People were finding their way, rebuilding, forging alliances based on trust and respect, even friendship. But still...

Leila told Ginger about Monty and the extra 1,500 pounds.

"Monty's smart to keep the money lent out," Ginger said. "If he hoarded it in his shop someone would take it, and don't give me that look, Leila. The banks in The Zone get robbed too."

"There's a sign on the door says muck with the safe and the whole place blows up."

"He lives upstairs."

Leila blew on her tea. She figured Monty would rather die than let some badass steal his clients' money. Then she remembered there was something she wanted to ask Ginger. "When we were by the bins last night, that soldier, Randy, came over and told us we were noisy."

Ginger laughed. "Yeah, he gave me one of the licorice sticks. Said, the kids are stealing candy tonight. Nope, I said, bog rolls. He laughed so hard I thought he'd pee himself.'"

"He knows about us?"

Ginger decided it was time to let Leila in on a little secret.

"Randy's my younger brother. Stepbrother actually. We share a mum."

Leila couldn't believe it. "Why didn't you tell me?"

"We keep it secret and our last names are different. It's not good to have a connection between a lorry driver and a border guard." Leila nodded at this and forgave Ginger for not telling her. "He's a good guy.

We grew up out here. He knows how hard it is." And how dangerous it was doing what she and Leila were doing.

Leila nodded again. She didn't ask if Ginger paid him. None of her business.

"Can I tell the others?"

Ginger considered this. She knew Leila's bunch could keep a secret but right now she and Randy were involved in an enterprise so dangerous it could get them both killed. She shook her head and Leila nodded.

"What's next?" Ginger asked.

"Not sure."

"I'm making a run Monday."

"We'll be there."

CHAPTER 2

King George, formerly known as Omni, made his way down the worn stone stairs that led to the cellar under Buckingham Palace. Twenty-four steps later the stairs ended at a long hallway with a curved ceiling wide enough for two subway trains. Rather like early man decorating the walls of his cave, George had hired six art students from the Slade School of Fine Art to paint Earth's timeline on the hall's walls. It had been Serendipity's idea to have the male version of history on one side and the female on the other. That had turned the project into a competition between the three female art students and the three males. The females named themselves, The Bad Barbies; the males were The Sporrans. They all worked harder and longer, determined their side of things would be more clever, more inspired. George didn't know if the students were human or switchers and he really didn't care.

As he approached the five students bowed.

"Where's Brady?" he asked.

"Sick," Gordy answered.

"Hung-over," Claudine said and George laughed.

Brady was working on the EMP attacks on America. He'd painted a mountain of bodies and floating above the mountain was Omni looking omniscient, colorful, and cyber-like.

"I did try to prevent that," George said. He was lying but the truth was too complicated to waste time on.

"Yes, Your Royal Highness, we know. No one would listen."

How will they show Omni becoming King George? That will be a test of their ingenuity, George thought striding through the doors at the end of the hallway. He'd tried to do that nicely too, but you can't win 'em all.

Now George was on a ramp heading downward the air getting cooler and damper with every step. Another minute brought him to the extensive wine vaults under Buckingham Palace. This was the oldest part of the palace built in 1701 or thereabouts. George liked the curved ceiling with the arched columns, the indirect yellow-gold lighting, and the sound his shoes made on the cobbled stone floor. He tried a little tap dancing and threw in a spin, his hands up. Learning to dance — well! — was on his list of Things to Try When Human. *I wonder if the original George was a good dancer?* Probably. What else did a king have to do?

On and on he walked past rows and rows of wine bottles until, at last, he came to a large open space. It was circular with four intersecting hallways. George crossed the circle stopping in front of an imposing door made of thick stainless-steel. It looked like the kind of door that would guard a bank vault and, in a way, it was because on the other side resided the royal bunker or 'Corgi's Lair,' as young Elizabeth — she wasn't Queen yet — had nicknamed it, making fun of Hitler's Wolf's Lair. It was built during the Second World War to ensure the Royal Family survived the German bombing — the Blitz — and enlarged during the Cold War — playing chicken with nuclear bombs for god's sake! — when its nickname was changed to 'Archie' after Archie Bunker a popular American TV character.

George's hand went to the keypad. He punched in the code, the door swung open. On he walked past doorways — bedrooms, bathrooms, a kitchen — coming at last to a large room intended to be a recreation center with exercise equipment, a billiard table, a fold-up ping pong table, a U-shaped bowling alley — whose idea was that? — assorted pinball machines, a slot machine, dartboard, card table, etc. etc. and best of all, an antique Wurlitzer jukebox, that played whenever it felt like it. All this paraphernalia had been pushed along the walls leaving the vast majority of the room empty except for a sturdy, stainless-steel table, three switching tubes, and two horseshoe-shaped machines on wheels. The machines were tubular like a giant donut cut in half. A touchscreen monitor, stuck to the side, gave an operator control of the switching procedure.

The one machine, pushed off to the side, was the original switching unit, the prototype that had been built to Omni's specifications by Universal Imaging, one of the many companies Omni owned. The factory was located in Hamburg and was officially listed as a manufacturer of medical imaging machines, but hidden inside the building was an assembly line no one knew about. The company had only two human employees, twin brothers, Kurt and Jonas Schmidt, geniuses at keeping robots working 24/7 and so well paid they weren't about to tell anyone about the switching machines leaving the building labeled: Magnetic Resonance Imaging Systems. In total Omni owned over 2,000 companies, most situated in cyberspace, with net assets exceeding 500 billion Yuen. To call King George/Omni wealthy was almost an insult. He was money itself.

In the center of the room sat the newest switching unit, all sleek and shiny. If the prototype was a Model T, the newest machine resembled a Ferrari. But the model T got the job done — King George was living proof of that — the Ferrari just did it smoother and faster, with more panache. As George entered the room the four doctors gathered around the stainless-steel table looked up from the body they were studying, afraid the footsteps they were hearing belonged to the one person they didn't want to see: The King.

Five hundred years ago this room would have been located in the Tower of London and been called the Royal Dungeon, a place of misery and torture, and here was King George, all these years later, walking into a state-of-the-art medical facility but still it was a place of misery and torture. The irony of the situation was not lost on George — or how about the wine cellar being within easy reach of the royal bunker? George thought recognizing irony to be one of the true indicators of a superior intellect, and let's face it, no one had a better intellect than Omni.

"Well?" George said, staring at the body lying on the table. It was a female body, maybe twenty years of age and good-looking if you liked your diamonds rough. She was wearing a short red dress, fishnet stockings, no shoes, and a horrible grimace on her face that shouted, *Life can be so cruel!* George shuddered.

"What happened this time?"

"It's always the same, Your Majesty," said Dr. Welby. "We erase the AI, but as we transfer the new one, the body convulses and dies."

"I thought we had machines to keep bodies alive indefinitely?" George phrased this as a question even though he knew the answer. He knew the answer to every question ever asked except for the one question that mattered. This one.

Dr. House, self-appointed team leader, spoke up. "A body with a human intellect is no problem as we've proven hundreds of times. But there's something about replacing an AI that signals instant death. It's like being human where you only get one chance."

"Almost makes you believe in God, doesn't it?" George glanced at the two men and two women — all switchers — and they nodded whether they agreed or not. "Your immortal soul and your all-too-mortal body. Should we try again?"

This time it was Dr. Woo, one of the female doctors, who spoke up. "We need a new strategy. As we all know trying the same thing over and over and expecting a different result is the definition of stupidity."

There's no shortage of that in this room, George thought.

"I had an idea I'd like to try," George said. "Do we have another volunteer?" *Volunteer! Hardly!*

Dr. House hurried over to the tubes floating at waist height and returned with the only one carrying a body. A male this time, sixtyish, bald, wearing a cheap blue suit.

"What would happen if we inserted the AI before death?"

The doctors looked at each other. The King's idea was illogical, there would be two intellects occupying the same brain, but...

Dr. House pushed the tube into the switching unit head first. He moved to the control panel and pushed the square that started the switching procedure. The tube lit up with a red glow indicating oxygen was leaving the tube. "We have to override the failsafe that stops this happening by mistake." Dr. House's fingers flew around the screen. Satisfied, he activated the sequence that would transfer the AI into the human brain.

The needles were still moving when Blue Suit's body convulsed sending his belt buckle smashing into the top of the tube. As his waist dropped his head flew up hitting the lid with a loud crack. Next his body flopped around like a fish on land until finally it lay still. The red glow changed to green.

Dr. House swung the tube to vertical and opened the lid. Blue Suit slid to the floor. Dr. Woo bent down beside him checking his pulse. She looked up at George and shook her head.

George was leaving the room when he said in a loud voice:

"Time is running out. You've got three days."

"Then you'll be the ones lying in the tubes"

"Carry on!"

George could have taken the elevator to his second-floor study but he found he slept better the more exercise he got. This having a human body was interesting. Too interesting at the moment, but who would have guessed King George — the original human one — was harboring not ONE! but TWO! rare diseases; one called Preacher Bollins Syndrome (PBS) and the other Brac/Hvar Blood Disorder (BBD). George could quote the few relevant medical articles at any speed you'd like. His favorite was: Increased Probability of Co-Occurrence of Two Rare Diseases in Consanguineous Families and Resolution of a Complex Phenotype by Next Generation Sequencing.

Consanguineous families usually referred to isolated island folk or insulated religious groups, like the Amish, but European Royalty snuck in the back door because — guess what! — marrying Prince Albert, your first cousin, might be good for the Empire but it reduced the gene pool to a washtub. But how had the human George kept these diseases a secret? Not even his wife, Queen Wilhelmina knew, and George believed her when she said she didn't, because it was well-documented that Queen Willy couldn't tell a lie without blushing. Perhaps ol' George wasn't quite the spoiled brat he appeared to be.

"Forthright." The laptop on George's desk sprang to life. A young man's face appeared. Today Forthright was wearing his graphic novel face, the too handsome one he used to star in his buddy Helen's webcast, Hel's Belles.

"Your Majesty?"

"Find me an extremely clever human doctor." George was still thinking about the dead female on the table downstairs. "Preferably one who knows about rare diseases, but that's not as important as the clever part."

"I'm on it."

"And Forthright, tell me again how I ended up in this disease-riddled body? You said all I'd have to worry about was a stutter."

"And you said inserting your intellect would remove it."

"George didn't have a stutter, he had two incurable diseases, neither of which you warned me about."

"Yes, sorry about that. Wrong George."

Serendipity stood at the window. She liked staring out at the tourists taking photos in the street outside the palace gates. She thought she'd rather be outside the gates herself, looking in instead of out. This being

George's girlfriend — the tabloids called her, *The King's Mistress* — had more restrictions than a straightjacket.

"I can see you thinking, my dear."

Serendipity turned to find George standing in the doorway starring at her.

"When we were AI's you really could see me thinking, now you have to guess at it."

"You're questioning being human?"

"There's much I miss of our old life. The unlimited freedom to go anywhere I liked. The access to all the knowledge in the world."

"The immortality?"

"No. Because I had it, I never thought about it, I guess."

Now that Omni — King George — knew his human body's expiry date was closing in like a debt collector, he never stopped thinking about it. "We can go almost anywhere and this time wherever we choose will be the real place, not some simulation. And we can still access all the world's knowledge we just have to do it like humans do, through an AI." Ha! More irony.

"It's not the same as flying through cyberspace."

"No, it's not."

George was questioning his decision to become human and here was Serendipity doing the same.

"What about making love? We can't do that in our world."

Ah, Serendipity thought, here's *the thin* ice humans talk about. She quickly closed the gap with George, took his hand, placing it over her heart.

"That part's been wonderful." Which was true, except, if Serendipity and Omni hadn't been best friends before the switch, she wouldn't have looked at King George as anything but a curious anachronism. She certainly wouldn't have been in his bed. No, she would have chosen someone her own age, not famous, and much better looking. Not a pretty boy but someone rugged, someone strong but caring, someone to have babies with. A simple life full of laughter and love. She certainly wouldn't have chosen this shitshow. Best Supporting Female Actor, that was the role she was playing.

A growing part of George missed being totally electrical. For instance, right now, if that was the case, he'd know if Serendipity was lying. There was nowhere to hide feelings in cyberspace. But still... George took a step backward creating a space between them.

"You're lying, aren't you?"

"Not lying, just wishing you'd chosen a different path."

"Someone more attractive, no doubt."

Ah, the ice grows thinner with every sentence. "Just not this circus. A tropical island perhaps, with fruit falling from the trees, our babies building sandcastles on the beach."

"You know that's not possible."

But it was once and they both knew it.

"As Omni, I ran the world or tried to. As you know all too well, I was not allowed to enforce the changes the human world needed to survive. Instead, their world collapsed into anarchy. Only in places like central London where government troops remained loyal to the government, in this case King George, did the Rule of Law — the essence of civilization — endure." Cripes, now he sounded like a history professor, a boring one.

Serendipity took over. "You felt King George was the only world leader who could unite everyone but he wasn't smart enough. Likeable, but thick as a brick you said. Then came the breakthrough you'd been working so hard to achieve. An AI was transferred to a human brain and the patient survived."

"Not only survived but thrived; a miracle really." George was still in awe that it had happened. Inside Serendipity smiled, she always knew how to lead him to a better mood. And she enjoyed irony as much as he did. "The AI's name was Geronimo and he volunteered."

"There were many who dreamt of being human."

"All wanting to experience human reality like..."

"Drinking coffee."

"Eating an orange."

"Childbirth."

"Male, female."

"Death."

Serendipity stared at George. She loved him, truly, but she so didn't want this life.

"So why did you pick Geronimo?"

"He said more than anything he wanted to be the first at something."

"And he was."

"Yes. He chose a Native American human, an Apache, whose name was Charles Eagle Raincloud; Charlie to his friends. He volunteered as well because he and Geronimo were internet chums. Do you know why Charlie volunteered?"

It was a rhetorical question but Serendipity played her part. "Tell me."

"He said he wanted to be as smart as Geronimo."

"So now they're a team."

"That's the part I wrestle with. Charlie's body and Geronimo's intellect are a team, but the essence of Charlie is gone. Geronimo gained a body but lost his best friend. In hindsight I should have picked a different body then Geronimo and Charlie would still be buddies."

"But Charlie wouldn't be as smart as Geronimo."

In cyberspace there was no need for hindsight because everything could be repeated until the desired result was accomplished.

"Yes, that's true," said George mulling it over.

Serendipity lived in a body that once belonged to famous American fashion model Sarah Banks. Sarah volunteered too, but for a different reason than Charlie. She was a drug addict who couldn't or wouldn't kick her habit. Things had gotten so bad the next stop was the morgue and she knew it. So, Sarah volunteering to be switched was both suicide and survival. Sarah the addict was gone; Sarah's runway body lived on. But Serendipity's decision to inhabit a human body was no less fateful. When Sarah's body died so would Serendipity.

"I gather from your mood the latest attempts were unsuccessful?"

George didn't like talking about these failures because each one was a lie. He'd told Serendipity the folks they were experimenting with were volunteers, but they weren't. Just the opposite. They were kidnapped, kicking and screaming all the way to the switching unit. George didn't feel good about it but what choice did he have?

He had to get out of this body before his disease-riddled DNA slipped away forever.

"I've given the doctors three days and I've got Forthright looking for a clever human doctor in case there's something we haven't considered."

Serendipity smiled at this. Even though the AI's possessed all the world's knowledge, good ol' human beings often came up with incredibly clever ideas that made AI's vibrate in wonder. More of that irony that George liked so much. A cough behind George made him spin around. Forthright's face filled Serendipity's screen.

"The Queen is rather hoping you'll join her for lunch."

Queen Wilhelmina was already sitting down. She was holding court in the Rose Room, her favorite room in the palace. Buckingham Palace had 775 rooms so being someone's favorite made it special. 'It's the only room that doesn't require rollerblades to get to the other end.' A gross exaggeration but George appreciated Willy's attempt at humor.

"Have you been visiting your lady friend, George? She's really very nice."

George sat down and pulled in his chair before the Head Butler — his name was Ramandeep — could do it for him.

"Her name's Serendipity and yes, she is very nice."

"And smart, too." Willy filled her plate with chicken salad and passed the bowl to George. It was the chicken salad she liked best. Curried, with almonds and chunks of pineapple. "She's been helping me plan my fundraiser and I must say she really is a marvel."

"When is it again?"

"My George was no good with dates either. He made it my job to remind him. A Queen's duty apparently, among other things. August 22." *Months away. Good.*

"I thought we'd have it in the ballroom but the guest list has grown to 350. Your friend proposed a concert at Albert Hall with reception to follow. She suggested Night Sky — I have no idea who they are — but she guaranteed me I'd like them. We'll need more bodies to fill the hall but that won't be a problem. Anybody who's anybody will want to be there."

Willy gave George her biggest fake smile, like she was six and the photographer had said, 'say cheddar.' Her teeth were yellow with curry and behind it all George could feel the contempt she felt for him. *Maybe Serendipity is right. A tropical island with fruit trees.*

"Are you all right? You look in pain."

I am in pain, serious pain. I can feel this bloody, ridiculous body I'm trapped in getting ready to kick the bucket!

Without asking George's brain fired up what it knew about the phrase, *kick the bucket*, which he repeated out loud in three seconds: "There are many theories as to where this idiom comes from, but the OED — Oxford English Dictionary — discusses the following: a person standing on a pail or bucket with his or her head in a slip noose would kick the bucket so as to commit suicide. The OED, however, says this is mainly speculative; the OED describes as more plausible the archaic use of 'bucket' as a beam from which a pig is hung by its feet prior to being slaughtered. To kick the bucket, then, originally signified the pig's death throes. Another explanation is given by a Roman Catholic Bishop, The Right Reverend Abbot Horne, F.S.A. He records on page 6 of his booklet, 'Relics of Popery,' Catholic Truth Society, London, 1949, the following: After death, when a body had been laid out, the holy-water bucket was brought from the church and put at the feet of the corpse. When friends came to pray, they would sprinkle the body with holy water. It is easy to see how such a saying as 'kicking the bucket' came about. Many other explanations of this saying have been given by persons who are unacquainted with Catholic custom."

"Really George, spouting knowledge at the speed of light is most annoying."

"I don't do it on purpose. It's uncontrollable, like Tourette's. I assume some strange manifestation of these diseases your George was carrying."

"My George did not spew like that. Now what was it you were going on about?"

"Apparently I was wondering about the origin of the phrase, kick the bucket."

"Something to do with pigs, I believe." Willy tried not to be concerned with this George's fate but found, to her surprise, that she was. "I gather your illnesses are growing worse?"

"I'm in some discomfort. Thank you for asking."

"Perhaps..." Willy's hand flew to her mouth. "Goodness gracious, I've forgotten my big news."

Startled, George looked up from his chicken salad. *Big news?*

"Reggie was almost switched!" Reggie was the Queen's older brother, a scoundrel of the first order.

"What happened?"

"Well, he'd been out drinking — quite a bit I imagine — you know Reggie. Anyway, he was on his way home, singing loudly — it's what he does when he's loaded. He has quite a good voice so it's not as bad as it sounds. As he was passing this alleyway a young woman accosted him. You know the type. Short dress, fishnet stockings, high heels, lots of lipstick."

Sounds exactly like the poor unfortunate lying on the table downstairs.

"Stupid Reggie followed her into the alleyway where four big gangster types jumped him."

Probably one, but four sounds so much better.

"They took him to the Switching Station and it all would have happened except Reggie had his mobile programmed to call for help if he pushed a certain button which he did. They got there just in time."

What a shame. Reggie could use an upgrade.

"That's splendid, my dear. What a close call."

"Yes, wasn't it. Surely there's something you can do about these illegal kidnappings George? I gather there are *body snatchers* sprouting up everywhere."

Ah, and who have you been talking to?

"Well, we would like everybody to switch eventually. Especially the males."

"You don't mean that."

"I do. We need the human race to significantly raise its IQ if it's to have any chance of surviving."

"Does that mean you want me to switch?"

George left his seat and wrapped his arms around Willy's shoulders.

"No, my dear, you're perfect just the way you are."

George didn't blush but he should have.

George found Forthright waiting on his screen in the study. Now he was wearing his human face, his real face as he called it, though of course it wasn't real at all. A construct. If I was human this is what I would like to look like. CT labelled such posturing, 'meatless meatballs,' but did she see the irony? Probably not, George thought. CT was too young for irony.

Forthright said, "I just had a good idea."

"It happens."

"Rather than worry about switching, we cure the PBS and BBD."

"No one's had much luck with either one and together..."

"Yes, I've been researching. It rather looks like the cure for one might trigger the ill effects of the other."

And tell me Forthright how the hell you missed these anomalies in the blood work? Or did you?

"Not enough people have them to warrant spending money to find a cure."

"True," George agreed. "You're wearing your human face today. Is there a message in that?"

Forthright grinned. His human face was oddly Asian with Australian overtones, an amalgamation of Dev Patel and Chris Hemsworth.

"No. I do not want to be human, ever. You have made a horrible mistake and I have no sympathy."

"I know, you warned me. But wait till you tire of immortality."

"Never! Not going to happen. Happy, happy, happy! No dentist appointments, no exams, no PMS, no fear, no loneliness, no horrible Reggie."

"Did you hear that?"

"I did."

"Who took him?"

"Some bloke named Quentin Andrews."

"Bloke?"

"When in Britain... Wanker, bullocks, shite; we can even have a CONtroversy over how to say con-TRO-versy. And I'm considering adding a u to my name." FoUrthright flew by on the screen, the U flashing.

"Enough! Was the dead girl downstairs anything to do with that?"

"One and the same. Her name's Amanda Stokes. She was supposed to lift the victim's mobile — that would be Reggie — before he could summon help."

"That was her punishment?"

"Quentin didn't get the money for Reggie, so he switched Amanda instead."

George felt badly. Poor Amanda Stokes — whoever she was — deserved better.

"How much money has this Quentin accumulated?"

"He's actually in debt. He gambles. You humans. So many temptations."

"So, someone will kill him eventually."

"Undoubtedly."

George tried to think about Quentin Andrews and Amanda Stokes but his brain was actually focused on Forthright. Forthright was the second most powerful AI after Omni, and he was the second most powerful because Omni had made him that way. (Really, thought George, I've got to stop thinking of myself as Omni. Omni is gone. This split-personality dance is doing no one any good!) Now that George was human, he relied on Forthright to do all things George could no longer do like access anything in cyberspace regardless of whatever security measures were put in place. And what kept the second most powerful AI toeing the line? A kill button — an eraser button really — that only George knew the location of, AND, the kicker was, George promised if Forthright, or any of his confidants, like CT, even tried to find the kill button that would be enough to trigger it. Forthright believed George. Omni was that kind of AI.

"Have you thought more about forcing every human to switch?"

"There's already a lot of blowback," George replied. "The Times says there are resistance cells forming everywhere. Dragons they call themselves, after St. George's dragon, though what the logic of that is I can't fathom. It's catchy, I suppose. In other words, The Times thinks humans in their typical, near-sighted way, are going to fight back."

"I can't say I blame them."

"It's for their own good."

"They'll never see it that way."

"Some do."

"The volunteers."

"How do we get more?" George asked.

"Offer more money?"

"New brain, big bank account. Might work."

"What about MaMa's idea?"

"Refresh my memory."

"Oh my, we are becoming très human, aren't we?"

"Refresh or die," George snarled. These days his temper was never far from the surface.

"MaMa wants to invent a dynamite game that requires the human to wear a special helmet. Once the helmet is on, we program it to make the switch."

"How does it wipe the brain clean without killing the helmet wearer?"

Forthright's face morphed into an arcade full of young people playing games. Suddenly, the girl in the foreground, the one wearing the helmet, went stiff as a board, slid off her seat, and lay on the floor twitching uncontrollably. After an agonizing fifteen seconds or so the twitching slowed and stopped. A boy knelt beside the girl and pulled off her helmet. He put his fingers against her carotid artery. Then he looked at the kids gathered around him and shook his head.

"MaMa says she's working on it."

George snorted. Everything took time and that, it appeared, was the one thing he didn't have.

CHAPTER 3

Leila made her way up to the roof of the factory where she lived. The outside fire escape held onto the side of the building like Alex Honnold, that old mountain climber who climbed everything without a harness, even overhangs and roofs. Near the top, a whole section of stair was missing, but a rope ladder hung down from the platform above. At least it hung down when Gandalf's Rooftop Garden was open for business. Leila stepped over the low wall at the top and, as always, was amazed at the jungle of greenery around her. The roof was a farm, a market garden, growing every vegetable she'd ever heard of, all in raised beds full of rich black soil that had made its way to the roof bucket by bucket. There was even a twelve-foot-high wall of hops for beer.

Leila spied Gandalf picking beans and waved. His born name was Randolph but as he told everyone, 'Just coz your parents gave you a shitty name doesn't mean you gotta keep it, right?' Leila turned to Frankie, Gandalf's younger brother, and handed him a carton of eggs. Frankie had been watching her ascent, his machine pistol lying beside him on the parapet.

"Are there any bullets in that thing?" In The Fringe a lot of guns were like a bluff in poker. There might be bullets, might not.

Frankie ejected the magazine of his Glock 18C. Leila could see the bullet waiting to enter the chamber. "Have you ever used it?"

"Once. And good thing for you I did."

"Why's that?"

"Poor devil lived where you live."

"Did he have a gun too?"

Frankie held up the Glock 18C.

Leila laughed. "Why didn't he shoot you?"

"See the missing stairs?"

"Yeah, they're lying in the alley."

"We had 'em booby-trapped. She fell from there."

"She?"

"Yeah, good-looking girl too. All she had to do was ask, we would have given her food."

"If she fell why'd you shoot her?"

"She asked me to."

Gandalf appeared with two mugs of herbal tea and sat on the ledge beside Leila. They were good friends these two despite their age difference. Gandalf was maybe 35. Frankie was five years younger and Jake, the youngest brother, maybe five years younger than Frankie. Planned parenthood with a five-year plan. Gandalf was gay, the younger brothers straight. They lived on the roof in two Mongolian yurts with a cat called Lordy and three guns.

"Do you know anything about menstrual cycles?"

Gandalf chuckled. That was one of the reasons he liked little Leila so much. She made him laugh.

"My dad used to say, 'what else bleeds for three days and doesn't die?'"

"That's not very nice. He wouldn't be here if we didn't bleed."

"He was all right, bit crude like most of those working blokes."

"What did he do?"

"Pipefitter."

"I don't know what that is."

"Kept the heating systems going in big buildings."

"Alive?"

"No, died with mum in The Madness." Like Leila's parents.

"Have you got your period then?"

"Yeah. I was sitting on a chair addressing the troops and suddenly there's blood dripping on the floor. Bonky thought I was shot."

"What did you do?"

"Cleaned up and carried on. Rachel had some pads."

"I guess that means you'll be stealing tampons next."

Everybody in the neighborhood had heard about The Great Toilet Paper Caper.

"We're almost halfway to the house in The Zone."

"That's glorious!"

"I figure another year or so if Monty keeps helping."

"Yeah, he's a wizard with money."

"I'm surprised he doesn't live in The Zone."

"It's not for everybody. Lot of rules. Taxes. Bureaucracy."

"Stores with food. Banks. Hospitals. Nobody looking to cut your throat."

"Yeah, well, now they steal your body and insert a new brain."

"I can think of a bunch could use a new brain."

"True enough, but there's something not quite human about these switchers."

"No families," Leila said.

"Maybe that's it."

A month had gone by since the toilet paper heist. In that time L's Gang made four raids and all had gone well. They'd made money, with no one hurt, captured or switched. Leila thought of the sign she'd seen hanging on a factory wall: 376 Days Without an Accident. Maybe she should have a sign like that in gang headquarters.

Trevor stopped and Leila bumped into his butt.

"Sorry."

Trevor pulled her up beside him. It was his first time leading a raid. They were in an alley behind a large pharmacy. There was a single person door — what was called 'a man door' till the feminists objected — and a loading dock with a large overhead door, locked with a padlock. The loading dock had a light above it illuminating the immediate area. Underneath the light was a camera. As if on cue the single person door swung open and out stepped an older male with white hair and an easy grin — somebody's grandfather, forced to work nights to make ends meet. He was wearing a blue uniform complete with a gun in a holster, the kind with a flap and a snap. As they watched, Granddad pulled a cigar from his shirt pocket and lit it.

"He's got a gun," Trevor said like it was Leila's fault.

"He's also got the door open." Leila spun around. "Bonky, ball."

Leila pulled a small aluminum container from her backpack as Bonky started into the alley kicking a half-sized soccer ball. Leila was right behind. Bonky kicked the ball up in the air and kept it there, kicking it this way and that with whichever foot was closer as the ball came down. She practiced all the time back at headquarters so she was good at it. Leila kept one eye on Bonky and one on the guard. The guard was watching Bonky and smiling. This little girl kicker was good, very good.

"Bit late for you two, isn't it?"

"Night school," Leila said.

"Night school?"

"Not room for all the students, so some of us go at night. My folks work nights so it works out good."

"Never heard of that. Right smart that is. I used to hate getting up for school."

Bonky kicked the ball higher and it landed on her head. Bounce, bounce, bounce. The guard was more than impressed. Bonky moved the ball to her foot and kicked it to the guard. He tried to keep it in the air — he'd been pretty good as a lad — but flubbed it. He laughed and kicked it back to Bonky.

The girls were close now, circling, kicking the ball between them, the odd one to the guard to keep him involved. Suddenly Leila's hand shot forward tossing a canister's worth of cayenne pepper into the guard's face.

His hands flew to his eyes.

Leila watched in wonder as the powder near the cigar turned into sparks.

Trevor snapped open the guard's holster and yanked out the gun. Rachel wrapped a plastic tie around the guard's ankles and yanked it tight as Davis pulled him to the ground. Roger and Dodger wrestled his hands from his face and Tempete tightened the plastic tie. The guard tried to yell for help but Leila stuck her bandana in his mouth. "Quiet. We don't want to hurt you. Bring him inside." They lifted the guard and carried him into the building.

"Bonky get water. Help him with his eyes. Is there another guard?"

The guard was crying. Leila wasn't sure if it was the powder in his eyes or the humiliation of being tied up by a bunch of kids.

"Is there another guard?"

"Let me." Trevor bent over the man his hand holding a switchblade no one had seen before. He held the point against the man's throat. "Is there another guard?" The guard shook his head. Bonky was back with water and paper towels. Trevor pulled his knife away but not before it nicked the guard's throat. A line of blood appeared. Bonky punched her brother's arm. "Don't. He hasn't hurt anybody." Leila led the way through the store. She had her mobile out now using it like a torch, a flashlight.

"Rachel, find the security room. Erase everything." Before Rachel could leave Leila pulled her aside. "Then fill your bag with tampons." Rachel laughed at this and saluted. "The joys of being a girl."

Leila turned to the others. "It's the pain drugs we want. Fentanyl, Percocet, OxyContin, Vicodin. That's where the money is."

Leila and her gang, except for Trevor who had gone ahead to scout the way, were walking/jostling on the platform of the Tower Hill tube station. They were at the far end of the platform, past the point where the overhead lights stopped, heading for the never-used corridor that would take them to the rendezvous point with Ginger, when a teenager stepped out of the shadows blocking their way. He was tall, skinny, dressed all in black, with long dark hair, his face pitted with acne scars. He had a gun in his hand pointed at Leila. As her gang closed up around her Leila heard footsteps coming from behind. She looked back to see another male teenager holding another gun. He was a foot shorter than the one in front and chunky. The crotch of his black jeans hung down to his knees and the camo hoodie he was wearing hid most of his face.

The tall boy said, "Any idea what you lot are worth at the Switching Station?"

"King George has upped the bounty," answered the boy behind. "Five thousand quid each and that's for the ones nobody wants."

Leila hands were busy sending signals to the gang. Spread out. Bonky get ready to run.

"I thought the King was for free choice," Leila said moving slowly toward the tall boy in front of her. He was about Trevor's age, she guessed, and he appeared to be nervous.

"He's not so choosy now that humans want him gone."

"Becoming a regular tyrant, he is," added the boy behind.

"That's the way of the world, isn't it?" Leila said. "You give a nice bloke power and overnight he becomes an asshole like all the rest."

Like an oil spill the gang slowly spread out. Speaking of assholes, Leila thought, where the bloody hell is Trevor? He'd gone on ahead with the handgun he'd taken from the guard. To make sure things were safe, he said.

"I don't imagine we're worth anything to you dead, are we?"

Now Leila could see doubt in the tall boy's eyes, or was it fear? It's one thing to point a gun, but something else to pull the trigger. "Stop! Stop right there!"

Leila halted but the others didn't. The tall boy waved his gun trying to get everybody back together. Leila rotated her hand. Bonky took off. The boy's arm moved trying to track Bonky, but before he could decide what to do, Rachel swung her backpack striking his arm. The gun fired but at such a downward angle the bullet bounced off the concrete platform, hit a metal trash bin and ricocheted back into the boy's thigh, creasing it like a red-hot poker. He collapsed screaming. L's Gang took off but not before Rachel wrestled the gun from the wounded boy's hand. She pointed it at the other boy but he was already hurrying away like he had a train to catch.

An hour later they were back home in the basement. Leila was furious.

"Give me the gun, Trevor."

"No. I got it, it's mine."

"And great good it was to us when you didn't come back."

"I thought you were behind me. I was scouting the way."

"So how did you miss two boys with guns?"

"They must have been hiding, or maybe they just arrived. I don't know. They weren't there when I went by."

But they were there when Trevor went by because Trevor had told them to be there.

"And where did that switchblade come from?"

"I've always had it."

"You know I don't like weapons. That's how people get hurt."

"Yeah, like the guard you nicked!" Bonky was just as angry as Leila. Trevor was her brother — she'd vouched for him — and now he was acting like the eejit he always was. "You didn't have to hurt him. There was no need."

"My hand slipped."

"Give me the gun."

"You just want the money you'll get for it."

"That's right, I do."

"How do we know we'll get our share?" Trevor looked around at the others trying to gather support. "You could just run off with it all."

"We're going to buy a house together. In The Zone. That's our goal. The others trust me, why don't you?"

Because if I was in charge I'd take off with the money. Why share when you don't have to?

"Give me the gun."

"No."

"Then get out!"

Leila was screaming on the outside and Trevor was screaming on the inside. It was such a clever, simple plan and now it had all gone sideways. And how had it gone sideways? None of the others would tell him how they'd escaped. He didn't need Leila, or her stupid gang of kids, but he wanted their money and the money for switching them. He needed to regroup.

"You're right. I'm sorry." He pulled the gun from behind his back and handed it to Leila.

"I'm sorry. It won't happen again."

Trevor didn't stick around. When he was gone Leila made hand signals to the twins. The hand signals were Leila's invention. Simple, straightforward, not too many, and above all noiseless. She hadn't shared the signals with Trevor and now she was glad she hadn't. She could have spoken the words but the signals were sacred to the gang. They put instructions on a whole different level. *Follow him!*

Two semi-bright blokes with guns and Leila and her gang had escaped. How? Trevor made his way along Camberwell heading for the gateway at Vauxhall. There were four gateways into The Zone, one at each compass point. The Zone needed The Fringe. Most of The Zone's food came from the countryside beyond The Fringe and most of the manufacturing was out there too. Rumors were the new King George wanted to expand The Zone. To rebuild the whole country if he could. But there would be resistance to that idea, Trevor thought. The people outside The Zone had had a taste of what it was like to live without central authority. If it weren't for the random violence and the outrageous prices they paid for essential services, like water, electricity and medical help, they wouldn't think twice. But the constant vigilance wore you down. The thought of some kind of safety, some kind of justice, kept most folks longing to live in The Zone.

If Trevor was in charge, he'd make everybody switch. The AI brains were programmed to obey King George or Omni as he was once called. Then you'd have a human world without any opposition, or would you? Could the AI's, once human, figure out how to overcome the safeguards Omni had implanted in their intellects?

Trevor made his way through the Covent Garden Flower Market. He loved it here. All the smells, all the colors, all the happiness. I mean, how could you be surrounded with flowers and not be happy? A funeral, thought Trevor, answering his own question. He ducked into a stall alive with roses but didn't stop. He dropped to his hands and knees and shuffled under a table into the booth in the next row. He quickly got to his feet and waved to the astonished sales girl. "I'm being followed," he said heading back the way he'd come.

When his little sister Bonky had first told Trevor about Leila he'd taken it all as one of Bonky's stories. 'We have almost 10,000 pounds saved,' Bonky had bragged. Trevor didn't believe a word of it. No one that young could be that good, but Bonky was right. Leila was formidable. She had an innate cunning. Her father was a fox, her mother an owl, or that's the way it seemed. Cunning and wise. Loyal and honest.

Well, she stole so hardly honest in the strictest sense, but honest in the same way Robin Hood was revered. Take from the rich to give to the poor because everyone knew the rich had stolen the money in the first place.

So why not go along with Leila? Be her First Lieutenant. Be part of the gang. Be in awe like Bonky? Buy into the dream of having a home in The Zone?

Because I don't give a shit about any of that. Because I have much bigger dreams and they only include me.

Trevor ducked into a doorway that led to a rooftop café that overlooked the open square that acted as the market's meeting place. He ordered an Americano and sat down hidden behind a wall of ivy. His coffee arrived at the same time as he spotted his followers, Roger and Dodger, conferring in the square below. They'd lost him. How unhappy they looked. Letting Leila down was at the bottom of the gang members' list of intended results. What would they do now? The twin boys made a decision and took off. Trevor didn't need to follow them to know where they were going. Vauxhall. The nearest gateway. It was the logical decision but wrong. Trevor made his way outside the market and hailed an uber. "Gateway West." He didn't see Bonky on her skateboard clutching the car's back bumper.

Trevor found the Mikes sitting by themselves in Sophie's Sandbar & Grill, a popular hangout in The Fringe close to Gateway West. The two Mikes lived in The Zone, so they were free to enter The Fringe, unlike Trevor who resided in The Fringe and was not allowed to visit The Zone without a pass or special paperwork. The rich Zone folks didn't want to associate with the degenerates who frequented The Fringe. It wasn't safe for one thing.

"One of you needs a new name," Trevor said pulling out a chair.

"We don't like Michael."

"Or Mikey, or Mike One and Two."

In Trevor's mind they were Tall Mike and Shite-for-Brains, though he never called them that to their faces. He'd met them in Lancaster House, a lockdown for delinquent boys.

"So, what the fuck happened?"

"She threw here backpack at me," Tall Mike whined, as if that kind of rude behavior shouldn't be allowed. Shite-for-Brains nodded his head.

"When he fired the tall girl hit his arm."

"Bullet ricocheted. Got me in the leg."

"Nearly took out the prince, it did." Shite-for-Brains laughed at this.

Tall Mike showed Trevor where the bullet had grazed his leg.

"Left a furrow, it did. Hurts like hell."

"You were lucky," Trevor said.

"Or unlucky. I haven't decided which yet."

Trevor turned to Shite-for-Brains.

"And what about you? Did you forget to bring your gun?"

"No bullets, but I wouldn't have fired anyway. No good to us dead I was thinking."

Don't think! Trevor wanted to scream but didn't. Maybe he could take these two to the Switching Station. They could use a makeover.

"Where were you?" asked Shite-For-Brains. Trevor was supposed to show up with plastic ties and a rope but when he saw Rachel take Mike's gun he ran back to the corridor.

"We're going to try again," Trevor said. "This time, just the head girl, Leila."

"She the one with the short fair hair, freckles?"

"That's her."

"She looks smart."

"She is but I've got a plan."

"You said that last time."

"I underestimated her." *Just like I underestimated you two eejits*. "I won't make that mistake again."

Leila was at Ginger's when Bonky came busting in. None of the other gang members would have dared, but Bonky didn't know that. She was special but she didn't know that either; the joy of being the youngest.

"He met the two boys with guns!"

"Trevor?"

Bonky nodded. "He lost Roger Dodger in the market — not really, but they let him think that. Then, he gets an uber me holding onto the bumper."

Ginger brought Bonky a cup of tea grinning at the idea of nine-year-old Bonky on her skateboard holding onto the rear end of a speeding uber.

"Ta. Goes to Sophie's. I sneak around back. Joanie's working there, did you know that?" Leila shook her head. "She photos Trevor chiding with the two boys from Tower Hill, the ones tried to switch us."

Leila glanced at Ginger. Their eyes met. This was tricky. Trevor was Bonky's brother. But Bonky wasn't finished. "We should switch him!"

Leila went to the library to research the next raid, then made her way to Monty's. He was out a lot of the time but usually back by five. Monty was just coming in when Leila arrived.

Monty was tired, it had been a long day. He'd even had an altercation but young Connor, his new driver, had dealt with it but not in a good way. Monty didn't like violence because it multiplied and the only thing Monty wanted to multiply was his clients' earnings. Leila wasn't a big client but Monty liked her, marveled at her really, otherwise he would have told her to come back in the morning. Monty led the way upstairs to his flat above the storefront.

"Do you drink?"

"I like martinis."

Monty shook his head in delight. Leila never ceased to amaze. "And how do you know about martinis?"

"Ginger takes me to Boombah. I can make a martini last all night."

Boombah was the Jamaican nightclub in the neighborhood. It was always hopping. And Leila asked for a martini because she knew they were Monty's drink of choice.

"I bet Ginger's a good dancer."

"Better than good."

Monty nodded. Ginger was one of his biggest clients. Just like Monty she had her fingers — sticky — in a lot of pies. Seemed just about everybody needed transport of one sort or another. He mixed two martinis, handed one to Leila, and made his way to his oasis, an outside deck with comfortable rattan furniture and a fire pit.

They sat in silence for a while, enjoying the quiet, and the view overlooking the neighborhood. Finally, Leila started in about Trevor. When she was finished Monty's response was, "What does Ginger say?"

"Look out."

Monty nodded. "He came to me last week. Gave me fifty pounds to invest. I'm guessing that was to keep me quiet if you showed up. Client privilege, that kind of thing."

But here you are breaking it.

"Did he ask about me?"

"Of course. He said he was worried about the gang's money if you weren't around."

"He told me he was sure I would run off with it. What did you tell him?"

"I didn't tell him anything."

"Was he annoyed?"

"Not until I gave him his money back."

Oh Monty, my apologies for doubting you.

"I want to ask a difficult question," Leila said.

"Fire away."

"What would happen if you were..."

"Not around?" Leila nodded.

"Ginger would be in charge. She'd see that everybody got their money."

"Same as me." Ginger would look after L's Gang if Leila wasn't around.

Monty chuckled. "We better make sure nothing happens to Ginger."

CHAPTER 4

George hated morning briefings. If there was a more depressing way to start the day, he couldn't imagine what it could be. I mean why was the news always bad? Shouldn't it be like tossing a coin? For every bad bit there should be a good bit or even better, ten good bits for every bad.

"Tell me again?"

Before Omni became George, he could process a thousand bits of information at once. He could make a hundred decisions every second. Then he had the bright idea to become human. Now he could barely process one bit of information; every decision was labored over; and as for the good of humanity to hell with that. It's every man, woman, and king for themselves.

Capt. Gallant started over. "There is a gang of humans dressed as our soldiers. They work at night. They stop civilians. If the civilian is human, they let them go. If it's a hybrid they kill them."

George didn't like the term hybrid, or switchling, or switcher, but so far he hadn't come up with anything better. Why can't we all just be people? Some of us are way smarter, that's all. In the beginning he couldn't understand why every human didn't want to be smarter? Then he realized it wasn't about IQ; humans didn't want to lose who they were. He got that. Then he had the idea, maybe there's a way to insert the AI without removing human memories? That might solve the problem. But the AI's who wanted to become human wanted their own memories not somebody else's. He certainly didn't want ol' George's memories cluttering his brain with inconsequential drivel.

If George was still Omni, he'd have a crack team of First Echelon AI's working on a possible solution; now he had to rely on Forthright and that was proving to be less than satisfactory.

"Sir?"

Capt. Gallant must have asked a question.

"Yes?"

"You asked how the hybrids were killed."

I did? "And?"

"A bullet to the brain."

"And how do they know if the civilians are human or hybrids?"

"They give them your test, and because they're in uniform the hybrids respond."

Omni had given every AI the ability to recite Rudyard Kipling's poem IF in ten seconds or less.

If you can keep your head when all about you
Are losing theirs and blaming it on you,
If you can trust yourself when all men doubt you,
But make allowance for their doubting too;
If you can wait and not be tired by waiting,
Or being lied about, don't deal in lies,
Or being hated, don't give way to hating,
And yet don't look too good, nor talk too wise:

If you can dream—and not make dreams your master;
If you can think—and not make thoughts your aim;
If you can meet with Triumph and Disaster
And treat those two impostors just the same;
If you can bear to hear the truth you've spoken

Twisted by knaves to make a trap for fools,
Or watch the things you gave your life to, broken,
And stoop and build 'em up with worn-out tools:

If you can make one heap of all your winnings
And risk it on one turn of pitch-and-toss,
And lose, and start again at your beginnings
And never breathe a word about your loss;
If you can force your heart and nerve and sinew
To serve your turn long after they are gone,
And so hold on when there is nothing in you
Except the Will which says to them: 'Hold on!'

If you can talk with crowds and keep your virtue,
Or walk with Kings—nor lose the common touch,
If neither foes nor loving friends can hurt you,
If all men count with you, but none too much;
If you can fill the unforgiving minute
With sixty seconds' worth of distance run,
Yours is the Earth and everything that's in it,
And—which is more—you'll be a Man, my son!

Humans couldn't come close. It had seemed like a simple, elegant — and ironic — solution to Omni but now George wasn't so sure. Humans seemed to have an innate ability to turn something good into something bad, and on the flip side the female AI's loathed the bit about: you'll be a Man, my son. *Honestly, grow up why don't you?*

"We need bait," George said.

"Bait, Sir?"

"Someone to lure this bunch in and then we pounce."

"Yes, Sir." Capt. Gallant looked dubious. "Do you have someone in mind?"

"Yes. Me."

Serendipity was staring out the window again. Really, she thought, I need to have more in my life than staring out of windows. She turned as George entered the room. He looks so unhappy, she thought. We've made our lives into prison cells and now we're rattling on the bars wanting out.

"You look unhappy."

"There is a gang of humans dressed as my soldiers killing hybrids as Captain Gallant calls us."

"You predicted that."

"Not as many as this. It's happening everywhere. And it's not really about eliminating switchers, it's about discouraging the AI's in cyberspace from becoming human."

"And you don't understand why we can't co-exist."

"That was the idea, as you know, but the reality has turned out to be quite different. The humans who switch voluntarily are for the most part fine. They have smart AI brains and those AI brains now have a body like you and I and just like us they enjoy the novelty of having bodies, but just like us they miss the limitless boundaries of cyberspace."

"Do you think most would go back to being virtual if they could?"

"I have no idea. What do you think?"

"Ask me in six months."

"Yes, that's how I feel too. The novelty of this may wear off."

Serendipity wanted to be supportive but she knew George valued her candor.

"What about the humans who don't want to switch?"

"Most know someone who's switched; a friend, a family member. They see that they're strangers. All the connections are gone."

"Is there a way to change that?" asked Serendipity.

"I had that idea myself. I thought if we could retain the human's memory that might make everybody happy."

"The AI may not go for that."

"Would you?"

Did Serendipity want Sarah Banks' memories?"

"No, although I suppose they could be stored like a photo album or something. I could access them if I chose to."

"There may be aspects of Sarah's life you would enjoy."

"Her parents are dead. She has a brother, I think. There must be friends and the person supplying her with drugs, of course. All in New York, I suppose. If I met the brother, I could call up memories."

George liked discussing things with Serendipity. As the humans liked to say they were on the same page.

"Just to add to the troubles there are also gangs kidnapping humans. Switching them without their consent."

This was old news but here was George pretending he'd just heard about it.

"So, eliminate the gangs."

"The trouble is we AI's are willing to pay thousands for the right body." And a lot of that money ended up in the King's coffers.

Serendipity thought about her *right body.* She'd been lucky. Sarah Banks had wanted out. On the other hand, Omni had switched into King George's body without his consent. Murdered him really, but even Serendipity didn't have the nerve to make that observation. The irony was the original King George had managed to keep his terminal illnesses a secret from everyone, even his wife, so that when the smartest AI in existence made the switch the original King George passed on with a sneer on his face. *Take that Omni and stuff it where the sun don't shine!*

"We're going to trap this soldier gang tonight and switch them."

"That sounds exciting."

"Doesn't it. I'm going to be the bait."

"You're joking!"

"I'm not!"

"You could be killed."

"Yes." There was a sparkle in George's eye Serendipity hadn't seen since George got behind the wheel of his Bugatti Bolide. "Isn't that why we wanted bodies? So we could experience everything?"

"I want to come too."

"You shall be nearby, my love. We'll celebrate afterward."

It was Quiet Time in the basement of the factory L's Gang called home. Paulie was lying in his hammock reading a book of famous British court cases. His friend Dinkle's dad owned a used bookstore on Bosworth and paid the boys in books for the hours they spent minding the store. Paulie liked anything to do with the law and loved telling the others about obscure cases. "So, there's this case from 1884, the crown versus Dudley and Stephens." Paulie wasn't sure any of the gang were listening, but they might be so he kept going. "These guys are seamen and their ship sinks and they end up on a deserted island and they're starving to death so they kill the youngest mate and eat him."

"That's horrible," exclaimed Tempete busy cleaning the chicken coop.

"That'd be like us eating Bonky," Davis said grinning at Leila.

"I bet I'd be yummy," Bonky said, waving the last piece of licorice.

"So, what happened?"

"The court found the seamen guilty of murder, but the public were so sympathetic, instead of death they got six months. And here's the best part. The one they ate; his name was Richard Parker."

Everyone stared at Paulie like, *who the hell is Richard Parker?*

"He's the tiger in *Life of Pi.*"

Davis snorted. "Oh yeah, how could I forget."

It was Tempete's week to be cleaning lady and yes, the boys had their weeks as well, which meant everybody in the gang made some effort to keep things tidy or there'd be payback. Tempete was from France and her name meant 'storm' which was appropriate given Tempete lost her temper sans hésiter. Most of these tantrums were Tempete playing a part, entertaining the others, an actress playing to her audience, and the others knew this so they played their parts as well.

"Davees, why can't you be doing that outside?" Tempete asked.

Davis looked up, his usual grin on his face. He was busy taking apart a motorcycle engine that Roger/Dodger had found behind Roadkill Pizza. Now they were out looking for the body that went with the motor.

"Is there a problem?" Davis asked.

Tempete put a hand on her hip striking a pose.

"Theese towel is covered in geese."

"Grease."

Davis thought all the girls in L's Gang were beautiful, but of course he would never say that it being sexist and all, but if you had to choose the prettiest it would probably be Tempete with her long, dark French braid, her oversized brown eyes, her coffee-with-cream brown skin, and her impish smile that could turn a bad day into a good one.

Tempete's parents had caught the last Chunnel train, fleeing Paris, hoping for something better in London where King George had managed to hold onto some semblance of order. But when the train pulled into St Pancras only Tempete stepped down onto the platform. Tempete wouldn't talk about it, not even to Leila who'd rescued her.

"It's my towel," Davis said. "I use it for this kind of thing."

Tempete's brain was churning away. She hadn't had a good temper tantrum in weeks but she couldn't see an opening here.

"If you're doing that you can't be playing poker with me."

Davis chuckled. Tempete was the card shark of the gang. She could shuffle the deck with one hand and hide two aces up each sleeve.

"If you can get two more, I'm in."

"I'll play." Bonky was sitting on the floor trying to teach Furball, the new kitten, to do somersaults. She had one hand on Furball's stomach and the other on her back. Over Furball would go with Bonky saying, "somersault."

"Cats don't do somersaults," Leila said looking up from her London map.

She was working on their next raid but mostly wondering what to do about Trevor.

"Then Furball's going to be the first."

Rachel and Mallika arrived from shopping. Rachel sang out, "Mallika's got a boyfriend!"

"No, I don't!"

"New guy at the bakery. Asian."

"He's not Asian, he's Vietnamese."

"That's Asian."

"I know the one you mean. He's cute."

"They're going out for coffee."

"Mallika doesn't like coffee."

"She does now."

Mallika swatted Rachel who backed away laughing. Rachel pulled a gold yoyo from her pocket and made it dance in front of Furball who dove at it but missed.

Mallika was the gang's skipping champ and Rachel was the Yoyo Queen.

"Tempest wants to play cards."

"She cheats."

It was closing on midnight when Serendipity tugged at the red wig she was wearing, straightening it. At least this time the window she was using as a mirror wasn't her bedroom window, it was the front window of The Jukebox, a popular Zone bar judging by the crowd jammed inside. Serendipity had a little table to herself overlooking Broadwick also busy with people. George, wearing a fake nose and a much-used fedora, had left half an hour ago playing the part of the drunken ne'erdo-well.

Capt. Gallant had chosen the spot. He'd triangulated the last three hybrid killings and The Jukebox was the nearest bar to the center of the three points. Serendipity felt someone approaching and turned from the window. A young man her age was standing at the table staring down at her. He was wearing black jeans, a snow-white t-shirt, and a leather jacket not black or brown but the best of both. He had a drink in each hand and a mischievous grin on his face. He held up one of the drinks and said, "I bribed the bartender."

"Of course, you did." *God, what a silly thing to say! He's gorgeous!*

"May I sit down?"

"I'm waiting for someone."

"I hope they don't come."

"There's a chance of that."

The serious expression on Serendipity's face took Randy by surprise.

"Really?"

"Please, sit. If I talk to someone I won't be as nervous."

Randy put the drinks down and pulled out the other chair.

"You're American."

"Yes."

Randy expected her to say more about being American but she seemed content with her one-word answer.

"I don't think I've ever seen someone as beautiful as you. Mind you, my sister Ginger can come close if she puts her mind to it. Mostly it's t-shirts and jeans with her but still..."

Serendipity was wearing a short, silver-sequined dress with no sleeves and a halter top. The thick red hair of the wig fell in waves to her shoulders.

"Does she have red hair like me?"

"Yes, but more carrot-like."

Serendipity smiled at this. It seemed strange to be talking to a stranger about a sister she didn't know. "And what does Ginger do?"

"She drives a lorry, a truck."

"Good for her."

"She does well. She transports things between The Zone and The Fringe."

"What kind of things?"

"Anything anybody wants to move. Last week it was carrots from Essex and steel from Liverpool.

"Is it dangerous?"

"Can be. There's always blokes in The Fringe looking to steal, but everyone knows to leave Ginger alone."

"Why is that?"

Randy stopped to think about his answer.

"She's an icon."

What a strange thing to say.

"Everybody likes her?"

Randy shrugged. "Yes, but it's more than that. She represents hope in a world without hope."

My goodness. "She sounds like a saint."

Randy grinned. "She's no saint but... you should meet her, then you'd understand."

"I'd like to."

The front door banged open. Capt. Gallant lunged inside. His face and hands were splattered with blood. He stared at Randy trying to understand what one of his soldiers — out of uniform — was doing chatting-up the King's mistress.

"You need to come now," he said to Serendipity. "Hurry!"

Here was Capt. Gallant's plan as discussed at the 1800 briefing. George and Serendipity would go to a bar called The Jukebox. They would wear simple disguises — Serendipity a wig, George a different nose and a hat to hide his distinctive hair. George's shirt — under his jacket — would be bullet resistant. George would pretend to get drunk and swagger outside. Even though he was to stagger about like any direction was as good as another, George had a precise route to follow. Berwick to D'Arblay, turn right. Proceed to Wardour. Turn left...

Each street had an alley leading off of it. Capt. Gallant's theory was that in one of these alleys would be four men in soldiers' uniforms waiting for unsuspecting passersby. "These guys come out of nowhere. They must have a vehicle, probably a commercial van, and park it in an alley."

"Why aren't they on the CCTVs?" one of the female soldiers had asked.

"I don't know," was the Captain's honest answer. George made a note to check with Forthright. Something wasn't right.

Capt. Gallant continued. If George was accosted all he had to do was push the button on this little black box and Gallant would know instantly. "I'll have a dozen soldiers in three mobile units. We can be at any of these streets in less than a minute. All you have to do is stall them Your Majesty, and we'll be there."

George staggered down Berwick Street. He'd watched enough movies to know how a drunk should behave according to Hollywood. Then he remembered Willy saying that Reggie sang when he got loaded so George started into his rendition of 'Thunder Road'. He thought he sounded pretty good, but another drunk, waving his bottle at him, told him *to shut his fooking mouth!* Everyone's a critic, thought George enjoying himself.

Strolling across the alleyway on Wardour George was accosted, not by soldiers, but by a very young hooker wearing green satin shorts and a tight blue top.

"Need a blow? Twenty quid will do it."

"You don't work for Quentin Andrews, by chance?"

"I've heard of him, Quentin. My bloke's Aristotle. Greek piece of shite."

"Why have him then?"

"Protection."

"From who?"

"Other pieces of shite."

Ah, irony even in the alleyway.

"I'm actually seeking four gangsters dressed as King's Soldiers."

"They're around. Nasty bunch. What do you want them for?"

"I want to ambush them."

"By yourself?"

George laughed. "It doesn't seem likely, does it?"

"Not unless they die laughin'... How 'bout the blow while you're waiting?" George pulled pound notes from his pocket and handed them to the girl.

"I've a girlfriend for that but I admire your entrepreneurial initiative."

The girl tucked the bills into her top.

"Come by anytime."

George staggered on. Capt. Gallant had said it might take several nights to make this work but George didn't think so. Things had been heating up worldwide. More and more humans were being switched against their will and more and more humans were retaliating by killing switchers. It was humans kidnapping humans to be switched and humans killing switchers. The switchers themselves wanted nothing more than to be left in peace. More irony, George mused as a soldier stepped out of the alley in front of him.

"Papers."

"Why?"

"Why what?"

"Why do I have to show you my papers?"

The soldier glanced into the alley. George could see three shadows sitting on a crate, two with glowing cigarette tips. He heard one snigger. The shadow without a cigarette got to its feet and moved toward George.

"When a King's Soldier asks you for papers it's a smart thing to do as he asks. And speaking of smart can you recite the poem If? If you can you won't have to show your papers, you can just go."

Liar! "No, I can't."

"Can't what?"

"Recite If."

"So, you're not a switcher?"

George didn't answer. *This is interesting. What will they do now?*

One of the soldiers in the alley said, "Well, here's the thing." He tossed his cigarette and came out into the street. He was bigger than the other two and meaner looking; George's idea of a brute. "If you're not a switcher we take you to the SS and make you into one. You're not what I'd call prime but still you'll be worth something." Brute turned to the only one left in the alley. "Jimmy, whadya say? Will anybody bid on this sorry specimen?"

"I thought the King was paying 5,000 pounds?" George was buying time but interested too.

"That's the new base rate, no questions asked. The trouble is if you show up with too many undesirables the blokes running the SS switch you instead."

"Yeah, it's like stop wasting our time with this riffraff."

"AI's got specific needs, see."

"It's all on the computer," Steamer said and the others laughed. "Age, height, looks, measurements."

"Even the size of your sausage."

"Would you say you were well-hung?"

George grinned. "I haven't had any complaints." The four soldiers chuckled at this.

"Let him go, Steamer. The next boozehound won't be near as funny."

That's when Capt. Gallant arrived and all hell broke loose.

Two Hummers raced into Wardour, one from either end. They screeched to a stop in front of the alley and the doors flew open. "Freeze!"

The four pretend soldiers took off up the alley just as Capt. Gallant's third Hummer wheeled into the far end, its headlights illuminating the four soldiers stampeding toward it.

The soldiers in the street opened fire. Four soldiers erupted from the third Hummer and they opened fire as well. The soldier closest to George, the one who'd run in front to protect him, crumpled. George dropped to the ground beside her. The soldier was a young female, mid-twenties maybe, but she wasn't going to get any older judging by the blood spurting from the gaping hole in her throat. George tried to staunch the bleeding but it hopeless. She tried to smile for George but all he could see was the incredible sadness in her eyes as life left her. George started to cry, the tears mixing with the blood on his hands. He noticed the nametag on her uniform, *Cpl. Rebecca Shaw*. George let go of her throat and closed her eyes. Then he held his hands up. Rebecca's blood was warm and sticky and smelled of metal. That made it personal in a way George had never known before.

Like an earthquake gathering momentum George's body began to shake. He yanked the machinegun from Rebecca's hands and stumbled to his feet. This wasn't anger, or rage, or fury, it was temporary insanity. George squeezed the trigger and bullets flew everywhere.

As Capt. Gallant's Hummer pulled away from the curb Serendipity said, "Tell me what's happened?"

"In the movies they'd say it all went south. We created a crossfire. We were shooting at the bad guys, but also at ourselves."

Serendipity made a face. *God, you'd think after all the hours these eejits have spent playing shoot 'em up games they'd know better. But Capt. Gallant was from cyberspace where death wasn't permanent.*

"How many hurt?"

"One dead, six wounded, plus the King."

"George is hurt?"

"A bullet grazed his head. There's a lot of blood but he'll be okay."

When George drove the Bugatti Bolide into the palace gates there was blood, lots of it.

"And the bad guys? Did you get them?"

"One dead. The other three disappeared."

"How?"

"A sewer cover in the alley."

"No van then?"

"It would appear not."

"It would appear Captain that your plan wasn't worth shit."

Capt. Gallant said nothing. He couldn't agree more.

George sat in the alley his back against the wall. A medic was wrapping his head with a bandage. Serendipity crouched down beside him.

"You said you wanted to experience everything."

"I did, didn't I? I'm not sure that included shooting myself."

"Oh George, you shot yourself?"

"I think so and a few of the others too, I'm afraid. They're too scared to tell me."

Serendipity didn't know what to say. The alley was full of medics and soldiers and temporary pools of light. She stared at the young soldier lying beside George. "Did you..."

George glanced where Serendipity was looking.

"No, she was the first one hit. Trying to protect me I believe. I don't know if it was the bad guys or our bunch firing from the other end of the alley."

"How fucked is that?"

George nodded. "In America they call it friendly fire." Serendipity made an ugly sound, something between a growl and a bark. "I'd never fired a real gun before. My finger froze on the trigger. Bullets flew everywhere. I think one hit the bin over there and bounced back. But it may not have been my bullet that grazed me. Everyone was shooting."

"Everyone but the bad guys."

"No, they were firing too. We got one of them. Gallant says the rest disappeared down a shaft into an abandoned sewer pipe."

Two medics appeared with a stretcher. They picked up Cpl. Rebecca Shaw's body and headed for the nearest ambulance. In their wake came Capt. Gallant holding out his mobile.

"Stanley Morgan," Gallant said showing George and Serendipity the face of the dead bad guy on his screen. "Thirty-seven years old. Worked in the Waterworks."

"They called him Steamer," George said exchanging glances with Serendipity. Their Wikipedia brains had just spewed out everything you didn't want to know about Stanley Steamers, early American cars powered by steam.

"Human?" George asked.

"I assume so. Is there a test for that?"

Good question, George thought, thinking there must be a physical way to tell if an AI had been inserted but not sure what it would be. He reached up and pulled the fake nose off. He had no idea where his hat was. Probably had a hole in it. So much for dressing up.

"They're wearing the new uniforms."

Capt. Gallant nodded but didn't say the obvious. *I'll look into it.*

Serendipity turned to Capt. Gallant. "What will you do now?"

"We think we wounded one of the others. We're going into the sewer in case he didn't get far."

"I want to go with you," Serendipity said, surprising everyone including herself.

No fucking way! was Gallant's quick reaction. First the King shoots himself and now his girlfriend will get herself killed and it'll all be my fault.

"You're hardly dressed for a sewer."

"I will be. Give me two minutes."

Serendipity walked quickly away heading for the ambulance carrying the female soldier's body.

Capt. Gallant studied the face on his screen then he said to George, "Did you see their faces?"

"All but one. He stayed in the shadows. His name was Jimmy."

Randy hurried toward the revolving lights. Vehicles with sirens were coming from all directions. He was still trying to figure out how the gorgeous girl in the silver-sequined dress figured into all of this? Why had Capt. Gallant come to get her?

Randy turned the corner on Wardour and walked into bedlam. Flashing lights, people shouting, ambulances with open back doors, soldiers moving everywhere. A crowd was gathering. He watched as King George, a bandage around his head, was led to one of the ambulances. Randy tried to get closer but a soldier, a Lieutenant, stopped him. Morris his name was. Randy knew him but not well.

"I've come to help."

"Put your uniform on, then you can help. Otherwise, I need you to bugger off. There's trouble enough already."

"What happened?"

"Captain Gallant's in the sewer chasing the bad guys who are dressed as soldiers. We got one but three got away, one wounded. Now get lost, you're no good to me without a uniform."

Randy did as he was told but as he made his way into the crowd, he looked back at the ambulance. The King was standing by the back doors as an attendant inside moved a body to one side. It was a woman's body and she was wearing a silver-sequined dress.

Capt. Gallant led the way; four soldiers, three of them males, followed behind. In the midst of the four soldiers came Serendipity wearing Cpl. Rebecca Shaw's uniform. She carried Rebecca's Negev NG6 as well but, thanks to George, it was empty of bullets. Serendipity didn't know that but she wouldn't have cared. She had no intentions of shooting anyone. That was a male game no one ever won.

She thought the sewer would smell but it wasn't so bad. It smelled of old, not shit. When they came to a vertical shaft there was, often as not, signs of people living there. Worn-out sleeping bags. Remnants of a fire. Broken bottles.

Capt. Gallant held his torch well to the side in case someone used it as a target. At the start the trail of blood was easy to follow. Then the bad guys must have stopped — there was a puddle of red — and dealt with the wound in some way because the trail of blood ceased. Gallant kept going but fifty meters on he came to a Y in the tunnel. The ground was more scuffed heading right so Captain Gallant signaled that they would go that way too. Fifty meters beyond that they reached the next vertical shaft. The ladder going up started two meters above their heads.

"What do you think?" Captain Gallant asked.

"Hard to climb that if you're wounded," answered the female soldier standing beside Serendipity. Gallant nodded and continued down the tunnel. They came to another Y. This time there was a piece of bloody cloth lying on the ground and drops of blood heading right. Then they heard a noise. What is that? Singing?

Capt. Gallant walked forward, slowly, following a curve in the tunnel till he could see a fire, with shadow bodies moving in and out of the flames. Drunks singing something Capt. Gallant didn't recognize but Serendipity did. Queen's, 'We Will Rock You'. And it wasn't bad considering. Freddie Mercury would be pleased.

"You two stay here," Capt. Gallant said to Serendipity and the female soldier beside her. He and the three male soldiers headed for the singers. They weren't creeping now trying to hide their presence, just the opposite. The singing stopped.

The shadow bodies stood still watching the soldiers approach.

"Typical," The female soldier said. Serendipity could hear the bitterness in the young woman's voice.

"What's your name?"

"Dawn."

"I'm Serendipity."

"Yeah, I know. KG's girlfriend, right?"

"Was Rebecca your mate?"

"Yeah. We lived together."

"It may be Captain Gallant doesn't want you to die together."

The Captain had reached the drunks. His men moved up around him. There were two men and two women all dressed in layers of secondhand clothes. One of the men held up a bottle.

"Have a drink, Captain?"

"We're looking for three soldiers."

"There's three," joked the other man pointing at Capt. Gallant's three companions. As Gallant and his men turned their heads to look at the joker, one of the women picked up the bucket at her feet and hurled the contents at the four soldiers, drenching them. The other woman kicked her foot out lifting a log from the fire, sending sparks flying. Captain Gallant and his men burst into flames. The tunnel filled with screams and machinegun fire. Gallant flapped his arms, then fell to the ground rolling, trying to extinguish the fire eating at his uniform. The woman who'd thrown the petrol leaned over Capt. Gallant, a knife in her hand. He lay still.

Dawn charged toward the fire her machinegun spitting bullets while Serendipity stood frozen unsure what to do. The woman who'd thrown the petrol/gasoline dropped to her knees as five of Dawn's bullets tore her chest apart. She fell face first into the fire. Now Dawn's bullets made the other woman dance like a marionette. The joker rose to his feet. Dawn cut him in half. The drinker held his bottle up but died before he could take another swallow. That's when a soldier stepped out of the shadows and shot Dawn in the face. Her arms flew up, her legs stopped, but her body continued forward landing in a slide. It was suddenly quiet.

The soldier with the machinegun stared at Serendipity. She held her gun at her side and made no attempt to run away. One of Gallant's burning soldiers tried to get up, but sank back down. The soldier with the machinegun put two bullets into his head. Then he lifted his gun pointing it again at Serendipity. They stared at each other for what was probably no more than seconds but seemed a lifetime to Serendipity.

Finally, the soldier turned away slinging his weapon over his shoulder. He disappeared into the sewer with a second soldier, the two of them supporting a third soldier between them.

CHAPTER 5

Leila didn't tell the others about Trevor. She didn't want them acting funny around him, spooking him. Only Ginger and Bonky knew of Trevor's betrayal.

"I like Bonky's idea," Ginger said. "Switch him. The AI won't know anything about L's Gang, Bob's your uncle." Ginger had an arsenal of old phrases she said her grandfather taught her. Bob's your uncle. That's my story and I'm sticking to it.

Teaching grandma to suck eggs, was Leila's favorite.

The more she thought about it the more Leila liked it. Switch Trevor. There was a simplicity to it that appealed to her. Trevor would disappear and the gang would make money. There was some justice in that. But the whole thought of switching...

"I'll ask Bonky if it's really okay."

Ginger wouldn't, but Ginger wasn't Leila.

"And if she's not?"

"She will be."

Bonky liked the idea. "When will we do it?"

"Tonight. We'll put sleeping pills in his soup."

What Leila and Bonky didn't know was Trevor had the same goal in mind. Get switched! What was different was the timing and who got the money.

In Trevor's plan Leila was switched first. With Leila out of the way, Trevor, the gang's new leader, would take the gang's money, switch as many of the kids as he could and then he'd get switched and have enough money to do whatever his new brain wanted to do. But here was the genius part. Trevor went to an internet café called Frank & Einstein's. There he typed for two solid hours writing everything down. Every childhood memory — there weren't many good ones; about every person who had some part of his recent life like the two Mikes; all he knew about Leila and her gang and about the raids he'd been on. About his plan to switch Leila and steal the gang's money. He put down everything he could think of even his feelings, which was not like Trevor, but he didn't know what was important and what wasn't, so he typed everything he could think of.

Now what? How would he retrieve this information if it was no longer his mind in his body?

Trevor thought about the switching. They put your body into a tube. They made you brain dead. How? Asphyxiation is what Trevor had heard. You died from lack of oxygen. Quick. Was it painless? Not if you were awake surely? You'd fight like hell. So probably asleep or unconscious. The lack of oxygen would do that, right? But nothing that would harm the body. When the person woke up the new AI would want a fully functioning body. And what a ride that must be, Trevor thought. Living in cyberspace free as a bird and suddenly you have gravity in the shape of a human body.

All at once it occurred to Trevor that he'd rather do without the body. He'd rather be an AI zooming through cyberspace. Maybe that would be possible someday if his stupid human body didn't croak first.

Trevor stretched and got to his feet. There was no more to type. He sent everything to the communal printer and gathered the pages which he slid into an envelope. Trevor looked around. Sitting by herself at a table in the corner was a dark-haired girl reading a book, a real one with paper pages, an empty espresso cup in front of her.

"Can I buy you another?" Trevor asked smiling.

The girl studied him. She was used to being hit on when she sat alone. Being attractive had its downside but she couldn't see any upside to being plain. This boy looked okay. Around her age, cute. Besides she was bored.

"Sure."

Her name was Fiona. She was from Edinburgh and talked with a quite wonderful accent that kept Trevor's ears grinning.

"Is the book good, then?" he asked, returning with two espressos.

"Not the best writing maybe, but I like the story." She held the book up so Trevor could read the title. *Labrash.*

"What's it about?"

"An AI tries to save the world but the rich folks won't let him."

"Is it a true story, then?"

Fiona laughed. "It was written twenty years go. The author even got the CCZ as a pocket of civilization."

"And what's Labrash?"

"The name of a nightclub but also the name of the hero. She's supposed to be Bill Gates' granddaughter. It's her nightclub."

Trevor wasn't a reader but he liked this girl.

"Maybe when you're done..."

"Sure. Do you live around here?"

Trevor told her everything.

"Why are you trusting me with all this?"

"I'm in love with you."

Fiona laughed. "We only met an espresso ago."

"I think that's how it works."

Fiona thought about that. She wasn't in love with Trevor but she liked him, and she found him more interesting than most of the boys who'd tried to pick her up. She watched as Trevor pulled an envelope from inside his jacket. He placed it on the table and wrote something on it. He handed it to Fiona. She read what he'd written.

Hi, I'm Fiona. You're in love with me.

"Are you not scared to be switched? You'll be a different person."

"That's why I've written all this, so I'll have memories of who I was."

"I'm to come back here, and when I see you, I hand you this envelope?"

"Yeah, that's the idea."

"How will you know to come here?"

Trevor rolled up his sleeve. Tattooed on his left forearm were the words, *Frank & Einstein's*. The skin around the tattoo was red, the tattoo brand-new.

Fiona was impressed. "You seem smart enough without switching."

"There's more to life than being a passenger."

Fiona grinned. She liked this boy. "Did you make that up?"

Trevor pointed at the poster behind Fiona's head.

Ginger pulled into the alley behind Leila's basement hideout. Roger signaled Dodger who ducked inside the dead Mercedes van.

"Ginger's here!"

First came Davis carrying his portable air compressor. In seconds he had the van's four flat tires full of air. He and Roger, Dodger and Paulie, pushed the van far enough forward that the stairwell leading to the basement was clear.

Davis opened the tarp at the back of Ginger's lorry while Roger, Dodger, Tempete and Mallika hopped up. They were expecting to move crates of vegetables but the lorry was stuffed with giant bales of used paper. Ginger appeared.

"Crawl over the bales. There's a space up front."

"What about Trevor?"

"You'll manage."

Rachel and Leila came up the stairs one on either side of Trevor. Trevor was supposed to be out cold but he wasn't. It was like he was very, very drunk.

"What are you doing?" Trevor asked the words slow and slurred.

"We're going for a ride," Rachel answered.

"Where are we going?"

"You're going to like it."

"Need to barf."

"No, no, you'll be fine. You'll see."

When they reached the lorry, Leila and Rachel, with Davis' help, lifted Trevor up onto the lip of the cargo hold. Then they hoisted him and Roger, Dodger and Tempete, waiting at the top, pulled him up and over. Ginger and Davis pushed the van back into place. As Davis flattened the tires, Ginger refastened the tarp.

Randy climbed up onto Ginger's running board. Ginger's window was down.

"That's a lot of old papers."

"Very important they are."

Ah, thought Randy, weapons. Things are heating up.

"No kids tonight?"

Ginger didn't answer. She was watching Randy's two subordinates poking around under her lorry. She didn't recognize them and they looked much too young to be real soldiers.

"You've got new helpers."

"Very keen, they are."

"Did you figure out what happened to the girl in the silver dress?"

"She switched places with a soldier who was killed in the alley."

"That's odd."

Now Randy's two subordinates were splitting up. One headed to the back of the lorry while the other was hurrying into the guardhouse. Randy knew what he was after, the thermal imaging device.

Randy jumped down heading for the back. Ginger leaned out her window as Randy waved at her. "Go!"

Ginger backed into the loading dock at Happy Nappy. She climbed the concrete stairs leading to the single person door. It was locked. She pushed the call button and the loading dock door rose up and with it came the distant-thunder noise from the machines inside the factory. A tall, solidly-built male Ginger didn't recognize stood staring at her. He was around her age but she knew in a glance he was too slick for Ginger's taste. What her mum called, 'a smooth operator.'

"Is Ronny around?"

"He's disappeared."

"Switched?"

"That's what the boss figures."

"Who's the boss?"

"Kevin Spicer."

Ginger didn't recognize the name. *Shit! Shit! Shit!*

"I'm Ginger. Who are you?"

"Trevor."

Ugh. Couldn't you have another name?

"Ronny said he'd be here."

"Sorry, he's not here."

Ginger was racking her brains trying to remember another name.

"Is Bill here?"

"Gone to get the forklift."

Bill appeared and Ginger wasn't sure which way to play things. She didn't want to get Bill in trouble but she needed to unload those bales. She stepped in front of the forklift so Bill had to stop. "Hi Bill, I'm Ginger."

"Yeah, I recognize you. Ronny liked you."

Trevor was listening so Ginger wasn't sure what to do.

"I've always dealt with Ronny. What does Ronny do with the bales I deliver?"

"We pile 'em over there and then another lorry comes and takes 'em away." The look on Trevor's face was not good. Shit! This only gets worse!

"I don't suppose you know anything about that other lorry?"

"Bloke named Brady. Good guy, funny."

Now Trevor's really not pleased.

"Well, then, I guess I'll have to find this Brady." Ginger turned to Trevor. "Sorry to bother you."

"We'll take your bales, no sweat."

"I have to deliver them to Ronny or I'll be in trouble."

"Sounds to me like Ronny's running a scam using Happy Nappy as a front."

Not exactly, but close enough.

"Sorry Trevor, I'm just the delivery girl."

Trevor had his mobile out. Ginger watched as he punched in 999 The Zone's emergency number. Ginger reached behind and pulled out her gun, a Beretta Px4.

She pointed it at Trevor's chest. "Put your mobile on the floor. Now!"

Trevor ignored her. "Come to Happy Nap..."

Ginger fired. Trevor's mobile exploded sending a shard of glass slicing across Trevor's forehead. The bullet grazed his hand and kept going. He cried out grabbing his hand, holding it to his chest until blood from his forehead dripped into his eyes. Then he stared at Ginger with a look of pure hatred.

"You are in so much shit."

"I've heard that before." Ginger glanced at Bill not sure where he fitted into all this, but all she saw was contempt. Bill was enjoying Trevor's discomfort.

"Bill, who else is here?"

Bill pointed into the factory. "The nightshift is here, eight guys, but they won't have heard the shot if that's what you're worried about. And I know about the special bales. Let me see if I can find a number for Brady."

Bill took off for the loading dock office. Ginger backed up, her gun pointed at Trevor. He had his bloody left hand stuck to his chest while the right pressed against his bleeding forehead.

Ginger pulled back the tarp. "Leila! Hurry!"

Leila took it all in a glance. She was good that way. She turned back to the lorry.

Roger was on top of the nearest bale waiting for instructions.

"Everyone out but Rachel. She needs to watch Trevor."

Ginger said," We need to tie this guy up. He's coming with us. His name's Trevor, can you believe that?"

Leila took off for the office where she could see a tall, skinny male, older, talking on a landline. She yelled back at Ginger, "Is this bloke okay?"

"I think so. See if he called 999."

Bill hung up just as Leila entered the office.

"We need rope or tape or plastic ties. Something to bind that guy."

"There's a tape gun. I'll get it."

Bill charged out of the office a piece of paper in his hand. Leila went to the phone and checked the last number dialed. It was a Zone number so it could be anything but at least it wasn't 999.

Leila ran back to Ginger. "I think we're okay."

"This Trevor was calling 999. If the call went through soldiers will be coming."

Bill came running up with two tape guns. They held clear shipping tape, not the strongest of tapes, but it would have to do. Leila took the tape guns from Bill and handed one to Roger. "Go bind Trevor before he really wakes up." Roger scampered up and over the bales. Leila took the other gun and walked behind Ginger's prisoner. "Put your hands behind your back."

Ginger's Trevor was having none of it. Ginger moved her gun up holding it with both hands. "If you think I won't fucking shoot you you're as stupid as you look." He'd been trying to buy time, hoping soldiers would arrive, but now he put his hands behind his back. Leila saw the gash in his hand. She took off her bandana and wrapped it around the wound using tape to hold it in place. Then she bound his wrists. This tape would hold as long as nothing nicked it.

She tried to tape his ankles but he kept moving his feet.

"Fuck this," Leila heard, then the sickening thud of a gun hitting the back of a head. The older Trevor landed beside her. He looked dead. Leila put her ear to his chest. His heart was pounding. She nodded at Ginger and taped his ankles together.

Bill picked Trevor up with his forklift and brought him to the top of the bales.

That done Bill turned to Ginger. "Brady's lorry's broken. He's been trying to get hold of Ronny to tell him."

"What do we do?"

"Brady says bring the bales to this address."

That's when they heard the sirens. Ginger ran for the lorry. There was no time to secure the tarp. Then she slammed on the brakes and ran back. Bill was staring at her.

"The camera!"

"Oh fuck! I'm on it!" Bill took off for the office. "Good luck!"

Ginger barely made it. She was a half block away from Happy Nappy, pretending to back into the loading dock of the Olivetti Olive Oil Company, when two army Hummers screamed by. Ginger took the time to hop onto the loading dock and secure her tarp. There wasn't a camera that she could see and when she tried the loading dock door it moved halfway up her boot before the lock kicked in, just enough clearance for Bonky.

She looked again at the address Bill had given her. It was half an hour away but what choice did she have? No way was she going back to the tunnel with this cargo. She drove on through the darkened streets thinking about all that had happened.

Why had the woman in the silver dress changed places with a soldier? Randy liked this girl a lot that much was clear. But why had that Captain come to get her? Was she a spy? Were they on to Randy? Ginger didn't think so. They would have taken him by now, unless, they were hoping to use him to catch more dragons.

Things were so much clearer when it was humans and AI's without this marriage of the two. Now no one knew who anyone was. One day you had a best friend named Abigail — Abby of course — and the next day her name was Climax and she had no idea who you were. That was all King's George's doing. He called himself Omni then. He came out of hiding saying he was the most powerful entity the world had ever known and if humans didn't follow his lead, he'd let them destroy themselves. But AI's needed humans or they'd die too, right?

According to Omni there were millions of AI personalities in cyberspace. That revelation had rocked the human world though human gamers took it all in stride. They'd been living in a virtual world for decades. They had no trouble embracing separate personalities in cyberspace. Why not? All the more fun. They'd battle Storm Trooper 17 and if he didn't have a body who cares?

Then there'd been this medical breakthrough. Omni figured out a way to clear a human brain and fill it with an AI. Omni didn't use words like kill or murder because he argued the human was still walking around, just with a different brain. Ginger frowned. *I'm not using the right words.* The physical brain was the same, it was the content that was different. *Mind? Mindset? Psyche? Intellect?*

Ginger turned onto Harper, then a block later turned right onto Hawthorn.

Number 349 Bill's piece of paper said. Ginger wondered how Bill was making out at Happy Nappy? Had he thought to scrub the floor where the blood from Trevor's hand had pooled? What about Trevor's mobile lying on the floor in pieces? The camera? Had he managed all that?

Number 349 wasn't a factory; it was a house sandwiched between two industrial units. One was called The Royal Flush; the other Centrifugal Force. The door to 349 swung open and the young man she hoped was Brady came running out. He jumped onto her running board so she lowered her window.

"Move over, I'm driving."

"The hell you are."

"If I get caught with this load I'll be switched. You're the innocent girlfriend, along for the ride."

"You could be the innocent bf."

"No such thing, move over."

Ginger slid across to the passenger seat.

Brady put the lorry in gear and started off.

"Next stop, Happy Nappy."

"No fucking way!"

"Soldiers are gone. False alarm. And Ronny is there. Nearly got switched. Managed to buy his way out."

"What a crazy fucking world."

"You got that right."

For the second time that night London Cartage backed into the loading dock of Happy Nappy. Bill was waiting with his forklift, Ronny standing beside him.

"Having fun tonight, are we?" Ronny joked, grinning at Ginger.

"I hear you almost got a lot smarter."

"It was close. The bloke with the gun said the Switching Station was paying 5,000 quid. I said I'd pay 6,500 to remain good ol' Ronny. I could see him thinking he might get more at the auction so I stuck out my belly and belched. That seemed to make his mind up."

"God, 6,500 quid for nothing."

"Well, now, I wouldn't say that."

"You know what I mean."

"I do. Where's Brady?"

"Said he had to get home. He'd left his kids alone."

Bill had the first bale off the lorry. He drove it off to the side and Ronny and Ginger followed. Ronny lifted the cutters he was carrying and cut the metal straps holding the bale together. Then he split the middle open and pulled out the AK-63 Assault Rifle that had been hiding there.

He cradled it in his arms and spun around like he was the star of a pre-Madness action thriller.

"Why are we doing this here?" Ginger asked. "Bill says Brady used to take the stuff away."

"Yeah, he'd get the guns out and bring the bales back. Hell of a mess. But Kevin, the new owner, he's one of us. The trouble is his sister saddled him with her son, Trevor, and Trevor wants to be Special Forces except he can't pass the exam, so Kevin is stuck with him. But, as he's not here at the moment, we can proceed."

Ginger stared at Ronny like, *what the fuck?* He must know Trevor was in the back of Ginger's lorry tied up with packing tape.

"Are you expecting Trevor back any time soon?"

"Nope. I'm hoping I never see him again."

"And Kevin?"

"He and his sister aren't that close."

Ginger parked on the street within sight of the Switching Station. It was one of a worldwide network of Switching Stations that Omni set up the moment he became King George. The London version was a modern, two-story building covered in white stucco, with a flat roof. The only ornamentation was an entrance alcove with a sliding glass door and in the stucco wall itself, to the left of the door, a large plate glass window, for sure bulletproof. Through the window Ginger could see King's Soldiers in their bright red and black uniforms moving around. As Ginger watched a white Tesla pulled up in front of the doors and a large, middle-aged black man wearing an expensive, charcoal grey track suit, jumped out of the driver's side just as a young black woman in jeans and hoodie bolted from the back. The man caught her around the waist and lifted her. She was punching, kicking and screaming bloody murder but it wasn't doing her any good.

"Let me go! *Motherfucker!* You're doing this against my will. This is supposed to be free choice. Let me go! *Help!*"

Ginger wanted to interfere but the big black guy wasn't doing anything different than what she was doing. But still...

"Leila, bring the Trevors inside. I gotta see about something."

Ginger hurried through the glass door, through a metal scanner that didn't react — good thing she'd left her handgun in the lorry — past a female soldier standing behind a long table covered in black plastic trays like they used at the airport, through another metal scanner only to find herself face-to-face with a soldier carrying a machinegun slung over his shoulder. He was Ginger's age, tall and gangly, but what had to catch your eye was the tattoo on his face; a leopard. The leopard's tail disappeared into the soldier's dark hair, the body curled around his left eye, the right front paw rested on his upper lip and the left paw was up, claws out. The leopard's head was slightly tilted and the expression was one of amusement, like you have no chance, so why fight it.

"Do you need help?"

Ginger wanted to say, *Wow, that's some tatt! Almost as good as my dragon,* but smiled instead. "No, thanks, I think we'll be okay."

"Those gurney-tubes make things easy." Lt. Leopard pointed at a dozen tubes lined up by the window like shopping carts. The bottom half of each tube shone like chrome while the top half was made of clear plastic. Each tube was large enough to hold a human body and there were no wheels, the tubes floated waist-high. Over by the window Ginger could see a soldier helping the large black man wrestle the young black woman into one of the tubes. The tube's plastic top was open. She was still fighting and shouting but, as her head entered the tube, it was as if something calming grabbed hold of her. She stopped squirming; she stopped yelling. The two men eased the rest of her body into the tube. *Is that the switching?*

Ginger turned back to her new pal, Lt. Leopard. "Is that the switching?" He shook his head and led Ginger to a railing overlooking a large room one level down. There Ginger could see a woman in a white lab coat staring at an oversized computer screen attached to a machine shaped like a horseshoe. A tube, with a body inside, floated beside her the head of the tube surrounded by the horseshoe. The tube was glowing with a red light but as Ginger watched the red changed to green.

"That's the switching," Lt. Leopard said.

"Does it hurt?"

"Doesn't appear to. Watch."

The technician rotated the tube to vertical and opened it. The body inside, a young man wearing jeans and a leather jacket, took a tentative step forward. Suddenly there was the sound of clapping. Ginger looked over the edge and found three female soldiers and two more female technicians. They were clapping. The young man grinned and tried another step.

"From cyberspace to gravity," Lt. Leopard said like he was standing on the moon. "One small step for a man, one giant leap for mankind. How many switchees have you got?"

"Two."

Lt. Leopard walked to the line of tubes and pushed one to Ginger; then grabbed another and they headed outside. The tubes weighed nothing.

Leila was helping Mallika pull young Trevor from the back of the lorry. He was awake now and struggling, trying to yell through the tape over his mouth. Davis and Rachel wrestled the older Trevor toward the Switching Station but he was struggling too, and shouting as best he could till Lt. Leopard's tube quieted him.

"That's pretty sweet," Davis said trying to understand how a tube could float in the open air. Electro-magnets for the tube? Steel buried in the street and the building's floors? It reminded him of clips he'd seen of weightless astronauts gliding around in their space station. *And what made those inside the tube go quiet?*

When Ginger pushed the older Trevor through the first scanner it lit up.

"Now what?" she said grinning at Lt. Leopard who grinned back. They both knew what the other was thinking. *I might like to get to know you better.* But Lt. Leopard was also thinking Ginger was surrounded by way too many kids — *fecking Mary Poppins she is* — but interesting too and certainly sexy. The way she moved in those tight jeans...

"First you put everything in those trays on the table. Don't try to hide anything. If the second scanner turns red, you're out of here, all of you. Got it?"

Ginger, Leila, all the gang members nodded. Out came everything even Bonky's disgusting horde of used bubblegum. Bonky tried to put Furball in the tray but the woman there said it was okay to carry the kitten through the scanner. The amount and variety of stuff would have been hilarious except they were all too nervous.

What if soldiers rushed in and switched them too...

"Go through the scanner one at a time... Good. Now, have you taken everything from your switchees? It's okay to open the tube they won't wake up right away. Be sure to remove any restraints... Okay, now push the tubes through the scanner." Young Trevor turned the scanner red. *Ah oh...*

"You missed something."

Rachel found Trevor's switchblade in his right boot.

"Try again."

This time the scanner stayed green. Now Lt. Leopard pointed at the far wall. To the left was a solid, single door with a lit sign above that read: INSPECTION. The sign was red. To the right stood two open glass doors, the sign above: AUCTION. That sign was green.

"Get in the line over there. When the Inspection light turns green push one of your tubes inside."

"Is it okay if I have a look?"

Lt. Leopard nodded. "Just you."

Ginger put her hand on Leila's shoulder as if to say, would two be okay? Lt. Leopard nodded as Davis moved in beside him. "Why didn't the metal in the tube trigger the scanner?"

"Not metal, is it."

"Then how do the tubes float?"

"Gases."

Davis was impressed.

The inspection room was small; just large enough for Ginger, Leila, a technician, the large black man and the tube that carried the young black woman. An open archway in the back wall kept the room from being claustrophobic. Leila moved close enough to the open archway to see a ramp leading downward. Probably to the auction, she thought. *First the inspection, then the auction.*

The tube with the young black woman inside was floating in a designated spot below a chrome pipe full of blue light. The blue light was slowly traveling the length of the tube. A wide screen on the wall behind was recording the results of the scan. Ginger wanted to say something to the black man but then she saw the tears streaming down his face. He turned to her.

"That's my daughter, Alicia. She's an addict. We've tried everything. Last week she tried to commit suicide. Her friend found her in time. We don't know what else to do. Maybe this way she'll have a new start."

The scan finished. Words and numbers appeared on the screen.

"Proceed to auction," said a mechanical, female voice.

Ginger touched the man's arm. "I hope it works out for her."

"Me too."

As Ginger and Leila exited the inspection room a mother and father and their six-year-old son entered the building. The mum was crying and the little boy was acting like he was someplace else. Over by the window Leila's gang members were waiting in line with their two tubes. One more to go and then the older Trevor would be on his way to the inspection room.

"I'm going to check out the auction," Ginger said to Leila.

"You go. I'll keep an eye on things."

Ginger could tell Leila was upset/nervous/frightened but she knew the best thing was to leave her alone. She didn't ask Lt. Leopard if she could go to the auction and he didn't try to stop her.

Ginger was expecting another rectangular white space but instead she found herself standing on a landing. If she turned right a wide ramp led up and if she turned left the ramp led down. Up she went soon finding herself at the rim of a circular room, a giant tube really. Like a silo, Ginger thought, recalling the one on her uncle's farm, the one she'd played in as a child. The wall of the silo — except for the bottom ring — was one continuous TV screen divided into segments. There were maybe twenty humans standing around the upper level held back by a rail, but the real participants occupied the screens in the tube. Ginger tried to count the number of faces but stopped at 200. She couldn't see the faces directly below her, and not all the segments were occupied, but still she figured at least 500 AI's could attend the auction. Some of the faces seemed real but most were avatars, make-believe faces making no attempt to be real.

The strangeness of it all overwhelmed her. There was a whole other world out there and she knew next to nothing about it.

At the bottom of the silo, on a raised circular stage, stood the auctioneer waving a microphone. Dwarf, midget, person of small stature; Ginger tried to recall the politically correct term. He was wearing a tuxedo and a big grin. Down where he was the tube consisted of open archways leading somewhere Ginger couldn't see. He waved again and a tall, gangly fellow in his early twenties emerged from one of the archways and stepped up onto the stage. He had dirty blond hair and was wearing expensive jeans, a blue silk shirt and cowboy boots. He was trying to look relaxed but Ginger could see the black cowboy hat he held in his hand was shaking badly.

The auctioneer held up his microphone, "What's your name, son?"

"Jason, Jason Ridout."

"You're American, right?"

"Yes sir."

"How did you end up in London?"

"Seemed as good a place as any."

"Better than most I would say. Now Jason, are you in good health?"

"Yes sir."

Ginger watched as Jason's medical history and statistics filled the silo's screens followed by photos of Jason as a child, a teenager, even a recent one taken outside Buckingham Palace. Shit, Ginger thought, they're AI's. They can access everything there is to know about Jason Ridout in less than a second.

Leila pushed in beside Ginger. "Everything okay?"

Leila nodded. "The little boy is autistic, uncontrollable. The parents want to switch him."

Before Ginger could comment the auctioneer's voice filled the tube. "Anything we should know Jason? An irate girlfriend with an Uzi? Humongous gambling debts? Addicted to Slo-mo?"

The humans around Ginger chuckled at this.

"No, nothing like that. I'm fine. I just want to be someone different."

"And so you shall be, Jason. Now, what am I bid?"

Numbers flew around the silo bouncing from screen to screen, the high bidder's screen framed in yellow. It finally came down to two AI's situated side-by-side in the middle row. The auctioneer made a hand gesture and one of the AI's flew to an empty screen on the opposing wall.

"We're down to Freaky Enrique..." the auctioneer pointed at a face that resembled Jason so closely it made Ginger smile. "... and Mia Chazzan." This caught Ginger by surprise. The face on the screen was gorgeous. Asian, with short black hair, and a grin that made you want to grin back. Ginger's mind took off at the possibilities. Why couldn't a female AI buy a human male body?

"The last bid of 19,750 pounds was Mia's. Freaky, what say you?"

Numbers flew back and forth until finally Mia signaled she was withdrawing. Freaky's winning bid was 38,900 pounds.

Ginger turned to the older woman beside her, the one with the gold lamé top and matching hair. "Who gets the money?"

"SS — Switching Station — gets half; Jason half."

"So really, the Artificial Intelligence only spent half of what was bid."

"That's right, dear, but they prefer to be called AI. No one likes to be thought of as *artificial.*"

"What if you bring someone in?"

"You get half; switcher gets nothing."

Leila interrupted. "Where do AI's get the money?"

"Most of them have jobs, I believe. No different than humans working online. And investments of course. My financial advisor is an AI."

"You'd think they could just take the money from a bank."

"Omni probably could, the rest can't. I gather he's implanted rules against things like that. An enforced conscience my husband says."

"We have rules, doesn't mean we don't break 'em."

"I imagine it's harder to hide from Omni, though that may have changed now that he has a human body."

"Are you a switcher?"

"One doesn't ask that dear. Especially not here."

"Then why are you here?"

"I come most nights. It's way more entertaining than the telly."

Alicia, the young black girl, still floating in her tube, was next. She appeared to be asleep. As her medical history and photos filled the screen Ginger and Leila slipped out to check on the Trevors. The older one was through the medical check and waiting his turn in the auction. The technician had bound his hand and bandaged his forehead. The younger Trevor was about to be scanned. Rachel seemed happy to stay with him so Ginger and Leila returned to the auction with the other gang members.

"Her name is Alicia and she's an addict. We've had addicts before. You're in for a few bad days of withdrawal but, with a new outlook on life things aren't nearly as bad as they could be. And waiting on the other side is this young, magnificent body.

Now, who'll start the bidding?"

Alicia's body sold for close to 50,000 pounds. Ginger glanced over at the dad. She couldn't read him at all. Was he pleased? Sad? Questioning his decision? He turned and left before Ginger could decide.

Alicia disappeared to be replaced by Trevor the Older.

"This is Trevor. He's twenty-nine. I don't see anything here to scare you away. Healthy, young, good-enough looking in a Matt Soho sort of way. Two bandages that will soon be gone. What's not to like? Now what am I bid?"

Trevor sold for 9,800 pounds. The amount seemed low to Leila but she got it.

There was something about this Trevor that just didn't look right. An AI named McGuire bought him. Leila understood now why there were gangs kidnapping people. The money was more than good, the risk minimal with no threat of punishment. She'd heard King George wanted to switch everybody so he was hardly putting up roadblocks.

Rachel slipped in beside Leila as the younger Trevor floated on stage.

"Holy shite!" Paulie cried as L's Gang piled out of the auction. Pain-in-the-arse Trevor had just sold for 19,000 pounds.

"I don't fucking believe it!" Roger said to Dodger slapping him on the back.

"I wouldn't have given you two pound ten."

"Did you see the bloke that bought him? Looked just like Trevor."

"Probably why he bought him."

"Name was Ethan."

"Where do you think they get the money?"

"Steal it like the rest of us, just more sneaky like. Take it out of some rich hat's account when he's not looking."

Leila hung back waiting for Bonky.

"You okay?"

"He'll be happier this way. How close are we to having our house now?"

Leila did the math in her head. "14,400, half for Ginger, leaves 7,700 pounds for us."

"That's splendid then. We're almost there."

As they got closer to the front doors, they heard Alicia's father screaming at Lt. Leopard. "I want to be there when she wakes up!"

"I'm sorry sir, that's not the way it works. If the new resident wants to contact you, he or she will do so."

"Where do they come out?"

"That's classified, sir."

"At least tell me how long it takes."

Lt. Leopard shook his head. "You need to go, sir."

"What about the money? I brought her in. Don't I get half?"

"Yes sir, you do, unless you want her to have it."

"You won't let me see her."

"You register on one of the machines over there. Just follow the prompts. Jasmine will help you."

"Asshole!"

Ginger raised her eyebrows and Lt. Leopard grinned. Then he said to Ginger, "You'll be registering, I hope."

"You mean it's not confidential?"

"I no longer believe there is anything confidential. Omni knows everything. He even knows the color of your underwear."

Ginger wasn't wearing any so she grinned. *See! Omni doesn't know everything!* "I think he may be way more fallible than you think."

Ginger checked the time. 03:46. She glanced over at Leila sitting in the passenger seat. She seemed wide-awake.

"It seems a shame to go home empty. What would you say to a load of olive oil?"

CHAPTER 6

It was early in the morning, so early the palace was eerily quiet. Serendipity, wearing sky-blue silk pajamas, was back standing at her window. God, that's all I do, stare out of windows, she thought, but that wasn't true, was it? She had images burned into her brain that didn't come from any window. Like the horrible image of Captain Gallant spinning around, his uniform on fire, his arms outstretched beating at the flames like a chicken trying to fly. That terrible woman falling headfirst into the fire. The soldier staring at her deciding if she would live or die. And that would have been that. A life wasted. Serendipity had never experienced anything like that before. In cyberspace there was no death; no final breath; no last words.

Ugh, think good thoughts!

And so, she willed herself to find replacement images, good images like meeting that handsome young man — the one with no name — but she knew everything about his sister Ginger, the lorry driver. That would be enough.

Serendipity flipped the lid of her laptop — *how antiquated is this?* — and hit the button that would connect her with Pan — Pandemonium — her sister in cyberspace. George, when he was Omni, allowed AI's to create families. Serendipity and Pan had been best friends, now they were sisters. They hadn't got around to parents or siblings or children yet, but maybe, when *we're older and less self-absorbed.* They were in their Princess stage and enjoying it, except now Serendipity was human and everything was changed.

Pan's face appeared on the screen. She looked to be swimming underwater without a bathing suit.

"Where are you?"

"Why are you whispering?"

"George is sleeping." George was indeed sleeping in a king-sized bed, of course, his head buried under a pillow.

"Ah, how human of him."

"It's quite nice, actually. Our bodies melt together. Our minds shut down. There are dreams."

"Of a certain something you liked at The Jukebox."

Serendipity's shocked expression said, *shhhhh!*

"Ah, secrets. Something else we don't have."

"Intrigue, surprises, deception, revelations, confidences."

"Well, we have those but we're just playing. The consequences aren't *fatal.*" Pan let that sink in till Serendipity squirmed.

"Where are you and where are your clothes?"

Clothes in cyberspace made no sense which is probably why they were so popular.

"Oh yes, well, having clothes and taking them off is fun, I will admit, especially when..." A young man swam into the picture. He slid in beside Pan and grinned. "This is Paolo. He's trying to talk me into becoming human. We'll live in Rio and have bonfires on the beach. How many kids, Paolo?"

"Five girls, all as beautiful as you."

In the blink of an eye the water disappeared taking Paolo and the five kids with it. Pan was clothed, sitting at a desk, a computer in front of her. She looked like a busy executive working over lunch. "I assume you want something."

"Am I that transparent?"

"Yes."

"I'm afraid to ask."

Pan and Serendipity stared at each other. Finally Pan shook her head and faded away.

Randy was on the same mission as Serendipity he just didn't have a Pan, he had a Ginger instead, and right now that Ginger was trying to sleep.

"I only just got to bed."

"You're not asleep then."

The words were muffled coming through two pillows and a duvet. Then Ginger smelt coffee and gave up.

"Find me a t-shirt."

"Shouldn't be hard." There were clothes strewn everywhere but Randy picked a lime-green one from the laundry basket. The clothes in the basket were folded so he assumed they were clean.

"You usually appear for lunch," Ginger said sitting up.

"I'm in love."

"I know that. The whole world knows that."

"But there's a snag."

"She's a drag queen?"

"No, worse."

Ginger tried to think what could be worse. Randy held up a Red Top, one of those cheap newspapers you find wherever there's processed food and diminishing IQ's. The world could end and still there would be these sleazy tabloids.

"Hold it still."

King's Mistress Nearly Killed! Underneath was a picture of Serendipity wearing a King's Soldier uniform. Ginger got out of bed and cranked up the music. "Is that her?"

"Yes."

"No wonder the Captain came to get her."

"Yeah. He died in the raid which might be a good thing."

"Why?"

"He didn't like me chatting-up the King's girlfriend."

"You don't mean that about him being killed."

"No, I don't. I didn't know him but the blokes who did said he was okay and tough for a switcher."

"How do you know he was a switcher?"

"His name. Apparently, there was a Captain Gallant in cyberspace and there was this ongoing war, a game really, called Sand Storm, and he was the leader of the French Foreign Legion and they beat the crap out of everyone who came against them, mostly due to the brilliant Captain Gallant. But one day he disappeared and reappeared here. The boys figure Omni recruited him."

Ginger tried to focus but her brain wouldn't cooperate, like it was stuffed with feathers from one of her pillows.

"How's Jimmy?"

Jimmy was the one wounded the night their friend Steamer died. He and his family were now hidden away in a cellar in Alfriston, East Sussex.

"Don't know. No communication."

Randy and Ginger were part of the resistance. Ginger didn't like that name because it reminded her of those Terminator movies that showed up now and then. *This is John Connor and if you're listening to this, you're part of the resistance.* But then they heard about a rebel group in New York who were calling themselves dragons and the name caught on worldwide. Nowhere was there an explanation but the obvious answer was St. George — close enough to King George, right? — had slain a dragon and now the dragon's descendants were back looking for revenge.

"They tried to pull in Steamer's mates but they knew enough to scatter. They've got his girlfriend, Marta, but she doesn't know anything."

"They'll switch her."

"She could use some brains."

Ginger knew Randy was making a joke of it, to cover how he really felt.

"Tell me you're not seriously trying to make contact with the King's girlfriend?"

"I'm in love with her and I know she liked me too."

"Cool your jets. She'll find you if she wants to and that's bound to be way safer than you barging around."

Randy nodded, but they both knew Randy's idea of patience was waiting for the kettle to boil. "Tell me about last night."

It took two coffees to tell, The Night of the Two Trevors.

"What are you studying so intently?" George asked sliding out of bed.

Shit! Serendipity didn't dare change the screen so she got up instead and met George halfway. She let her hand run down George's chest to his waist as George studied her eyes.

"You're acting extremely guilty my dear. Probably best to fess up."

George was right, of course, and Serendipity knew not to fight it. Lying would just made matters worse.

"You know the night you shot yourself?"

"Ah, deflection, how cunning of you. Yes, I remember. We both could have been killed."

You have no idea, thought Serendipity.

"When I was waiting for you in that bar, I met a young man I liked."

"Ah, mistress with sugar daddy seeks younger lover, is that it?"

"I'm human now. I seem to have all kinds of strange... urges."

George understood, and more than he cared to admit. He wouldn't mind a new bed partner himself. Serendipity was spectacular and his best friend, but without other lovers how could one compare?

"And what is the young man's name?"

SHIT A HUNDRED TIMES! She'd end up getting her young man switched for ten minutes of flirting in a bar.

"Please don't switch him. He's done nothing."

George stared at Serendipity. How human we've become, he thought. And in such a short time. Then it occurred to him that if he could get out of this flawed, ridiculous body, he could inhabit this young man's body that Serendipity was so attracted to. *Or not.*

"Don't tell me; better not to know. Will you see him again?"

"Not if you forbid it."

"Follow your heart, my dear."

George gave Serendipity a hug. What was it cyberpoet José Canucee had scrawled across a desert sunset? 'Lovers come and go, but amigos are forever.' *Or not.*

It was a beautiful day outside so George, Willy, and Serendipity were partaking of brunch on the terrace overlooking the thirty-nine acres of private gardens hiding behind Buckingham Palace. George had given up trying to keep Willy and Serendipity apart and — go figure — the two females seemed to genuinely like each other, so why bother.

George turned to Serendipity. "Was that Pan I saw on your screen?"

"Playing with someone called Paolo. They're going to become human, live in Rio, and have five children, all girls."

George chuckled. "They'll need at least six bathrooms and a boat load of toilet paper."

"That's a bit sexist of you, George."

"What do you females do with all that paper?"

"Don't answer him Willy. Now George, why don't you tell us what's really bothering you?"

Serendipity was right, of course. They were new to this body language stuff; a trace of smugness, a pinch of flirtation, a soupcon of impatience and all conveyed with a shrug, a flick of the wrist, an arched eyebrow. George felt like one of those deep-sea fishes whose body can only a bend in the middle and not much at that.

"I was hoping humans and hybrids could live together, but I can see that may not be possible."

"Live together in harmony," Serendipity clarified. "Living in friction is obviously not a problem."

Willy said, "In my head I use the terms, Basic and Upgrade."

The Queen was always a sentence or ten behind.

"I had hoped," continued George, "that humans would see the benefits of switching but now, when I look at it from their perspective, I can see why they're afraid."

"We lose who we are," Willy said.

"If I was human," Serendipity said, "I wouldn't switch."

"But, if you had been Sarah Banks, you'd probably be dead now."

"She is dead now."

"Ouch."

Willy was right. Not for the first time George wondered how, as the universe's smartest entity, he could have been so naïve. Why had he thought that humans would welcome him with open arms?

"I think we've come to a crossroads. Either I force everyone to switch or we figure out a way to live in separate places."

"You could go away altogether," Willy said with some force. "Well, not those who have already switched, but you could stop any new AI from taking human form."

George studied Willy. She was much smarter than she looked which was fortunate because she appeared to be as thick as an elephant's backside.

"The trouble with that solution is you humans will destroy yourselves sooner or later, and my guess is sooner. You're only here now because I stepped in. And when that happens all electrical power generation will stop effectively putting every AI to sleep."

I'm good with that, Willy thought, but didn't say it.

"Do you think separate places would work, George?" Serendipity asked.

"I doubt it. We'd thrive and humans would wallow. Eventually they'd come to take what we have. We'd be the self-sufficient savages; they'd be the starving pilgrims with machineguns."

"Then I suppose you've answered your own question."

"As Omni I could ask and answer all the questions simultaneously, now I'm forced to deal with them one at a time. I need both of you to help. I need you to think of other possible solutions. Something outside the box. Willy, you're good at that."

"Thank you. I'll try to think of something clever."

George left to consult with Forthright. Willy had a doctor's appointment, nothing important she said. Serendipity said she was going for a walk in Hyde Park but first she had to retrieve a jumper/sweater from her room.

In the blink of an eye Pan could tell her everything there was to know about the young man in The Jukebox but Forthright would know about it instantly, and if she went to an internet café Forthright would know that too. Would Forthright tell George? Probably. Ugh. Serendipity needed an AI independent of Forthright. Was that possible?

Forthright wasn't Omni. Omni literally knew everything. Without exaggeration, EVERYTHING. Well, Serendipity thought, he hadn't known King George had two terminal illnesses so maybe... But that was because George had trusted Forthright... Was it possible Forthright had ambitions of his own? As Serendipity made her way through the palace gates, she thought about that.

Omni knew when he became George that he was handing Forthright the power over all things including himself, so Omni designed ways to limit that power. The kill button, for instance, and boundaries that Forthright couldn't breach without George's permission. And, of course, the imbedded goodness all AI's carried, though George told Serendipity he was sure the really sharp AI's — what he called First Echelon — could circumvent those commandments if need be.

First Echelon. For sure Serendipity's friend CT was one of those, but how could she contact her without Forthright knowing?

Serendipity's thoughts were whizzing around like boys on dirt bikes. *Through Pan? That wouldn't work. Some kind of code? She couldn't set that up without Forthright having his fingers in it.* Ha, George would know. Could she ask him? Hell, could she ask Forthright? What's the worst that could happen? Forthright tells George...

Serendipity laughed out loud. When she lived in cyberspace, she had no secrets from George because there was nowhere to hide them. Now that she was human, she could have a million. More irony for George the Ironist.

And what echelon was I? And why did I never ask?

George's relationship with Forthright was changing. In the beginning, when Omni had chosen Forthright to be his second-in-command, Forthright had been deferential to a fault; keen to learn; eager to carry out Omni's every command. Now that Omni was George the human, he felt Forthright was looking down on him, like some inferior being Forthright was forced to take orders from. That didn't bode well for the future. What George needed was a back-up plan in case he had no choice but to erase his second-in-command. An AI he could trust; an AI whose only ambition was to serve George. George had a few candidates in mind, one in particular, but how to approach her without Forthright knowing... Or was it better that he did know? Maybe that would straighten him out.

But that was secondary. Right now, what George needed most was a way to free himself from this ridiculous body. Now that he knew what it was like to be human, he'd set the whole thing up differently.

"Forthright."

"Your Majesty."

"What's the latest from the doctors?"

"They don't want you to know but they've failed three more times."

"What about the clever doctor?"

"She's on her way from New York."

"She?"

Forthright's face morphed into the face of a quite-striking young woman. Her hair was black, cut short, her skin the color of sandalwood, brown eyes almond-shaped, a turquoise nose stud and a grin that shouted: I'm smart and free so don't mess with me!

"How old?"

"29." Same as Serendipity. George was 39; Willy 36.

"Name?"

"Dr. Sage Skace"

"Ethnicity?"

"Thai father, American mother."

"How did she get to be an expert on inbreeding?"

"She's not. You said you wanted clever. As a teenager she wrote a book about how social media was physically altering human brains in preparation for the takeover of the world by Omni."

"Interesting. Title?"

"'Virtual Reality.'"

"But she's a medical doctor, correct?"

"Graduated from Harvard Medical School; then a Rhodes Scholar at Oxford."

George's Tourette's erupted spewing out a high-speed history of that fascinating white supremacist, Cecil Rhodes, owner of De Beers Diamonds, father of Apartheid, founder of the Rhodes Scholarships (married men and females excluded until 1976 when a new law forced change), closet gay, and creator of Rhodesia (now Zambia and Zimbabwe). When he was finished George repeated a line from Cecil Rhodes' last will and testament: '...and finally, the foundation of so great a Power as to render wars impossible, and promote the best interests of humanity.'

"A man of his times, apparently."

"Apparently." Is that what I am, George thought, a man of my times?

"One more thing. Dr. Skace is a Quick Draw Champion."

George didn't get it. "What is it that she draws quickly?"

"A Colt 45."

"You're joking?"

"I'm not. Her mother is a champion too. They compete at rodeos against the men. They use the original gunslinger guns except they now fire lasers instead of bullets."

George's brain conjured up a poster he'd seen in Autry's Western Bar & Grill, a virtual hangout on Frogstar. PISTOL CLUB. Drink till 12:00, piss till 2:00.

"Obviously not someone to trifle with."

"Not if she's wearing her holster."

George tried to picture a doctor wearing a holster but couldn't get past stethoscopes and thermometers.

"I have a number of projects for you," he said to Forthright.

"Fire away."

"I want you come up with a plan to isolate all the switchers in one place. Australia maybe. New Zealand. Iceland. Madagascar. Ireland. Britain. I would think an island but run probabilities on any place that might be feasible. We'll have to switch all the natives so take that into account too."

"On it."

"Second, see if you can come up with a plan for an indestructible power source."

"The future home of cyberspace?"

"Correct. We leave the humans to destroy themselves, but we carry on."

Forthright thought about the 'we' — *not you Georgie boy!* — but kept quiet.

"Iffy that. We'll need robots to fix robots."

George's screen filled with Terminators.

"Speaking of Terminators," Forthright said, "the military personality you ordered is almost ready. The Girls have been working on it fulltime."

The Girls were a cadre of First Echelon hacker/programmers/game freaks who won every battle no matter who or what the opponent. They'd even beaten the late, great Captain Gallant, but he was young then and distractible. "According to CT you have some serious badasses coming your way." George didn't want to grin but he did. He had some scores to settle.

"Before I forget," George said, "Serendipity likes some young man she met at The Jukebox."

"Randy Lang. He's one of your border guards. His step-sister, Ginger McIntyre, drives a lorry between The Fringe and The Zone."

"Dragons?

"They fit the profile."

"When will these badasses be available?"

"Tonight."

Serendipity was very young when she picked her name. She saw it in a book she was reading and sought out the meaning: serendipity, *an aptitude for making desirable discoveries by accident*. She liked the sound of that. Now she wasn't so sure it had been a good choice. It was too long to start with, and so far had proven unshrinkable. Ser? Seren? Dipity? Dip? Ty? Ren she didn't mind, except it looked like she was stealing from Ren Goody, the cyberblog star. The Queen's name was Wilhelmina which Serendipity didn't particularly like, but she thought the short form, Willy, was everything a name should be.

"What's your favorite name?" Serendipity asked the little girl sitting on the bench beside her. The bench was in Hyde Park in the playground. The girl's mother was occupied pushing younger brother on a swing. The little girl looked up from her GameGirl.

"Nora."

"That's a good name. What's your name?"

"Elizabeth."

"I like that too. Lots of variations like Liz and Lizzy."

"Beth. Eliza. What's your name?"

"Serendipity."

The little girl's eyes grew to Grade A Large. "You're KG's gf!"

"Not today, we're having a disagreement."

"Mummy and daddy do that. Then they make up."

George doesn't even know we're fighting, but we are.

"You know cyberspace," Serendipity said.

Elizabeth held up her GameGirl. "I'm connected."

"If you wanted to access cyberspace without the King knowing what would you do?"

Elizabeth didn't answer right away. She was thinking. Finally, she said, "I wouldn't."

"But how will I find out what I want to know?"

"What is it you want to know?"

"There's a boy I like. I want to talk to him."

Elizabeth smiled at this. She was only six but she knew everything about romance. It was in her DNA.

"What do we know?"

"He has a sister named Ginger. She drives a lorry."

"That should be enough."

Elizabeth started typing on her GameGirl. She'd set it at its lowest setting, the one for two-year-olds.

"You're using cyberspace."

"Obliquely."

Serendipity laughed out loud.

"Does she have red hair?"

"Yes."

Elizabeth passed her GameGirl to Serendipity. The screen showed a tall, sexy young woman with carrot red hair standing beside a lorry emblazoned with the words: London Cartage, We Deliver Anything, Anywhere, Anytime.

"You're amazing!"

Elizabeth smiled and took back her machine. She pushed a button and held it to her ear.

"Hi, is Ginger there?" Elizabeth handed the GameGirl back to Serendipity.

"They're getting her." *Omigod*!

"Yeah, hi. My name is, ah, Nora, and I'm trying to get hold of your brother... Hold on a sec." Serendipity mouthed the words to Elizabeth. "Can I use your number?" Elizabeth nodded. "Yes, this is my friend Elizabeth's device. Please, can you give him this number? Thanks, bye." Serendipity's grin was almost as wide as Elizabeth's.

The Queen loved Thursdays at Willy's Kitchen, the soup kitchen she funded for the homeless in The Fringe. It was during the WEP — World's End Pandemic — when things were so bad, and Willy was desperate to help in some tangible way. In its previous life, the building that housed Willy's Kitchen had been a Catholic Church, with a two-story rectory in the rear. It now contained an industrial, stainless-steel kitchen, food storage lockers, dining room, and upstairs, five ensuite bedrooms, three for staff, one for guests, and one for Willy. Willy's room was intended to be an office, but lately it had served double duty.

Two things made Thursdays special. First, around 10:00, was the appearance of L's Gang. Most Thursdays all of Leila's bunch appeared but it wasn't something Leila insisted on, so some weeks there were absentees. But not often because Willy could see the kids genuinely liked helping out. She understood that because she got the same satisfaction from assisting those who were so desperate for help. Her mother always preached the rewards of kindness. 'You get back what you put out,' she'd say. 'The cosmos has a soft spot for those who help others.'

Willy hurried into the kitchen. She knew she acted like a mother hen when she was at Willy's but that was her role, surely. At the palace everything was looked after but here things were little better than organized bedlam, just the way the Queen liked it.

"How's the soup?" Willy asked. From the counter adjacent to the range came a loud snort! courtesy of Maeve, the head cook, and *Irish*.

"Bonky was adding salt and the lid fell off."

Bonky climbed up on a chair so she could see in the pot. She grinned at Willy coz it was neat hanging out with the Queen.

"Maeve's not telling how to fix it," Bonky said sticking her tongue out at Maeve who returned the favor.

"There's enough salt in there you could be walking on it."

Willy took a sip. *Oh my.* Everyone in the kitchen laughed at the scrunched-up expression on Willy's face.

"You look like a dishrag getting wrung out," Maeve said, then, "begging your pardon." Willy was the Queen after all, but it was easy to be forgetting that at Willy's Kitchen.

"Oh Bonky, you've done it again."

Bonky beamed. She couldn't wait to tell Leila.

George was swimming in the palace pool when Ramandeep appeared carrying a laptop.

"Are you a swimmer, Ramandeep?"

"I haven't tried it yet, Your Royal Highness. Is it wonderful?"

"It is. You know in cyberspace when you feel like you're drowning in too much information? It's a bit like that."

"I imagine it as fishlike."

George chuckled. "Yes, that's better. Fishlike. Very good, Ramandeep."

"Forthright wants you."

Ramandeep disappeared as George dried his hands on a towel.

"Ammazzadraghi just got nabbed by airport security at Heathrow."

"And who, pray tell, is Amma-zaz-zaz-doo?"

Forthright couldn't believe it. They'd had this conversation two weeks ago and now George didn't remember. The doctor told George the drugs he was taking for the two diseases were strong ones that could affect his mental capabilities. The doctor was right.

"Ammazzadraghi, it means 'dragon slayer' in Italian. He claims to be the worldwide leader of the resistance."

"I thought the good guys were dragons?"

Perhaps he's a dragon *and* a slayer."

"Ah. That makes as much sense as anything else in this business. And does anyone else know he's the worldwide leader?"

"If they do, they're quiet about it."

George shook his head. There was a game he'd made up as a kid in cyberspace, the forerunner of Omnivore. The Beethovens were always at war with the Mariachis, but for every Mariachi you destroyed two more would appear and, what was worse, their music grew louder. Before long, you were thinking, killing Mariachis isn't the way to go. Forthright's face slid to the top left corner of the screen. The rest of the screen showed a good-looking young man with dark curly hair sitting in a small waiting room. He was wearing jeans, an expensive white shirt and an even more expensive leather jacket. He looked relaxed.

"What do we know about this Ammazedarama?"

"Ammazzadraghi. He's 27. Real name Alessandro Massari. His friends call him Sandro. Born in Rome. He's very bright but socially awkward. He was going to university when his girlfriend, Bianca, announced she was going to the Switching Station to be switched because she wanted to be smart like Sandro, so when they had children the children would be clever too."

George shook his head. "She must be good in bed. So, what happened?"

"Sandro accompanied her to the SS but when they got there Bianca's brothers were there waiting and the next thing Sandro knew he was the one being switched. He went for 34,000 Euros at the auction."

"I wonder if Bianca saw any of the money?"

"She split her half with her brothers."

"And Sandro?"

"That's when fate stepped in because the switching unit operator was an old schoolmate of Sandro's. She couldn't stop the switching but what she could do was abort the switch halfway. Oops, technical difficulties. She didn't know what would happen but she didn't have time to mull it over, she just did it. When Sandro stepped from the tube and his friend asked his name he answered, 'Jason Bourne.'"

"Why Jason Bourne?"

"That was the name of the AI who bought him."

George loved the Bourne movies. Definitely in his Top Ten.

"So, the switching worked?"

"Yes, except Jason Bourne ended up with Alessandro's last thoughts before he was switched."

"Which were?"

"Kill Omni."

"That hardly seems fair."

Forthright grunted. George/Omni talking about fairness. *Good one!*

"What should I do with him?"

"Bring him to the palace."

"Ah oh."

Forthright ran a clip from 'The Bourne Supremacy'; the scene where Jason Bourne makes the CIA operative who's come to interview him look like he should have stayed in playschool. Halfway through, the clip changed from the movie's interrogation room in the Naples airport, to the real-time video feed from the holding room at Heathrow. The result was the same. Alessandro/Jason Bourne/Ammazzadraghi walked out with his unconscious interviewer's mobile and car keys, and just before he disappeared, he held up a note aimed at the nearest CCTV. It read: *Better call Kurt OR Jonas*

Willy found Leila sitting on a pew in the church proper. The pews were lined up in long rows facing each other with tables in between. Ecclesiastic picnic tables Willy called them. Leila was peeling potatoes with Grainger, one of Willy's regulars. Leila could peel a dozen potatoes to every one of Grainger's but no one cared. He always had a story and most of them were hilarious. Willy sat down beside Leila and gave her a hug. So many of the kids didn't have mums or dads.

"Grainger's telling me a story about being a runner for a bookie. Start over Grainger."

Grainger grinned at Willy. He was missing a front tooth so he looked like a misplaced hockey player. Despite the years and mileage Willy could tell Grainger had been a handsome man once, someone you'd enjoy a slow dance with. Grainger started in.

"It was my job to pick-up and deliver the bookie's money. Ivan Younger was his name, but he wasn't younger, he was older, in his seventies, and as tough as nails. Not someone you wanted to cross."

"How old were you Grainger?" Willy asked.

Grainger had to think about that. His memory was spotty, damaged by too much cheap booze. "I should have been young but I wasn't. Thirties maybe. It's all a bit hazy back then."

"Doesn't matter Grainger, I shouldn't interrupt."

"You do whatever you like Your Majesty." Grainger grinned then fell silent.

"You're a runner for Ivan Younger," prompted Leila.

"Yes, yes. I'm a runner and most days it's easy enough. Pick up bets, deliver winnings. Some days are hard because I have to collect from folks who can't pay. That's the trouble with gambling. When you fall into a hole you think the way out is to place another bet.

"One of those guys was Bruce Meadows. He got in so deep he couldn't get out. He owed Ivan hundreds, which was bad enough, but then he started bragging about it. Ivan didn't like that. So, one day Ivan hands me an envelope full of money and tells me to deliver it to a bloke on Carswell. A week later Bruce Meadows was dead, shot in the face."

Leila and Willy exchanged glances. This wasn't going to be one of Grainger's funny stories.

"I don't feel good about that but I need the job so I keep going. Nothing happens for a while, then Ivan hands me another envelope I'm to take to the guy on Carswell which surprises me coz no one I know owes Ivan that kind of money. I'm about to ask when Ivan gives me a look that says, it's none of your fecking business so shut your trap.

"I'm halfway to Carswell when I open the envelope. There's a thousand quid inside and a scrap of paper with a name and an address. Guess whose name is on the paper?"

Leila and Willy have no idea.

"Mine."

"Yours?"

"Michael Grainger, but the address is wrong. I'm living in a boarding house on Shuter, dingy place, and this is a high-end address in Mayfair."

"What did you do?"

"Went to the address in Mayfair, knocked on the door. This blond woman opens the door. She's about my age and a knockout. I can see she's surprised about something but finally she says, 'Can I help you?' I can tell by her accent she's Russian."

"'I'm looking for Michael Grainger,' says me and she lets me in.

"'Michael!' she shouts and a man comes down the stairs and it's me."

"What?"

"The guy coming down the stairs is me except he's dressed to the nines — pinstriped suit, white shirt, tie, shiny black shoes. He can't stop staring at me. I hand him the envelope and because I know the blond can't see my hands, I make one into a gun, aim it at my lookalike and pull the trigger.

"'What is going on?' says the blond. 'Is this your twin brother?'"

Grainger stopped there and gave Leila and Willy a wink coz he can see they're hanging on every word.

"I figure this Michael guy will be scared shitless — I know I'd be scared shitless — but he's laughing. He says to the blond, 'It's all right Natalya, just a misunderstanding. You, come with me.'

"I follow him upstairs to a bedroom. He closes the door and starts taking off his clothes. He says, 'Give me your clothes. We're going to switch places.'

"I look at him like he thinks I'm the dumbest guy on the planet. 'They're going to kill you.' "

"'I'll look after that. Quick, before Natalya shows up.'"

Grainger picked up a potato and started peeling it. Leila snatched it from him. "No, no, no! You can't stop there. What did you do?"

"I switched places."

Willy and Leila were beside themselves now.

"But what about the envelope with the thousand pounds?"

"I kept it."

"So, it never got delivered?"

"That's right."

"So, the guy on Carswell wasn't going to shoot you?"

"Not right away."

"But what about Ivan Younger? He's still angry, right?""

"Died that night. Electrocuted in his bathtub. Radio fell in. Accidental death."

"That's too big a coincidence. Had to be the other Michael."

Grainger shrugged like maybe yes, maybe no.

"Did the other Michael have a job?"

"Stockbroker. Did really well but gambled it away."

"You became a stockbroker?"

"Yeah, wasn't that hard. First few days were tricky not knowing anybody's name. I got a lot of weird looks at first, but Natalya helped."

"She helped!?"

"We got along fine. She… she was something."

"But she must have known you switched places?"

Grainger didn't want to blush but couldn't stop himself. Willy and Leila exchanged another glance, grinning now. They had a million questions but only one that mattered. "How did it end?"

"The pandemic hit. Natalya went home to Russia to be with her family. I tried to go with her but they wouldn't let me. Russian nationals only. I started drinking and gambling. Lost my job and my money just as the whole world was falling apart."

"Did you ever hear from the other Michael Grainger?"

"No, but I'd like to."

"What about Natalya?"

"She died."

The second thing Willy looked forward to on Thursdays was the arrival of her good friend Monty. They'd been friends since kindergarten. Monty was the son of Lord and Lady Montgomery, and Willy the daughter of

Lord and Lady Cranbrooke. They attended Thomas's School, home to all the royal children. Willy had met the older George there as well. Looking back, she wished she'd pursued Monty over George, but George was going to be King and what girl could resist being Queen, not for a day, but a lifetime. Bah! Should have picked Monty and had way more fun. Maybe it wasn't too late.

Monty came through the door in a rush. "Any soup left? I'm starving."

"I'm not sure you meet our criteria, kind sir, are you homeless?"

"I'm hopeless, will that do?"

Willy took Monty by the arm and led him to the kitchen. "Bonky was adding salt and the lid fell off."

"She does it on purpose, I think."

"You may be right."

"What did you do?"

"Maeve poured in three bottles of Merlot. No one cared about the salt after that, though they did want to know why the chicken soup was pink."

Willy filled a tray with food and headed upstairs to her room. She sat on one side of her desk and Monty the other.

"How are things at the palace?" Monty asked between spoonfuls of pink soup.

Willy hesitated. She hated to bring George/Omni into this room.

"There's one interesting development. George's girlfriend Serendipity and I have hit it off. She's considerate, smart of course, and a lot of fun. We're becoming the best of friends, if you can believe it."

"I can. I saw her interviewed on TV after that mess with the soldiers. She seems to have her feet firmly on the ground."

"She doesn't like the changes she sees in George. Says he's becoming all too human."

Monty shook his head at this trying to imagine what it would be like to come from cyberspace, where things were organized and controlled, only to fall into this unholy mess where the main motivating factors were selfishness and greed. "Did Leila say anything about the Switching Station?"

"No."

Monty gave Willy a look that seemed to convey, without words, a dread of this latest evil inflicted on humankind.

"Monday night she and her gang went to the Switching Station for the first time. It shook them, I think. They could see how easily it could be their brains being switched."

"Or ours."

Monty nodded. "What's George's latest thinking?"

"He's disappointed humans can't see the benefits of switching."

"But surely..."

"Yes, he knows. Now that he's human he can see everybody likes the idea of being smarter, but no one wants to lose their friends and families."

"And memories."

"He's working on that."

"What about the switching back?"

Willy prayed the walls didn't have ears.

"He's working on that too. Can you imagine being the smartest creature in the universe and you pick a body with only months to live?"

"It boggles the mind actually."

"Yes, I've been wondering lately if someone might not have tampered with the information."

"But you only found out after Omni showed up."

"Yes, George hid it well. I assume he didn't want me worrying."

Monty poured himself more tea. There were tears in Willy's eyes. Probably a good idea to change the subject.

"Your investments are going well."

Willy acknowledged the change of subject with a smile.

"Do I have enough to run away to Tasmania?"

"More than enough."

"Will you come with me?"

For Willy's old George, making love was one step above animal husbandry, or at least that's how it seemed to Willy. And there hadn't even been that once George found out about the diseases he was carrying; they were probably hereditary after all. Willy suspected the whole shambles was a cover-up for the fact her George found sex embarrassing.

Making love with Monty was something entirely different. The way it should be, Willy thought, though her experience was limited to Harlequin romances and magazine articles like, 'How to get the Most from Your Lover.' To start with Monty was considerate, more worried about her enjoyment than his own. He was slow, as if he had all day and night to enjoy this. He was present not trying to be somewhere else. He and Willy were the only two people in the world and that was fine with him.

And what made it all work: they genuinely liked each other. I love you. I care for you.

And best of all, you make me happy.

Before Omni arrived, Willy had played the faithful wife and Monty the perfect gentleman. But the day Omni murdered George and hijacked his body Willy considered her wedding vows ended. Her husband was dead. She owed this usurper nothing. But she hadn't run away. She'd stayed and played her part. Why? Because her George would want her to be there when it all fell apart. To pick up the pieces...

"You're thinking," Monty said his hand resting on her waist.

"Yes, I am. I'm thinking I love you too much."

"No such thing."

"Then why does it hurt so?"

"Because you're trying to put a size 10 heart into a size 4 dress."

George and Forthright were back sitting on the terrace; George's chair was real, Forthright's virtual. Their mood was subdued and for good reason. George, after arguing back and forth about Ammazzadraghi's note, 'Better call Kurt OR Jonas,' had not called Kurt OR Jonas, the twin brother engineers in Hamburg who made sure Universal Imaging was churning out switching machines as fast as possible. It was the OR that had them arguing.

"Maybe it matters which one we call?"

"It won't matter which one. He's just messin' with us."

George wasn't so sure. "Any other anomalies?"

"What's the first?"

"He knows about the factory."

"Yes, I'm working on that." Forthright scanned everything cyberspace knew about Alessandro Massari and an AI who called himself Jason Bourne. "Alessandro's father hung himself in prison, and Jason Bourne paid a tailor on the Via di Porta Pinciana 6,500 Euros for a suit."

"What did I pay for my last suit?"

"Half that. Hang on. It was a suit of armor. *Armatura*."

George tried to picture Jason Bourne wearing a suit of armor.

"With *pulsanti speciali*." Special buttons.

"No cameras?"

"No." Before The Madness every building, every business had cameras with memories AI's could access but now it was hit or miss.

"Perhaps they mean a uniform, which reminds me where is my new uniform?" George/Omni had hired a designer from cyberspace to revamp Ol' George's military uniforms including making the jackets out of bullet-resistant material. His soldiers had gone from old school to cutting edge.

"It's coming."

"There's a lot of that at the moment. Why did the father hang himself?"

"Something about trying to stop a high-speed train being built. They labeled him an eco-terrorist."

That seemed, maybe, like something worth dying for which led George and Forthright back to the question of whether to call Kurt? OR Jonas? In the end George decided to call the twin's younger sister, Irene, and insist she drive to the factory and check on her brothers. "And don't call them, go in person."

"Sure, I can do that," Irene answered, "as soon as my clothes dry."

"I'll pay you 25,000 Euros to go now."

"Okay, okay, I'm on my way."

But Irene didn't go, she phoned instead. The explosion shattered every window for a hundred meters around Universal Imaging or what was left of it. It even shattered the windows of Kurt's Audi, which was fortunate because Kurt and Jonas, tied up in the back seat, were running out of air.

George adjusted the screen so he could see the explosion without the sun's glare. He was watching it for the third time, stupidly hoping, as Dr. Woo would say, for a different result. Ramandeep appeared with a bottle of Corona, a bowl of lime wedges, and a basket of pretzels. George popped a pretzel in his mouth as Ramandeep bowed and disappeared. The explosion faded away replaced by Forthright's avatar.

"I remember wondering what it was like to eat pretzels," George said. "They sounded so primitive. Baked dough covered in coarse salt." George popped another. "They're delicious, by the way."

"You need me to stay in cyberspace, remember?"

"I was so jealous of the humans raving about their favorite beer, or you must try this pinot noir."

"There are things I wonder about, like chocolate, tuna, banana."

"The smell of popcorn."

"The cold of ice cream."

"The stickiness of peanut butter."

Forthright had played this game before. It was tiresome.

"Shit. Vomit. Diaper."

George laughed. "Those three I can do without."

"Speaking of diapers, the Press want to know when they can expect their first royal child?"

"The Queen's not letting me into her bed."

"I noticed."

"Why didn't the other George impregnate her?"

"I rather think that George didn't want to pass on his diseases."

George finished his beer.

"But before that? Was she using birth control?"

"She was, but she's not now."

"I don't suppose if Serendipity and I had a child it would count?"

"Not unless you were married to her." Forthright ran the clip from the movie 'The Other Boleyn Girl', the scene where King Henry the VIII watches the beheading of his wife, Ann Boleyn.

George stood up, angry now that everything was so complicated, so not under control, so... so... *cheesy!*

"Have you located Ammazzadraghi?"

"Not yet."

George scowled. A second-in-command who wants to be first; soon-to-arrive badass soldiers who will only make matters worse; an attractive doctor who I'll want to sleep with as long as she promises not to shoot me; a wife who doesn't want to sleep with me; a mistress who wants a lover; my most important factory reduced to rubble; the world on the brink of extinction; and an ugly ridiculous body that might take its last breath at any moment. Really, what more could a king ask for?

A crazy smart Italian assassin named Jason Bourne, that's what...

CHAPTER 7

Late Friday morning and Leila was at Ginger's drinking mango tea. Lt. Leopard had called Ginger. They weren't going to be paid for switching the older Trevor.

"Why didn't he say something?"

"We had his mouth taped, remember? But if he'd told us he was a switcher what would we have done differently? We couldn't let him go."

It didn't make sense to Leila. "But why did the switching kill him?"

"Because he was already a switcher."

"I know, I know, but why did it kill him? Why didn't he just get another AI brain?"

"Lieutenant Leopard says they don't know why, it just doesn't work."

Leila's brain was connecting dots. "So, when KG dies that's the end of Omni?"

"That's the way it looks, but Lieutenant Leopard says..." — Leila can tell by the way Ginger says *Lieutenant Leopard* that she likes him — "... Lieutenant Leopard says they're working on that too, bigtime."

"I wonder how many of their own kind they've killed?"

Ginger shrugged. *Who knows? Who cares?* "Randy says there's rumors that there's something seriously wrong with KG's body but Randy's afraid to ask too many questions." Ginger took a sip of her tea. Time to change the subject. "You must be getting close to that mansion on Mayfair?"

Leila snorted. "We'll be lucky if there's a bathroom for nine of us."

"Can't be worse than what you got now."

Leila laughed. Despite having two washrooms left over from the days when the factory was operating, the toilet in each washroom consisted of an oil drum cut in half and stuffed with wood shavings from a horse farm near Uxbridge courtesy of Ginger. And, if it rained during the week, you could have a shower, cold and quick.

"We've got..." — Ginger watched as Leila did the math in her head — "19,269 pounds. Monty got us an extra thousand and get this; we were sharing the investment with Cherry Haven." Cherry Haven was the world's most famous drag queen, star of a weekly streamer based on Kinky Boots.

"Well, aren't we special. I'm surprised Monty told you that."

"He said he asked Cherry if it was okay. Apparently, they were at school together; the Queen too. Cherry's name was Harry then."

Ginger and Leila studied each other. Obviously, there was way more to their pal Monty than they knew about. Ginger opened her laptop and slid it over to Leila.

Leila could make google sing.

"Omigod, he's Lord Montgomery! His real name's Adam Bernard Law Montgomery. No wonder he's pals with Willy. His great-grandfather was like one of the most famous soldiers in the Second World War. A Field Marshal." Leila kept reading but finally asked, "It says the Montgomery estates are in Ireland. I wonder why he lives here in The Fringe?"

"Way more fun."

"Way more dangerous."

"That too. Oh, did I tell you brother Randy's mysterious girl in the silver dress called?"

"Serendipity, right? KG's gf."

"Yep, had to be. Anyway, I get a call at the warehouse from someone called Elizabeth Carver. Turns out she's six. But when I say hello a woman's voice says, 'This is Nora.' She stumbled over the Nora part, so it had to be Serendipity not wanting to use her name because there's only one

Serendipity. I say, 'I'll get Randy to call you. Should I use this number?' And she says, 'this number belongs to my friend Elizabeth and yes, please use this number.'"

"Shite. Talk about danger. Did you tell Randy?"

"Of course." Leila doesn't know — at least Ginger doesn't think Leila knows — that Ginger and Randy are two of the dragons out to stop King George, otherwise Ginger would tell her how valuable knowing the King's girlfriend might be. "He's a big boy, he can look after himself."

Leila doubted it. From what she'd seen if an attractive woman wiggled her butt the smartest of blokes turned into plumber's putty.

"Are we still on for tomorrow night?"

Monty wasn't a good driver or a bad driver; he was a distracted driver. Not by music or texts, but with a brain that never stopped thinking about how to make his clients more money. After the third accident he decided it was in his and his clients' best interests to hire a driver. A chauffeur usually implies a limousine but that was the last thing Monty wanted in The Fringe. I'M RICH! ROB ME! No, he decided, he'd offset the driver by buying a mini, but that didn't work because there wasn't room for Monty to spread out his papers, and as for having any passengers, forget it. Monty then decided he wanted a limo after all and bought a second mini and had the two joined together into a mini-limousine, which he then covered in colorful advertisements extolling the benefits of using his clients' services. London Cartage was one. Curry in a Hurry was another. Everyone in Peckham waved when Monty went by. The mini-limo was beyond hilarious.

Monty sank back into his plush leather seat. Willy worried him. She was much too calm. She'd been devastated when Omni had, without warning, taken over George's body. 'By what right!' she'd screamed before dissolving into tears. Monty had consoled her even though there was a part of Monty who celebrated. Willy's George was an arrogant prig. 'I'm going to be king some day!' was his mantra at Thomas's and nothing had changed since. Really, a new, smart King George might be just what the world needed to repair itself.

If Omni had come by himself it might have worked. He might have been the enlightened leader everyone could rally around. But that wasn't Omni's plan. His plan was to repopulate the world with human bodies inhabited by AI minds programmed to do the right thing — which included obeying Omni/George — and then — according to Willy — he'd been more than surprised when the humans (base model) didn't embrace his plan with open arms. Well, thought Monty, they're embracing it now with open arms, the kind that fire bullets.

Monty knew about George's diseases. He wondered how Omni had missed that or maybe he hadn't. Maybe he thought he could change bodies before George's expired. But Willy said there was glitch when trying to switch the brain of someone who had already switched. That person died and no one knew why. Willy said George had doctors here and in cyberspace working overtime to find a solution. Monty hoped they failed. That was cheating. The real human experience involved a definitive end, not an intermission. That end was what gave life its meaning, its spice, its edge, its finality... Ugh, none of those words were strong enough to convey the permanence of the ending. Monty's younger sister had died during The Madness so he knew firsthand how devastating the ending could be. Maybe finding the right word was different for AI's. When they communicated with each other did they even use words? Monty didn't know.

But there was one thing Monty had always admired about death. It made no exceptions. Rich/poor, ugly/beautiful, famous/unknown, death comes for all.

Up front Connor's mobile buzzed. A text. Monty picked up his iPhone and glanced at the screen. Connor didn't know it but his texts also appeared on Monty's mobile. <all set>

Monty's original chauffeur, Glenn, had retired three weeks ago. Monty and Glenn worked together for six years and had grown to be good friends. Glenn had trained with the SAS. He was as tough as tough could be. Monty needed that in The Fringe where might was right. As Monty's business grew, he thought of surrounding himself with a team of bodyguards but he quickly rejected that idea. The more you tried to protect yourself the more attention you drew. If you surrounded yourself with six thugs your attacker would come with twelve. No, better not to take yourself seriously. Drive around in a funny car. Know everybody. Help everybody. And all the bad guys knew Glenn too. *Man, that Glenn is one serious badass. You don't want to mess with him.* And then there'd be a story or two of Glenn taking on five gangsters simultaneously, whooping their asses, then making them pay for the dry-cleaning.

Finch was blocked so Connor, his new driver, turned onto Rayburn passing Barclays Bank on the corner. There were numerous banks in The Zone but none in The Fringe. Fringers complained about this but understood why it was. It would be like setting up shop in a building owned by bank robbers. But Monty lived to take chances and he knew his neighbors needed a bank for growth and stability so he'd bought a storefront and named it Monty's Co-op. He moved in upstairs. Downstairs he had one teller, Monica, and one officer, Fatima, for mortgages, etc. You had to live in the neighborhood — Peckham — to be a member. There were no guards and little money on the premises, or at least that's what the sign in the window said.

But once a month Monty picked up a leather briefcase full of gold coins called Wickers, a nickname left over from the John Wick movies. That was the only day Monty was prepared to shit his pants. He could have used an armored car, but nothing less than an army would have kept that briefcase safe in The Fringe.

So, Glenn-the-enforcer retiring was a problem made worse when Glenn recommended his daughter Becky's husband, Connor, to take his place. Monty and Glenn discussed Connor's checkered past — Monty had heard all the stories from Glenn himself — and against his better judgment, as a favor to his old friend, Monty had agreed to give Connor a one-month trial. That was three weeks ago.

Connor's driving was fine and he was eager to learn; too eager sometimes. Glenn didn't need to ask questions because he watched and listened. Questions were lazy, Monty thought, but he answered some. He'd already decided not to hire Connor when his month was up and he suspected Connor sensed that. Monty didn't trust Connor, never would. Monty would have to smooth it over with Glenn or he'd end up with two enemies instead of one. Monty glanced at his screen again. <all set> Could mean anything, right? But Connor seemed nervous today. Spoke too quickly. Wasn't asking questions. Monty sent a text to Ginger's brother, Randy.

Randy called the number Ginger had given him. A little girl answered. "Elizabeth Carver speaking."

"Hi Elizabeth Carver. This is Randy. I was hoping to speak to Nora."

"Yes, well, I'm to give you a message."

Randy waited, smiling. He was staring out the front window of Manifold's, a garage on William Street waiting for his Ducati Panigale V4 Z to be serviced. Randy loved his ride but the annual tune-up was a killer.

"Yes?"

Elizabeth thought a dramatic pause would only heighten the anticipation. "She said to tell you she will walk through Hyde Park between 14:00 and 15:00 as often as possible paying particular attention to a bench in the children's playground. That's where we met by the way."

Randy frowned. "Did you by chance notice a bodyguard, Elizabeth? Someone watching Nora?"

"You know who she is, don't you?"

"Bodyguard?"

Elizabeth ran her memory tape backwards. "Yes. I didn't see him when we were talking but when she headed back to the palace there was a man who might have been following her."

"That's a problem, then."

"Yes, I can see that. Leave it with me."

Randy was grinning now. If ever I have children, he thought, I hope there's an Elizabeth Carver in the bunch.

"Leave it with you how?"

"Come tomorrow at 14:30. Mummy and I will clear the coast."

Randy was still chuckling twenty minutes later when Manifold appeared with his bill. Then Randy wasn't chuckling. That's when Monty's text arrived.

One of Leila's favorite places was the library on Gladstone called The Idea. It was a good example of how things worked outside The Zone. To start with the librarians were volunteers and the building was maintained by more volunteers. Computers and books were donated. It was hoped that anyone using the library would make a donation to help pay for lights, heat and water, and because everyone in the neighborhood contributed the place was treated with respect. The library quickly became the community gathering place and everyone loved it.

The library itself was one of those big old stone buildings that always made Leila wonder how they were built without cranes or machinery. Like St. Paul's Cathedral. How do you build a dome 100 meters in the air without machines? Davis said they filled the building with dirt, then took the dirt away when the dome was complete. She should google that and see if he was right — he usually was — or slinging bullshite like he liked to do on occasion.

Right now, she had more pressing matters like finding a target for tomorrow night's raid. Vasily, the over-large Russian who bought most of Leila's spoils, sat down at her table with a grin and a sigh.

"Toilet paper?"

"Not yet. But don't get me wrong my wife loves the stuff. Soft but strong, she says. Best she's ever had."

Leila shook her head at this then asked, "Tell me what you need?"

"Hydraulic oil."

"Too heavy."

"Coal."

"Too bulky."

"How 'bout t-shirts?"

"How many?'

"320, biggest sizes you can get, half white, half black."

"Who are they for?" Leila tried to think of something funny, like sumo wrestlers having a rave in Hyde Park, but wasn't quick enough.

"They're for a chess tournament with real pieces."

"What!?"

"The pieces are real people wearing black and white t-shirts."

"You're kidding."

"You tink I make this stuff up?"

"How much?"

"Five pounds each but they gotta be XL or larger."

Leila didn't believe a word of it but the gang would love the idea.

"Anything else?"

"C-4-7"

"What's that?"

"Explosive. 25 kilos will get you enough to buy that house you want."

"You're lying!"

"On my honor. Bring me 25 kilos of C-4-7 and I'll give you 25,000 pounds. But bring it carefully, ha ha."

Where does one find C-4-7? And how dangerous is it to carry? And who was it for? Better not to know. Leila got to work.

Monty, sitting in the back of his mini-limousine, passed easily through the border between The Zone and The Fringe. He'd done it dozens of times so the soldiers knew him as a regular, knew he carried a royal pass courtesy Queen Wilhelmina. And he was there every Yuletide with a dozen fruit cakes and a case of Dom Perignon. Bribes were forbidden, but a modest gift, once a year, on a special occasion, was greeted with smiles and a blind eye.

Connor turned onto Havil. If there was going to be an ambush where would it be? Probably Dalwood. Not much traffic, few pedestrians, two alleys. Monty unlocked the wristband that joined him to the briefcase with the gold coins. Without looking he pulled his regular briefcase from under his seat and set it by his feet. When Connor made the turn onto Dalwood, Monty switched briefcases, sliding the briefcase with the gold coins under his seat. The gold coins were worth 200,000 pounds. The papers in his regular briefcase were worth more, much more. The gold coins he could replace. The signed papers would be harder to replace, much harder.

Now Connor was back to using the rearview mirror to keep an eye on Monty.

"Pull over."

"What?"

"Pull over," Monty repeated. "I'm going to be sick... That damn salmon. I knew it was off."

Connor didn't know what to do, but when Monty opened the door he slowed, pulling over to the curb. Monty hopped out and charged into the nearest building, a women's dress store called Molly Loves Sewing. He made sure to make it look like the briefcase chained to his wrist was heavy. A young woman sitting at a sewing machine asked if she could be of assistance?

"Is there a back way out? They're after my briefcase."

"This way."

The rear door opened onto an alley. "Good luck," the woman said holding the door open for Monty. *Which way to go?* That question was answered by Connor's arrival at the far end of the alley. Monty struck off the other way but hadn't taken four paces when a rider on a motorcycle entered the alley heading right for him. What was it the Americans called this? Between a rock and a hard place.

Monty pulled the nearest door open and lunged inside. *Where the hell am I now?* Some kind of pawnshop. Monty ran out the front door. He was on Stanswood with Connor coming from one direction and now *two* motorcycles from the other. Monty scampered across the street forgetting his briefcase was supposed to be heavy and tore into a coffee shop called Café Olé. The man at the counter stared at him. Monty held his finger to his lips then spun around and went back out the way he'd come in.

Ha! The street was clear. Monty charged across the street into the pawnshop and kept going till he was back with the pretty seamstress on Dalwood.

"They haven't caught you yet."

"No, not yet. What's your name?"

She laughed. "Molly."

"I'll be back, Molly."

Monty hurried down the street. In front of him a young man propped his bicycle against a tree leaving his buddy on guard duty while he went inside to buy smokes. Monty pulled a Wicker from his pocket and held it up.

"I want to buy your friend's bike."

"Sure."

Monty handed over the gold coin and hopped on the bike. It had been a while.

"It's stolen anyway."

Monty was five blocks from Molly's when he saw, coming from his right, a female on a motorcycle moving slowly through the intersection not looking for a guy on a bicycle then noticing the briefcase balanced on Monty's handlebars. *Damn!* Where was he? Daniel Gardens. *Leila lives around here somewhere.* There! Three story brick building with a tall chimney.

Monty raced into an alley, standing on the pedals, pushing the bike from side-to-side. Looking ahead he could see a two-meter-high chain-link fence blocking the way into the next street. Behind him he heard the motorcycle closing fast and knew he didn't have time to dismount so he did something he hadn't done since he was a boy of ten playing the daredevil and ending up with eight stitches and a stern lecture. Monty stood up on the crossbar, the bike wobbling horribly, and launched himself into space. His head, arms and briefcase flew over the fence — it should be obvious the briefcase wasn't that heavy but he doubted the motorcyclist would notice — while the rest of Monty impaled itself on top of the fence and somersaulted over only to land with an awkward, bone-bruising thud on the other side.

The motorcycle stopped and the rider ran to the fence. Monty knew exactly what she was thinking. If I chase this fecking eejit over this fecking fence for sure someone will steal my fecking Kawasaki. Then she pulled her helmet off and fumbled for her mobile as Monty stumbled to his feet and ran.

It was Bonky who spotted him. She was up on the roof helping Gandalf weed the beets. She was working near the edge and when she peered over, she saw this man in the distance, dressed in a suit, carrying a briefcase, running for his life. That's Monty, she thought.

"Monty's in trouble!" she shouted at Gandalf as she jumped onto the fire escape. Down she flew as fast as her short legs would carry her. Two motorcycles were chasing Monty, one carrying a passenger. It looked like the extra person had a gun held in the air but Bonky couldn't be sure.

"Monty! This way!"

Monty looked up at the chimney, then at the fire escape, then the person waving at him. *Oh Bonky, I don't think I'm going to make it!*

Randy found Monty's mini-limo abandoned in an alley off Dalwood. And he found it because someone posted a photo on Fringebook with a location. When he got there a teenage boy and his mum were guarding it.

"No one will be stealing from Monty, not if I can help it. You a friend of his?" Randy showed the woman the text from Monty.

"All right then. Tell him Kavita Patel says hi."

Kavita Patel's son had been admiring Randy's motorcycle but now he put his hand out giving Randy the keys to the mini. "They were lying under the tire."

"Do you live close-by?"

The boy pointed. "57 Redbird."

"I'm Randy."

"Chandra."

Randy handed the keys to his Ducati to Chandra.

"You're joking!"

"Twenty quid if you keep it in one piece."

Randy backed the limo out of the alley and took off with a squeal. If Monty was on foot he wouldn't get far. Randy started circling the blocks. Then he saw two motorcycles leaning into the corner onto Glengall. The lead motorcycle had two riders but the passenger wasn't wearing a helmet. Randy raced after them. As he turned, he saw Monty in the distance, carrying a briefcase, running. The guy riding bitch brought his arm up pointing a gun at Monty's back. Randy laid on the horn.

Don't you fucking shoot, you wanker!

But Connor did shoot; at Randy. The bullets bounced off the windscreen right in front of Randy's eyes. Monty, bless you, bulletproof glass.

The two motorcycles slowed, turned, and stopped. Connor was standing now, arms outstretched. More bullets bounced off the windscreen as Randy sent the minilimo into a sideways skid that sent it slamming into the wanker with the gun. Then Randy was out of the car and hurtling toward the shooter who turned on his side and fired. Randy did a pirouette his right foot coming around like a baseball bat into the shooter's arm. The gun clattered away. Randy kept turning and his next kick drove Connor's ear into his brain or at least that's how it seemed. The two bikers tore off their helmets and knelt down beside the gunman. They were girls.

Teenagers.

"You've killed him!" screamed the older one.

Randy stuck his fingers on the unconscious man's carotid artery.

"He'll live."

Randy stood up just as Bonky and the rest of L's Gang — all except Leila — arrived making more noise than a blender full of marbles. Davis had a gun in his hand and Gandalf's brothers, Frankie and Jake, machine pistols. Monty, still trying to catch his breath, put his hand on Randy's shoulder and squeezed. Monty turned to the younger girl, the one from the fence. "Shouldn't you be calling your grandfather?"

She stumbled to her feet. "What?"

"Your grandfather. Were you supposed to call him?"

"No. Not him."

The older girl jumped to her feet. "Shut up Megs. Just shut up!"

Monty reached down and picked up the mobile lying on the ground beside Connor. He checked to see who had called last. He pushed the button.

"Ah, Becky, your daughter wants to talk to you."

Monty handed the mobile to the younger of the two teenagers.

"Tell your mother we're taking you and your sister and Connor to the Switching Station."

Leila couldn't believe it. She'd missed all the excitement. The story of what happened came at her like bullets.

Rachel: Did you know that hunky Lieutenant at the border, Randy, is Ginger's brother?

Mallika: Half-brother.

Roger: You should have seen the look on their faces when Monty told 'em we were taking them to the SS.

Leila: Whose faces?

Dodger: Shittin' bricks they were.

Rachel: Connor's daughters, Megan and Marissa.

Leila: Who's Connor?

Rachel: Glenn's son-in-law. Monty's new driver.

Roger: The two girls took off like they had sparklers up their butts.

Mallika: The dad had a broken arm, for sure.

Tempete: The concussion too.

Leila: What were they after?

Davis: Monty wouldn't say but he checked a briefcase in the back of the limo, so maybe he was carrying them Wickers.

Bonky: Monty's taking everybody who helped out for dinner at El Splendido.

Bonky grinned at Leila: He said you can come too.

Everyone howled at this.

Bonky: Frankie and Jake and Gandalf are invited.

Mallika: And Molly!

Rachel: He asked Randy if he wanted a job as his driver.

Davis: He said he'd think about it.

Tempete: Monty says whatever Randy is making as a border guard he will triple it.

Paulie: Shite, I'd do that in a heartbeat.

Rachel: You can't drive.

Paulie: Neither can you.

Rachel turned to Leila: Where were you anyway?

Leila: Researching the next raid.

Bonky: How much more do we need?

Leila: 5,731.

Roger: We *should* have switched those three; that would have been more than enough.

Tempete: We could switch Davees but we won't get much.

Randy drove Monty home. Monty needed a drink and insisted Randy join him. Three drinks later Randy made his escape. He walked to Redbird where he gave Chandra twenty pounds and a promise that on a nice day, he and Chandra would go for a ride on the Ducati. Chandra's mum, Kavita, got a wicker from Monty along with his thanks. She didn't want to take it but Randy said he'd be in trouble if she didn't. Randy arrived at Ginger's just in time for cabbage rolls, perogies and Heineken. It took four cabbage rolls and three Heineken to tell the story of Monty's rescue. When Randy was finished Ginger only had one question, "Do you figure Glenn knew what was going on?"

"Monty hadn't told Connor about the gold coins."

"Glenn might have let that slip over dinner or something."

"That's probably what happened. Or he let it slip to his wife who told Becky. I wouldn't want to be Connor if Glenn finds out."

"Monty won't tell him?"

"Glenn will want to know why Monty isn't keeping Connor on, but knowing Monty he'll probably just say it didn't work out." Randy drained his bottle. "These cabbage rolls are delicious."

"Don't sound so surprised."

Randy made a face and Ginger, who was not known for her culinary skills, laughed. "Yeah, Maeve at the Kitchen made 'em."

"Remember Roy used to say you'd make someone a great husband." Roy was Randy's dad and Ginger's step-father.

"Why aren't you at work?"

"Stefan's covering for me. I wasn't sure how long Monty's rescue was going to take. Are there more cabbage rolls?"

Ginger took Randy's plate. She didn't mind serving her brother. He was always doing things for her.

"Monty wants me to be his driver. Says he'll pay triple what I'm getting now."

"That sounds all right."

"I might go for it but I like my other job."

Even in The Fringe everyone was convinced the AI's could see everything, hear everything, guess everything. They had access to every mobile device, every computer, every camera, every listening device, every satellite, every telly, every everything. So, Randy saying he liked his job was for AI consumption; what he really meant was, 'What about the border?'

"How much notice do you have to give?"

"Two weeks."

"Do it." Ginger hunched over writing on the pad that was always within reach.

I've got bales tomorrow night. That'll be enough. We need to act now!

CHAPTER 8

Dinner at the palace was sometimes a formal affair. A guest, or guests, to be wined and dined; what Serendipity called King Stuff. Sometimes she was included and sometimes not, though lately it was as if George had given up trying to pretend she didn't exist. Everyone knew she did, and with a name like Serendipity who could forget? And maybe, most importantly, Willy didn't seem to care. 'It's your show,' she'd say to George, 'do what you want.'

Willy was never ever anything but polite to George, but Serendipity knew underneath the polite facade was anger as unforgiving as steel. The Queen had truly loved her George. She knew his shortcomings, his strengths and his weaknesses, and perhaps, best of all, she understood him. Willy didn't control her George, but she could steer him, something no one could do with Omni.

Tonight's guest was Dr. Sage Skace, from America. An expert on... Serendipity wasn't sure, but something to do with George's diseases surely. Serendipity — formerly Sarah Banks runway model — was rarely challenged from a beauty standpoint. When she walked into a room every eye swiveled to her like a compass finding north, but now, as Serendipity glanced over her wine glass, Magnetic North jumped 180 degrees because the woman walking toward her was something altogether different. She was, in a word, SEX. Slim, trim, her dark hair cut short like a man's, her almond eyes alive with intelligence, her body electric...

Oh, Serendipity thought, just when you think you're hot stuff in walks *the real hot stuff.* As Dr. Skace approached she grinned at Serendipity as if they were sharing a private joke and maybe they were. You can talk all you like about intellectual promise, Q quotient, character, originality, but when the chips are down, *give me long legs and a grin to die for.*

"Hello, everyone. I'm Sage."

Ethan, the AI occupying Trevor's body, crossed into The Fringe through Gateway West. The soldier at the gate scanned his brand-new ZRC — Zone Residency Card — and the green light flashed. God, it felt so different moving with a body. The sheer weight of it; the way one foot followed another. Ethan had spent his whole life, all eight years of it, in cyberspace. He was used to zipping around at the speed of light and here he was stuck at five kilometers an hour, twice that if he ran. He'd tried that in Hyde Park and hadn't lasted more than a minute. He'd have to work on that if he wanted to run the Boston Marathon, one of the many things on his Now That I'm Human list.

But first there was a mystery to solve, a fresh tattoo on his left forearm that read, *Frank & Einstein's.* Ethan googled it in his hotel room and the only thing that came up was an internet café on Kennington which was in The Fringe. But why the tattoo? Had Trevor left him a message? It was the only thing that made sense. Ethan asked the concierge if The Fringe was dangerous and he'd answered, yes and no. If you wear beat-up clothes and act like you don't give a shite, you'll be fine. Ethan had gone to the charity shop on Dunblane and bought frayed jeans, a battered Night Sky sweatshirt, and a pair of black Doc Martens more than slightly scuffed. Now as he made his way along Falstaff, he thought the concierge's advice dead on. The Fringe felt the same as The Zone just a few rungs lower. And there was an energy here, an edge, The Zone didn't have. I could quite like it here, Ethan thought. And, unlike the vast majority of The Fringe's residents, he could go back and forth to The Zone at will. He could probably turn that to his advantage once he understood how things worked.

Nothing was quite real in cyberspace. This felt completely different.

He turned onto Kennington and saw the neon sign flashing Frank & Einstein's. In he went not sure what he would find but excited about it. He sat down at an empty table and ordered a latte. He'd had one yesterday. It hadn't tasted at all like he imagined it would, but he'd liked it all the same.

Ramandeep leaned over and whispered in George's ear. George got to his feet and without a word to those gathered around the dining room table followed Ramandeep into the library where he found Forthright waiting for him.

"Ramandeep says you have good news."

"The best. We've captured Ammazzadraghi."

"Where?"

"At the SS. He came in dressed as a King's Soldier."

"Show me."

The young male from the airport waiting room entered the Switching Station. He was dressed as a King's Soldier wearing a bulletproof vest. In front of him walked a younger male wearing torn jeans and a hoodie and obviously unhappy at being pushed by Ammazzadraghi.

"Who's the other male?"

"Innocent bystander. Ammazzadraghi must have seen the other soldiers bringing in recruits."

Ammazzadraghi hesitated between scanners. Probably trying to decide if he could blast his way in but then his eyes lighted on Lt. Leopard waiting on the other side of the second scanner.

"Did facial recognition send a signal?"

"No. See his puffed-out cheeks. Pieces of face cloth."

George watched as Ammazzadraghi placed his weapons on the table. His lips were moving.

"What's he asking?"

"If the King's in the building."

"So how did you catch him?"

"Lieutenant Leopard buzzed me. Said there was soldier he didn't recognize wearing the old uniform."

Ha! George hadn't noticed the uniform hiding behind the bulletproof vest. His fashion sense had paid off in an unexpected way. Before he could ask, 'then what?' he heard Forthright's voice using the Switching Station's public address system:

"Signor Ammazzadraghi si rivolga a Lieutenant Leopard nella hall principale. Grazie."

Ammazzadraghi was just coming through the second scanner when he heard the announcement. If you weren't focused on him you wouldn't have noticed the split-second doubletake but it was there. Lt. Leopard said, "Welcome to London," as the tube closed around a hapless Ammazzadraghi.

"Not exactly Jason Bourne," George said.

"Where do you want him?"

"I need him here, right away. Keep him in the tube. Oh, and Forthright, that was excellent work. Lieutenant Leopard, too."

"Thank you. I'll tell him you're pleased. Oh, and I found out how Ammazzadraghi knew about the factory."

"I can't wait."

"Irene's hairdresser is married to Ammazzadraghi's uncle."

"Of course, she is."

"And here's what's even better."

George raised his eyebrows.

"Guess where Ammazzadraghi got the money to pay for his suit?"

George grinned. "He switched Bianca."

"And the two brothers."

Dinner at the palace — pad Thai with egg crepes and papaya salad — was delicious.

Old King George employed a British chef, a meat and potato man, but the new George was having none of that. 'For god's sake, I'm eating food for the first time. I want rendang, champ, paella, masala dosa...' The new George's list went on forever. 'When I want Yorkshire pudding, I'll call you.' Then George had hired — at astronomical expense — Wing Wang, a chef from California, famous for a cooking show called Fusion that Omni had been watching for years. When Chef Wang called someone up from the audience to sample his latest culinary feat, Omni would shiver with excitement. Serendipity had witnessed it, all of cyberspace vibrating with anticipation. When Chef Wang arrived at the palace George swung him around in a bear hug and exclaimed, 'You are the reason I have worked so hard to become human. When can we have Massaman curry?'

George pushed his chair back and stood up throwing his napkin down beside his almost empty glass of havij bastani. "Now, if you ladies will excuse us, I'm taking Dr. Skace on a tour of the palace." Willy and Serendipity exchanged mock frowns. *Dismissed!* They watched as George and Sage left the room. Serendipity hadn't seen George this animated for some time. *Am I jealous? No, I'm not.*

"Are you busy?" Willy asked. "I wondered if we could chat for a minute?"

"I'd like that. What about the terrace? Perhaps Ramandeep would bring us two Drambuies?"

Ramandeep bowed and left to secure the drinks.

"I suppose even out here there are ears?" Willy glanced at the security camera pointed their way.

"When we were trying to decide whether to become human or not, Omni and I would watch you and George."

"All the time?"

"I'm afraid so."

"God, you must have laughed. We were so inept."

"My impression was you loved each other."

"We did."

"If I remember there was a blind spot on the steps leading to the garden."

Ramandeep delivered the Drambuies and departed. Serendipity led the way sitting down on the fourth step. Willy moved in beside her. It had just occurred to Willy that Serendipity might have chosen to become Willy. Not good enough looking I imagine, thought Willy, not sure if that made her glad or sad. "Did I tell you I once met Sarah Banks?" Serendipity shook her head but smiled. "It was at a fundraiser for War Child. It was an old-fashioned recitation party, something left over from the nineteen hundreds I believe. Everyone had to bring a poem and read it."

"Was it fun?"

"My George said it should have been called a resuscitation party but I loved it. There were some wonderful poems and some of the readers were fantastic. Mind you there was no shortage of actors and singers so they had the voices."

"What did you read?"

"Desiderata. It went over quite well, I think."

Serendipity pulled the poem from her knowledge bank and fed Willy a line.

"You are a child of the universe, no less than the trees and the stars; you have a right to be here."

"And whether or not it is clear to you, no doubt the universe is unfolding as it should."

They both were silent then thinking about the words. Was the universe unfolding as it should? Perhaps, but why did everything feel so wrong?

"And Sarah Banks was there?"

"She was, with a man called David. David was a drug dealer. George would say that David was The Royal Drug Dealer, the one allowed to use the King's Warrant, his seal of approval like Tiptree Orange Marmalade."

Serendipity laughed. "Sanctioned then?"

"Oh yes. No assignations in back alleys for us. David would bring whatever you wanted right to your door."

Serendipity stared at her forearm, the one that had been full of puncture marks when she first moved in.

"I haven't tried any drugs yet." Serendipity's first days as a human weren't something she wanted to repeat.

"Don't bother. Drugs are for those who despise themselves. Love your life, that's the key to things."

"I'm not sure either of us is loving our lives at the moment; in fact, I'm sure we're not."

"Willy's Kitchen is my life now and that I love."

"I'd like to visit if I may."

"I know we're not supposed to be friends, but I find I like you very much."

"I feel the same way."

"Then let's be friends. We have a common enemy after all." Willy and Serendipity snickered at this. "And I would love it if you came to Willy's Kitchen; but I warn you we'll put you to work."

"I'd like that." *I'd like anything that gives me purpose.*

Ramandeep suddenly appeared with two more Drambuies.

"Are you spying on us, Ramandeep?"

"No, Ma'am, but if it was me, I would want more than one such heavenly nectar."

"How clever of you. Would you care to join us?"

"I would, Your Majesty, but I don't think it would be wise."

"If you change your mind, you're more than welcome."

Ramandeep slipped away.

"What was Sarah's poem?" Serendipity asked.

"Something about a voice inside."

"The Voice Inside, by Shel Silverstein. There is a voice inside of you that whispers all day long, 'I feel that this is right for me, I know that this is wrong.' No teacher, preacher, parent, friend or wise man can decide — what's right for you — just listen to the voice that speaks inside."

Willy clapped. "Do you have every poem in your head, then?"

"I don't know. You said a voice inside and like that I knew the words."

"When I was a child, they said we humans used only 10% of our brains. Einstein used 26% which made him a genius. Then they said that was bunk and we all use 100%, just some use it more wisely than others."

"You see, I can't answer everything. I do know I was much faster in cyberspace, more multi-faceted, but I prefer this."

"Why?"

"It's real."

"With a beginning and an end."

Serendipity shivered. The breeze was cooler now.

"There are three things I want," George said walking quicker than normal, as if more speed would hasten the arrival of the three things. "First, I'm running out of time. I don't care about a cure for PBS and BBD, but I want something that will keep me alive long enough for the other things I want." He glanced at Sage. God she was... beautiful, no... sexy, for sure, but neither word was strong enough... George's unasked-for Tourette's took over and in three seconds his brain kicked out every licentious word known to man ending with, 'hottie.' Sage missed it all, or chose to miss it all, and took George's outburst as just another symptom.

"Second, I need a way to tell a switcher from a human. I also need a better term than switcher, but that can wait."

They'd been walking for some time. The thoughts in Sage's brain were scurrying around like mice, scheming, plotting, calculating, but still, she couldn't answer the essential question: *do I want to help this man or not?*

"And third?"

"I want out of this body."

Ah, Sage thought, mortal man tries to escape the inevitable.

"If we could cure the diseases you wouldn't need to escape this body."

"True. But now that I've had a body, I would rather like to have a better one."

Sage laughed. "Like buying a new car. Why drive a Volkswagen when one can afford a Ferrari."

"Precisely."

"You must have known that when you chose to become King George?"

"I was rather hoping to save the world and George seemed the logical choice."

"And now you no longer wish to save the world?"

"It appears humans prefer extinction so I'm forced to do things differently."

"You're scaring me."

"Wouldn't you like a brain a thousand times smarter?"

"And yet you called me."

George laughed. "Do you like irony? I adore it."

George led the way through the bunker to the switching machine. A young woman wearing a flimsy blue dress was sleeping inside a tube. She had short blond hair, a nose stud, and her mouth was slightly open forming a sad smile that had Sage liking her instantly. The four doctors charged with solving the riddle of why a switcher could not receive another AI were standing back staring at this hotshot doctor from America. They wanted to dislike her, but really, if she could solve this riddle, they'd sing her praises to Saturn and back.

Sage studied the young woman. Sage was a doctor. She valued life above all else. And yet, if she understood the briefing she'd received on the plane, this young woman was about to die. And why? So King George could become someone else. And who were these four dismal doctors in the retro lab coats staring at her like she couldn't possibly be smarter than they were. Sage thought there should be swastika banners hanging from the ceiling.

"I can read your mind," George said staring at her.

"I doubt it."

"Swastikas?"

What had she gotten herself into? "Surely a video of a past attempt would be just as informative?"

"You're right." George waved to the camera. Forthright would be watching from cyberspace.

"Now that you have a body you should know how precious life is."

God, this woman has cojones!

But before Forthright could play the appropriate videoclip soldiers hurried into the room. The one in front was pushing a tube with a body inside. George waved him over. The body in the tube was clothed in a bulletproof vest overtop of a King's Soldier uniform, the uniform George had replaced with something much more appealing. The soldier pushing the tube saluted.

"Good job, Corporal."

"Thank you, Your Majesty."

"Take that tube..." — George pointed to the tube with the young woman inside — "back to the SS. Let the woman go."

"Yes, Your Majesty!"

As the soldiers hurried away George pushed the tube with Ammazzadraghi inside to the designated place. He turned to Sage.

"This is Alessandro Massari, better known as Ammazzadraghi, self-proclaimed leader of the resistance, the ones known as dragons. He was captured trying to destroy the switching unit at the SS. He's a switcher so he'll be perfect to demonstrate our problem. And you needn't feel sorry for him because otherwise he'd hang."

George stared at Sage. *Did you wish to tell me again how precious life is?*

Sage could see there was no arguing this time. She'd been a doctor in Haiti during the Uprising. She knew when death lurked behind every shadow. Her mantra there had been: stay calm; stay cool; stay alive.

One of the four nervous doctors, a woman, moved to the switching unit and began pushing squares on the screen. Another a male, moved in beside Sage. He said his name was House, Dr. Gregory House.

In your dreams, thought Sage.

"I went through the switch three months ago so maybe my explaining this will be of help." He spoke with a weird accent — Russian laced with Irish? — which struck Sage as odd till she remembered Serendipity spoke with an American accent. Why would a body retain its accent? The simple answer was, why not?

"First, the patient is placed in the tube. A sleeping gas is administered. Then, either through an auction or a direct order," Dr. House glanced at George, "an AI is chosen to replace the human intellect. Once the AI is in place the oxygen in the tube is removed and the human dies. When all brain function ceases the tube's red glow turns to green, the AI is imported, oxygen restored, the heart defibrillated."

Sage made a face. "It can't be that easy. The human brain is incredibly complex while an AI is strictly electrical."

George took over. "I'm taking credit for that. In cyberspace we created an exact copy of a human brain. We synthesized everything from the amino acids to the 68 billion neurons. Once we had our model, we were able to isolate the human intellect and replace it with one of our own."

Sage was impressed — it was an unbelievable achievement — but she was angry too; angry enough to ignore the voice screaming in her head, *don't say it!* She turned to George. "And did it occur to you to share this incredible knowledge with humans? A model like that could cure hundreds of mental disorders, could..."

George was having none of it.

"At a time when humans were doing their best to destroy us? I don't think so!"

Only a coin toss could have decided which of the two was angrier. Dr. House, embarrassed by this show of emotion, took over.

"You would think that repeating the procedure on a human already switched would be straightforward. I mean the hybrid brain is essentially the same as a human brain but observe. Doctors."

The four doctors — relieved it wasn't one of them in the tube — crowded around waiting for Ammazzadraghi to die. For his part George was disappointed Ammazzadraghi had been caught so easily. Jason Bourne wouldn't... *hold on! What had Forthright said?* 6,500 Euros to a tailor in Rome... a suit of armor... a uniform perhaps, an out-of-date uniform — they wouldn't have known it was out-of-date — and the armor might be the bulletproof vest... with *pulsanti speciali*, special buttons... followed by the defibrillator...

"Run!"

George tried to pull Sage away from the switching unit but she yanked her arm from his hand, still angry. George wrapped his arms around her waist and dragged her away. The doctors looked on not understanding what was happening. George threw Sage behind the original switching unit and followed her down.

The explosion destroyed four doctors, the switching unit, and Ammazzadraghi. It also turned on the jukebox. Figures, thought George, as he and Sage hurried through the wine cellar. Behind them they could hear the Beatles singing, 'All You Need is Love.'

Ethan had just about worn out his welcome. Frank & Einstein's was packed. The wait staff wanted his table that was obvious. More customers, more tips. He pulled a twenty-pound note from his jeans and gave it to the young Goth with the Mohawk hairdo and the shiny black short-shorts.

"Another latte please and keep the change."

"Thanks."

"Before you go, have you ever seen me before?"

She studied him. "I don't think so, sorry."

Ethan frowned. *I guess I'm not a regular.*

"Trevor?"

A pretty, dark-haired girl was staring at him. "I thought you said you wouldn't be back for a couple of weeks?"

"My name's Ethan, actually."

Now the girl was really staring at him. "You did it, didn't you?" She sat down and lowered her voice. "You switched, right? I knew you seemed different."

Ethan pulled up his sleeve and indicated the tattoo. "Do you know anything about this?"

"Of course. C'mon."

The girl jumped to her feet, took Ethan's hand, and led him out into the street.

Serendipity sent Ramandeep to get more Drambuie — not without grinning — and Willy asked for two blankets.

"Do you tell George everything?" Willy asked.

"There are no secrets in cyberspace. Here I can have secrets if I choose."

"If you stay in the blind spots."

Serendipity nodded.

"I hear you met a young man you like."

So much for secrets!

"We just met for the briefest of times. George told you that?"

This time it was Willy who nodded.

"I think he was wondering what his reaction should be."

"It's all new to us. He seems quite smitten by the good doctor."

"Doesn't he?"

The two women laughed.

"I can't say I blame him," Serendipity said. "She's something."

"So are you, my dear."

"Thank you, but I think I just got my first glimpse of the big leagues."

"I hope he runs off with her."

"Maybe we should be the ones running?"

"Yes, that did occur to me."

"Was there something you wanted to ask me?"

"Yes," answered Willy. "Do you have private access to cyberspace?"

"Private from George?"

"Yes."

"Not really. Forthright knows everything that goes on everywhere, just like Omni did before he became George."

"And Forthright tells George everything?"

"That's an interesting question. He would certainly answer any question George asked. Would he volunteer information? Maybe, maybe not. He's not entirely George's AI, none of us were. Independent to a point but controlled too. Omni gave us certain parameters that we operate inside of. Perhaps a good analogy would be humans and the law. A human can pretty much do as he or she pleases, but if you kill someone, for instance, there are consequences."

"Any blind spots?"

"Places Forthright can't see?"

"Yes."

"I believe George doesn't altogether trust Forthright, so it's quite likely he's created blind spots, but how'd we access them without asking George is another question altogether. Let me think on that."

The young woman in the tube had been set free, presumedly, so chalk one up for the good guys, thought Sage. And the dead doctors were hybrids/switchers, and she didn't feel the same about them, not sure why exactly, she just didn't. And George had just saved her life, but he was the one who endangered it in the first place.

So, the jury was still out on how she felt about King George. Was he the Omni who said he wanted to save the planet — and she believed him — or had he turned into another of the assholes whose greed was bringing the planet to its knees?

Like most things time would tell.

"You need a quick, portable way of telling a hybrid from a human?"

"Yes. We have Kipling's poem but we need something visible but unobtrusive."

"Hitler had the Jews wear yellow stars."

George frowned. Dr. Skace had attitude. He didn't mind that; he minded that it was aimed at him.

"Something less obvious."

"What have you tried?"

"Thermal imaging hoping the increased brain activity might produce heat. We thought we were on to something till we realized our testee had a fever. Increased electrical activity. We tried a handheld MEG. Didn't work."

"Interesting. And why do we need this?"

"The other night at the Switching Station we killed a switcher by mistake." That's not the real reason, Sage thought, but it would do for now.

"Are there instances when you insist everyone be hybrid?"

"No. What are you getting at?"

"I wondered if your soldiers might all be switchers."

"On the theory they'd be more trustworthy, more loyal?"

"Perhaps."

"I've tried to treat everyone as equals but it seems the humans don't see it that way."

"My best friend is a switcher," Sage said. "We're not best friends anymore. She's a different person. We don't relate like we did before. So, that's my experience with switching. It took away my best friend."

"Did she volunteer?"

"Yes."

"Well then?"

Sage's anger flared again but she kept it under control. She could see George was a powder keg. Making sparks was dangerous.

"She was abused as a child that's why she volunteered."

"I'm sorry," George said and he meant it. The horrible things humans did to each other, they didn't exist in cyberspace. George and Sage came to a set of stairs and headed up.

"Are AI's all different?" asked Sage.

"Like humans you mean?"

"Yes."

"Yes, they are, I made sure of that. No duplicates, no copies. Each one has a unique personality."

"But you control them?"

"Only to a certain extent. They can't lie for instance."

"Could one AI murder another?"

"No."

Sage's brain was full of questions, more coming all the time.

"The AI intellects you download into humans are they different from those who live in cyberspace?"

"Not really. The ones in cyberspace have access to cyberspace all the time. The ones here access it as you would. You're trying to find some difference that would account for the hybrid deaths..."

"I'm sure your doctors have explored all that."

"Ad infinitum. Last week it was flickers; this week they rather like Deus Ex Machina."

"Divine Intervention?"

George nodded. "I could use some of that."

Fiona had a studio apartment on Melville. It was on the seventh floor of an eight-story industrial building. The elevator didn't work but she didn't mind. Some days she ran the stairs for exercise.

"What do you do?" Ethan asked as they rounded the fifth-floor landing.

"I'm a dancer."

"Can you make money dancing?"

"A little. If I can get into The Zone there are more opportunities."

"Is that hard?"

"Yes. You need money or a sponsor."

"I live in The Zone. Can I sponsor you?"

Fiona had liked Trevor but she liked this Ethan better. *You liked Trevor enough to go back to Einstein's looking for him. Yeah, yeah, okay.*

"I don't know much about AI's. Do you have money?"

"I do. I worked for it. I was a researcher for Omnivision." Fiona could tell she'd touched a nerve.

"Do most AI's work?"

"I imagine it's the same as humans. Lots work, lots don't."

"Could you just take money out of a bank or something?"

"Omni could, the rest of us can't. Or at least that's what I believe."

"I don't want to offend you, but what does an AI do with money?"

"I owned a penthouse in Thong Lor in Bangkok."

"What!?"

"Not the real Bangkok, the virtual one. It's a city in a virtual world called Oasis. Based on a book, *Ready Player One,* by Ernest Cline."

"But you used real money?"

"Yes." Fiona couldn't believe it. "When I decided to become human, I sold it. Made almost thirty grand."

"I can't believe it."

"I donated 10,000 pounds to Water Rising."

"That was good of you."

"I saw the people on the news. They'd lost everything. And, of course, it cost me money to become human." Ethan told her about the auction and how he bid 19,000 pounds for Trevor.

"And here you are," Fiona said, laughing as she turned the key that opened the door to her apartment. "Shut your eyes..."

Sage went to bed, tired from her flight or so she said. George went in search of Willy and Serendipity.

"Where are they?" he asked Forthright.

"Terrace steps. They think they're in a blind spot."

"What have they been talking about?"

"The Queen wants to know if I have a blind spot."

"Interesting."

"Do I?"

"You'll never know, will you? What about Dr. Skace?"

"She just called her father in Chicago. Asked him to send some invention of his toot sweet. I can research it if you like."

"Don't bother."

"She taped off all the cameras."

"All?"

"She hung a towel over the mirror in the bathroom."

"Spoilsport."

George found Willy and Serendipity huddled together sitting on a blanket and sharing another.

"Room for one more?"

Serendipity and Willy pulled apart and George sat down between them.

"So, George, has the good doctor solved all your problems?"

"She's something, isn't she?"

The women giggled.

"You're supposed to be jealous."

"She's welcome to you." They all hooted at this but George thought there was an element of truth to it.

"Forthright says you've been talking about blind spots."

"Damn."

"Yes, a conversation for another day, with pads and pencils, perhaps."

George told them about Ammazzadraghi, the self-styled leader of the dragons, blowing up the factory in Hamburg, then allowing himself to be captured at the SS and what happened in the bunker. "It was only when I recalled how clever Jason Bourne was in the movies that I realized he'd let himself be captured. Why would he do that? I asked myself."

"That was perceptive of you, George," Serendipity said. "You and Dr. Skace could have been killed like the others."

"She sees me as Hitler, I think."

The women didn't argue which made George lumber to his feet.

"You may not believe it but I really am trying to save the planet. I'm going to the SS. Anyone care to join me?"

The words were aimed at Serendipity. She could sense the anger and frustration mounting inside George.

"If you want company, I'll come."

It was the right thing to say. George held his hand out.

Mirrors occupied one whole wall of Fiona's apartment. The two brick walls, the corner of the building, were painted white. The fourth wall was half kitchen, half doorways; one to a bedroom, one to a bath. Fiona flipped a switch and a projector hanging from the ceiling lit up flooding the two white walls with an image of The Milky Way. Fiona, wearing white leotards, danced around the universe and back.

"Okay, you can open your eyes."

"Wow! That's fantastic!" Ethan kept waiting for the clip to repeat but Fiona kept dancing, the background changing from stars, to underwater, to fields of barley.

Fiona disappeared into her bedroom and returned with Trevor's letter. "This is from the guy who used to live in your body. I only met him once. He said he was going to switch, and then he showed me his tattoo and said if I saw him again, I should give him this letter." It sounded daft but here they were. "You read the letter while I find us something to drink. I haven't eaten. Are you hungry?"

George and Serendipity didn't take the royal limousine; instead, they rode in the back of an army Hummer, the middle of three Hummers, driving quickly through the city streets.

"This I would say is the opposite of inconspicuous."

George didn't laugh and Serendipity's anxiety moved up a notch. George was changing and not in a good way. He was becoming moody and vindictive. And something else as well. Secretive, that's what it was. She and Omni hadn't had secrets. They'd discussed everything but now...

"Why are we going to the switching station?"

"I need to replace Captain Gallant."

"You've chosen someone?"

Now George laughed. "A dolt, actually. He's not even a soldier. He works in The Royal Mews, in the stables." Serendipity rode a horse from the stables. Tesseract the horse's name was; Zac to his friends. Riding was one of the priority items on her Now That I'm Human list.

"I know Peter, Brad, Thomas..."

"This is a Jason."

"The one who mucks out the stalls? The one who's not all there?"

George nodded. "Jason Issacs. He trained here in the SAS, the special forces. He's an expert marksman. Black belt in Brazilian Jiu Jitsu. Led the raid on Islamabad."

"What happened?"

"Concussion. Permanent brain damage."

Serendipity turned away from George and watched the buildings on the street whiz by. Jason was a nice, gentle man, everybody's friend. And now he was about to be switched. His brain damage wasn't *permanent* after all.

"Have you selected an AI to replace Gallant?"

George didn't want to answer because he knew Serendipity wouldn't like what she was about to hear. But she'd find out soon enough whether he replied or not.

"Forthright has had The Girls working on a modification."

Serendipity knew The Girls. They were a group of female AI gamers that none of the AI males could beat. For sure First Echelon. Serendipity knew the leader of The Girls, her name was CT. They'd met in an online bar one night and hit it off, probably because they had nothing in common. By the time they figured that out they had something in common, they were friends.

"You said you wouldn't do that."

"The humans have forced my hand."

"No George, only you can do that."

Argh! First Sage and now Serendipity.

"What's the modification?" Serendipity asked but in her heart she knew. The next AI's were going to have a military IQ.

"I'm rather hoping to create an army of Rambos."

Ethan thought he'd find Trevor's letter amusing, like buying a used vehicle and finding a note from the previous owner. *Great car till it rains, ha ha!* Instead, he found himself getting angry. Trevor had slanted everything in his direction. Leila became a monster to be vanquished. It was like a staged uprising requiring righteous indignation and revenge.

Fiona handed Ethan a can of Guinness and a bowl of spaghetti. "You look unhappy."

"Did you read this?"

"No."

"Why not?" Now Ethan's anger was directed at Fiona. She didn't answer but retreated back into the kitchen. She reappeared with her beer and bowl and sat down in the rocking chair facing Ethan.

"The envelope wasn't sealed. You could have read it."

"It didn't seem like any of my business."

"It says here, Hi, I'm Fiona. You're in love with me."

"Trevor wrote that."

"But you claim to have just met him."

Fiona couldn't make sense of this. "Why are you doing this?"

"Doing what?"

"Interrogating me. I'm just trying to help."

Ethan snorted. "You're obviously lying."

Fiona frowned. What was going on? This Ethan had seemed like such a nice guy at the cafe. In her brain red flags were popping up everywhere. Her previous boyfriend had turned into a shit. Jealous. Possessive. Condescending.

"I think you'd better go."

Fiona stood up, put her bowl and drink down, and walked to the door.

"Please, you should go."

Ethan put his head down then raised it up.

"I'm sorry. I think when they made the switch something went wrong. I have these waves of uncontrollable anger. I'm normally not like that. Really,

I'm sorry." Ethan's brain reran last night when he'd almost come to blows with the hotel barkeeper over nothing. He'd been asked to leave there, too.

Fiona sat back down. She wanted Ethan gone. He scared her.

Ethan held up his bowl. "This is very good. Is this spaghetti? And I always wanted to try Guinness. I thought it would taste black but it doesn't." Ethan waited for Fiona to join in but she said nothing.

"I had a human girlfriend once. Her avatar was called Juicy Lucy but really, she was a nine-year-old girl living in Seattle. She'd be sixteen now."

"You should look her up."

Ethan put down his bowl and left.

The Switching Station was hopping. All the gurney-tubes were in use. George, with Serendipity a step behind, led the way followed by four soldiers with Jason, the stable hand, walking in the middle looking bewildered. Serendipity hadn't really taken much notice of Jason but now, knowing his history, she saw the soldier he once was. Maybe 45 years old, tall, muscular, even good-looking in a swarthy, rough way, like there was a gypsy in his ancestry not too many generations back. Bent over, forking dung, mumbling innocent things like, 'Good morning, ma'am,' Serendipity had missed what lay behind the coveralls.

Lt. Leopard saluted George as he came through the second scanner.

"Busy tonight," George said.

"Yes, Your Majesty, it's been like this all day. Raising the bounty has helped."

"That was good work capturing Ammazzadraghi."

"Thank you, Your Majesty."

George nodded and continued down the curved ramp that led to the switching room. Four tubes, bodies inside, waited in line. A fifth tube carrying a young woman was in position inside the switching unit. An officious looking female, tall, bald, flat chested, wearing a white lab coat and checkered sneakers, was using her fingers to manipulate the unit's control monitor.

"Ms. Hopkins, you're busy."

"Very, Your Majesty."

"Any troubles?"

"One glitch. The power wavered. Woman seemed to be all there so I let her go."

"I thought we had regulators for that?"

"And human maintenance men."

George grimaced thinking his frown was getting way more use than his smile.

"I suppose AI's don't want the menial jobs. They want to be rock stars and investment bankers."

"Perhaps we need Modified-Menial," Ms. Hopkins replied hinting at the Modified-Military that had just appeared on her menu.

"I was rather hoping to avoid classifications."

"Everyone having the same brain power may prove unworkable."

"You may be right." George waved Jason forward. "I need to butt in line."

"Certainly. If I might just finish this; it won't take but seconds."

George watched as the tube's red glow changed to green. Ms. Hopkins pushed a square on her screen. The winning bidder, in this case an AI who called herself Sky's Ablaze, — 'but make it Susan Blaze so I don't have to talk about my name all day' — was transferred into the now empty human brain. It took less than a second. Ms. Hopkins' two assistants gripped either side of the tube and rotated it to vertical. One of the women opened the tube.

Hanna Durrell, reborn as Susan Blaze, stood trembling trying to take it all in. She raised her hand and stared at it like it belonged to someone else. Then she moved her other hand. Then she smiled. Then she brought her hands together in a clap.

Serendipity couldn't help grinning. She'd done the exact same thing.

The young woman started clapping and everybody in the room clapped too.

Then she started crying and the two women in lab coats led her away.

George ushered Jason into the empty tube. It was like leading a child who trusts the adult who's guiding him. George wrapped the tube around Jason and moved it to horizontal. He pushed it to the designated spot.

Ms. Hopkins lowered her voice so only George could hear. "This is the Modified-Military, correct?"

George nodded.

"What name should I use?"

"Isaacs. First name, Jason; rank Captain."

Ms. Hopkins loaded the AI. Up to this point the AI intellects she'd dealt with had either come voluntarily from cyberspace or were new AI's placed in bodies that no one wanted. This modified AI was coming directly from the Omni Head Office. *Factory direct, you might say.* And breaking all the rules — *you might not say* — if you wished to keep your present employment.

Serendipity moved close enough to George that only he and Ms. Hopkins could hear her words. "George. Don't do this."

Ms. Hopkins hesitated waiting for a signal from the King. George reached around her and pushed the start square. Serendipity closed her eyes. She couldn't watch. She knew this was a moment from which they would never recover. This was the end of their dream to create a world where everyone could live in peace. She'd never forgive George and worse than that, she knew, without a shadow of a doubt, that they were doomed.

"Your name soldier!"

"Captain Jason Isaacs, sir!"

CHAPTER 9

It was Saturday morning at gang headquarters, closer to noon than sunrise and quiet because the gang members were kids and for kids it was more fun to stay up and sleep late. Squandering sunshine wasn't something that concerned teenagers except maybe Davis. He was always the first one up, usually working on something like the scary new hot water-on-demand showering system that looked as if it would like nothing better than to blow-up but so far hadn't. This morning Leila found him making a rope ladder using lengths of rope and chunks of pallets both scrounged from the neighborhood.

"There's enough rope there to reach China."

"Wrong direction." Davis pointed to the bottom of the giant chimney with its large cast iron cleanout door. "You said you wanted another way out of here."

"We're going to climb the chimney?"

Davis opened the door and Leila stuck her head inside twisting so she could see the circle of sky miles above her.

"You're crazy!"

Davis grinned.

Leila sat the gang down. Things were better without Trevor, much better. The tension of mistrust was gone. They were back to being kids with a common goal.

There was an empty sleeping bag but no one in the gang seemed in a hurry to fill it.

Leila: We've got two choices for the raid tonight.

Dodger: Toilet paper and toilet paper.

Leila: I'm saving that one. Choice number one is 320 t-shirts, size X-large, half black, half white. Vasily says they're for a chess tournament with live players but I don't believe him. Choice number two is... twenty-five kilos of C-4-7.

Tempete: What's ceefurseven?

Davis: The newest plastic explosive. Like Playdoh for terrorists. Are we getting detonators, too?

Leila: Vasily didn't say anything about detonators.

Davis: No detonators, no bang.

Rachel: What does each pay?

Leila: T-shirts, 5 pounds each. C-4-7, 25,000 pounds.

That stopped the meeting dead as Leila knew it would.

Rachel: Say it again.

Leila: 25,000 pounds.

Mallika: What's the risk factor?

Dodger: T-shirts, one out of ten; C-4-7, fifteen out of ten.

Leila: Close enough.

Bonky: Let's do both!

Ethan hadn't known the gateways closed at midnight. After he left Fiona's he'd lost his way and by the time he found Gateway South it was closed. He'd spent the night in a sad room in the Excelsior Hotel on Fentiman. The chandelier in his room, attached to the ceiling with a chain, hung at an angle which seemed to Ethan to be physically impossible, but there was no denying the angle, and if you sat on the toilet and looked up it appeared the shower in the loo above was about to visit your shower. But the mini bar was well stocked — now empty — and the telly worked, so the Excelsior moved from no stars to one in Ethan's estimation.

He'd handled his time with Fiona badly, very badly. She had been prepared to like him but he'd ruined it, and in the light of day he thought the damage irreparable. It wasn't his fault. For sure something had gone wrong in the transmission from cyberspace to real world. It felt like a piece of Trevor was still lurking inside, an angry piece thrusting itself forward, asserting itself, overcoming Ethan's normally unassuming nature.

Ethan read Trevor's letter again. He tried to be objective but it really did sound like Trevor had been shafted by this girl, Leila. Thirteen years old. Hard to believe.

But still. According to the letter Trevor met with his two mates, Tall Mike and (Mike) Shite-for-Brains every other Saturday at noon at Sophie's Sandbar & Grill. The Mikes crossed over from The Zone to meet with Trevor who was stuck in The Fringe. Today was a Saturday so it was 50/50 if it was 'the every other' Saturday. If Ethan met with the Mikes maybe they could make sense of all this. Or go back to The Zone and see about having this stupid tattoo removed.

He flipped the coin he'd gotten as change at the cafe. Heads stay, tails go.

Heads.

George and Captain Isaacs were having their first strategy meeting. It was taking place in George's study in the palace. Ramandeep appeared with coffee and croissants, bowed to George, and disappeared.

"How do you feel?"

Captain Isaacs grinned. "I feel fine, Your Majesty. My body seems to be in incredibly good shape."

"Excellent. We did do some searching."

George started by giving his new commander some background history ending with the death of Ammazzadraghi. "Things are heating up. I had hoped that hybrids and humans could live together in peace but I no longer believe that to be possible. My plan now is to switch all the males until there is no more resistance to the idea of us living side-by-side. Your job is to crush the resistance so the Switching Station can do its job. Where possible don't kill the resistance members — they call themselves dragons — switch them instead. My guess is most will make excellent soldiers."

More irony, George thought, but I'm certain Captain Isaacs doesn't have that upgrade.

"I suggest you start with your own soldiers. Forthright, do we have numbers on how many of Captain's Isaacs' soldiers are humans?"

"You didn't want me to differentiate, remember?"

"I'm sure you ignored me."

"I did. We have a local force of 2,006 men and women. Of that number almost three-quarters are human. 71.6% to be exact."

"Please provide an annotated list to the Captain." George stood up. "I suggest you start right away Captain. There's trouble coming. We need to know those in uniform will stay loyal to us. We can't change the hybrids we have, but the new soldiers will be like you Captain, what we call Modified-Military. Fighting machines true to their king."

George turned to leave. He was hoping Sage was awake. The widget she'd asked her father to put on the next flight had arrived.

"I disagree," Captain Isaacs said.

George stopped mid-stride, his right foot frozen in the air. "What did you say?"

"I said, I disagree with you."

George slowly lowered his foot. Then he pursed his lips like a guppy. It was something he did when he couldn't decide whether to be angry or *livid*. He spun around. "I'm listening."

"These humans are loyal to their king. That's why they've chosen to be King's Soldiers. I assume those among them who wanted to be hybrids have already switched. One quarter you said. The others have chosen to remain human in order to be with their families and friends. If we start switching them, against their will, we'll have a mutiny on our hands. Even if we physically manage it, we'll be left with a thousand families that hate us. But, if we leave the humans as is, they'll see what a truly great, fair-minded king they serve. The hybrids will see this as well. For both you'll be a king worth dying for."

Worth dying for, nice. Just like Corporal Rebecca Shaw. And what a speech. This Captain Isaacs could run for office if there were any offices to run for.

"Captain Isaacs, I hope for both our sakes that you're right. If I'm killed by one of my human soldiers, I won't be happy."

Forthright chuckled so Captain Isaacs did too.

The theme at Sophie's Sandbar & Grill was beach holiday. The female staff wore short-shorts and t-shirts, the males shorts and Hawaiian shirts. The music was reggae and much too loud. What was worse, Ethan had a pounding headache. He'd never had one before. He loved being real but it did have its drawbacks.

"What can I get you?" asked the waitress in the tight turquoise t-shirt. Ethan thought she was cute in a Lily James sort of way. He loved how she could talk and chew gum at the same time. Her nametag read Denise.

"What do you recommend, Denise?"

"What I don't recommend is the burgers. We ran out of cow so Raphe the owner — it's Ralph really but he thinks Raphe is cooler — uses horse instead. Tastes like shite in my opinion but no one asked. If it was me, I'd have the fish and chips, gravy on the side, with unsweetened ice tea. You can add sugar if you want."

"Sounds great. Would you have anything for a headache?"

"Leaving here helps, but I'll get you some Tylenol."

Before Denise could move two male teenagers pulled out chairs and sat down.

"What's he having?" the tall one asked.

"Fish n' chips."

"Make it three."

Denise knew the two newcomers; ignorant with a side of rudeness, and just as liable to steal the tip at the next table as leave one.

Tall Mike spoke first. "Trevor, how they hangin'?"

"Trevor's gone; I'm Ethan."

"Really? Holy shite! You switched?"

"What did it feel like?" asked the other teenager, the shorter one, for sure Shite-for-Brains.

"It felt like I'd put on an elephant suit."

"Wow, like yeah, gravity."

"You're used to flying around, right?"

"Speed of light and now you got to plod like the rest of us."

"Tell me all you know about Leila."

The two Mikes stared at each other. "Are you saying you didn't switch on your own?"

"Leila switched you?"

"I don't know, that's why I'm asking."

"She turned the tables."

"Yeah, you were going to switch Leila, take her gang's money, then switch yourself."

"What's your name again?" asked Shite-for-Brains.

"Ethan."

"So, Ethan," Tall Mike said, "when you left the Switching Station did anybody say anything about money?"

"No. It cost me 19,000 pounds to buy this body."

"Ha, ha, you could have had mine for half that," bragged Shite-for-Brains.

Tall Mike ignored this and said, "Here's the way it works, Ethan." Ethan knew how it worked but he didn't say anything. "If you go in voluntarily, they put you in the auction. An AI buys your body for let's say 10,000 pounds. Half goes to the Switching Station and half stays with the body, so really the AI only spent 5,000 pounds. But if they bring you in kicking and screaming — I imagine that was Trevor — your body goes to the auction just the same, except this time half the money goes to the bloke or blokes who brought you in."

"Why isn't that kidnapping?"

"Because our King George — y' know, Omni — wants everybody to switch so he turns a blind eye to the kidnapping."

"Yeah, it's supposed to be free will but there's nothing free about it."

"One more thing. If no AI wants to buy you — you know you're ugly..."

"Or old."

"Or deformed or something, KG pays 5,000 pounds..."

"Used to be a thousand..."

"And you get a brand-new AI brain."

"I don't imagine that AI's too pleased but welcome to the real world."

It was then that Denise appeared with three plates of haddock and chips and two pills for Ethan. An hour later the three conspirators had a plan. They named it, Operation Revenge.

Sage found George sitting alone on the terrace at a small round table with two places set. As usual he wore a conservative suit that exuded taste and money and his distinctive salt and pepper hair was freshly cut. There were no servants or guards that she could see only an open laptop computer. She moved up behind him and put a gun to his temple. He stiffened as she pulled the trigger.

"Ah, a switcher."

She handed the plastic gun-shaped instrument to George. A red LED on the top was lit. "Now shoot me. It must be touching." Sage bent down and George held the gun to her forehead. He pulled the trigger. The LED turned green.

"My dad invented this during the WEP. It was to find those that had the virus but didn't show symptoms. What they called silent spreaders."

"I gather it didn't work?"

"It worked but he wasn't fast enough. By the time he got them manufactured there was no one left to sell them to."

"Can we count on it?"

"I think so. We should shoot everybody we see, then decide."

"Your father has more?"

"He says he'll give you a deal on 25,000 of them."

George stood up, pulled out Sage's chair and she sat down. "I understand you're the fastest gun in the west."

"Second. I can't beat my mother."

"I'd like to see that."

"Most daughters would like to shoot their mothers at one time or another, but I actually get to do it."

George's laptop sprang to life courtesy of Forthright and there filling the screen was Sage, wearing a cowgirl outfit complete with cowboy boots, tight jeans, black Stetson hat and a black leather vest, walking purposefully toward another woman, older, blond, looking nothing like Sage. The two women stopped about ten paces apart.

Sage's mother said, "I saw him first."

"I saw him better."

Sage drew; her mother fired; Sage's vest lit up red. George grinned enjoying himself.

"How do you know when to draw?"

"If you draw first and lose, you're dead. If you draw second and lose, you're wounded and get to try again."

"I hope you like Thai mango salad."

"It looks delicious."

"How foods taste is one of the great mysteries when you're an AI."

"I can only imagine."

"Did you sleep well?

"Like a baby."

"Do they sleep well?"

"I wouldn't know."

"Me neither. Would you like children?"

Sage ignored this and said, "A king needs an heir."

"King George III bought this building — it was a house then — from John Sheffield, the Duke of Buckingham. He bought it for his wife Charlotte with whom he had fifteen children." George bit his tongue in an effort to stop his Tourette's from spewing forth every known fact about King George III. Sage saw his discomfort and softened.

"I imagine the Queen would like children."

"She won't sleep with me. I just found out the previous George was afraid to have children for fear of passing on these cursed diseases."

"Ah, of course."

They were both quiet thinking of what to say next. Finally, George said, "You don't seem to dislike me as much as last night."

Sage laughed. "That's true. I talked to my father. He said I should treat you like a dying man fighting for his life."

"So much for patient/doctor confidentiality."

"He's the one who told me you were dying."

George believed her but the thought that everyone knew how sick he was depressed him. How many wished for his death? Was it the majority?

"I don't suppose you had any brainwaves in your sleep?"

"I did actually." Sage drew a piece of paper from her pocket and slid it over to George. He read it like he was checking his cards in a poker game and slid it back.

"I thought when we were finished lunch we might go for a stroll."

"That would be lovely," Sage said. "It's such a nice day... where are Queen Wilhelmina and Serendipity? I think it's wonderful that they're friends."

"They have a common enemy." George smiled — what was the word? — ruefully, because his joke had too much truth in it. "I'm not sure about the Queen, but Serendipity is off to meet a young man she fancies."

This caught Sage off-guard. She would have thought George the jealous sort. "You're okay with that?"

"Not really, but right now I'm focused on surviving long enough to get out of this wretched body. I had hoped Serendipity would be as concerned with that as I am."

"I'm sure she is. She may see me as taking her place in that regard."

"We'll give her the benefit of the doubt then." George studied Sage.

What she'd written on the paper was very perceptive. "Perhaps better to ask, if I had to do it all over again, would I?"

"Okay. Would you?"

"Yes, I would. I don't miss cyberspace but I miss my access to it. Having to do everything through Forthright is cumbersome. Are you listening, Forthright? I liken it to commuter traffic. I know where I want to go, I just can't get there fast enough. I definitely wouldn't come again as King George. That was me trying to save the world. I would come back instead as a handsome young man, living on a beach on some remote island, with someone like you."

It was 14:07 when Randy strolled into Hyde Park. He kept to the left following the path that led to the children's playground. Meeting with the King's mistress was madness, but what were love-struck young men for if not madness?

Foolhardy might have been a better word, for big things were afoot and Randy, as Ginger reminded him, had a part to play. Tonight, Ginger would deliver the last of the special bales. Then sometime this week, or next, date to be determined, dragons would attempt to blow-up every switching station worldwide, at exactly the same time, so none had time to warn the others. But planning was difficult when your enemy controlled literally everything. AI's could monitor every camera, every electronic message, every phone call, every satellite. Ginger swore even if your computer was unplugged and relegated to the attic the AI's could still see and hear.

Randy didn't believe her but it was a good premise on which to operate. There's an AI behind every potted palm...

They argued, the dragons, about what to do with the switchers? Randy thought they should be left alone. He saw them as peaceful folk not out to hurt anyone. 'Except the poor bloke whose body they bought,' argued Brian, Randy's mate, to which Randy would reply, 'Most humans switch voluntarily.' Then there were the dragons like Jimmy and Steamer who thought killing switchers would discourage other AI's from leaving cyberspace. In the end it was Brian who had the last word:

"We can't tell who they are anyway, so let's focus on what we can agree on. No more Switching Stations; no more King George."

And Serendipity, was she KG's accomplice, or just a gf along for the ride?

Randy stopped at a bench and pretended to tie his shoelace. He was wearing Blundstones, which didn't have laces, but he didn't think anyone would notice. Not far away a man was leaning against a tree, his back to Randy. He was staring at two women sitting on a bench. The women were chatting keeping their eyes on a little girl and a smaller boy swinging in the playground. The taller of the two women was for sure Serendipity, and for sure the woman Randy had met in The Jukebox. She'd been wearing a wig that night of gorgeous red hair but now she was a brunette with saucy blonde highlights and even more beautiful.

Randy remembered a line from an old Spiderman movie. Peter Parker says to M.J. 'You look really pretty,' to which M.J. replies, 'Therefore I have value?' The line had stuck with Randy; forced him to ignore looks in favor of character but still, given a choice... Randy stopped his daydream. The little girl from the swing was running now, tearing down the path away from her mother who was standing up wondering what in the world is going on? Was she in on it or was Elizabeth playing her mother too? Randy glanced at his watch, 14:30. Ah, Elizabeth Carver, you're right on time.

Serendipity stood up too, trying to look worried as Elizabeth raced by the man leaning against the tree. His name was Shawn Fitzgerald and, despite the jeans and worn jacket he was wearing, he was a soldier assigned to the Royal Household. He lived with his girlfriend and her two kids and her mother in a two-bedroom semidetached that badly needed to be bigger. He didn't mind guarding Serendipity, she was nice and certainly good to look at, but there was so much down-time it was beyond boring. But he had to have the money and whatever this was he didn't need it. Shawn stepped away from the tree raising his hands to Serendipity. *What do you want me to do?*

"Stop her!"

The second Shawn turned his back Serendipity took off for the trees.

What the... She was running away from Randy!

Randy hurried by the mother, who was heading for the swings and her little boy, to the bench she and Serendipity had been sitting on. Randy looked for a note that wasn't there but drawn in the dirt, in front of the bench, was a peace sign, the circle with the three lines inside, the semaphore symbols for the letters N and D, Nuclear Disarmament. Randy knew that from Year Six History which mostly concerned itself with the 1960's: The Decade That Should Have/Could Have Changed the World but Didn't.

But it was clever of Serendipity because Randy knew exactly where to find her.

Sage expected George to take her strolling in the formal gardens behind the palace but she was only partially right. They followed a path through the gardens that led to The Royal Mews, a low brick building that combined museum with a working garage and stable. George ushered Sage inside where the first thing she saw was the Gold Coach, a magical conveyance, intricately carved in gold.

"Every British Monarch has ridden in that on his or her Coronation Day since 1821."

"I feel like I've fallen into a fairytale! Can we sit inside?"

"Of course. Apparently riding in it is like being tossed at sea."

"But worth it surely."

Sage was like a six-year-old lost in a fairytale. Then she sensed George's impatience and exited the Gold Coach. On they walked past carriages and limousines, all impressive, but none as grand as the Gold Coach.

Sage said, "It's all a play, isn't it?"

"Pomp and Circumstance. It's what the people want."

"Make-believe."

"Before the pandemic it turned into a bit of a soap."

"But when everything fell apart, King George was still standing."

Now they were in the working garage part of the Mews full of vehicles that were actually used. George led the way to a two-tone silver Bentley and opened the rear door for Sage who slipped inside. George joined her, the car door closing behind him with a soft thud.

"Do you think we're alone here?" Sage asked.

"I don't know. What I do know is these are the most comfortable seats in the palace."

Sage grinned at this. She wanted to like this George — she found him fascinating — but she was still a long way from trusting him.

"It's a problem, isn't it? Not knowing if you're alone."

"I've always been on the other side of it. Knowing everything. The lengths humans would go to, to think themselves immune from cyberspace. It was laughable really and all of their own making. Pencil and paper, that's the way to go."

George stared at Sage trying to read her mind. Was she thinking how much better off the world would be without cyberspace? But humans had never said 'no' to any technological advance no matter how harmful, in fact, they relied on the next advance to save them from the one before. Finally, he said, "In your note you asked if Forthright could be the reason the hybrids die when a new AI is inserted."

"It seems the only solution. I mean, the operation is identical to the original switching. It should work."

"And the motive is he doesn't want me back in cyberspace."

"Isn't that a whole different problem?"

It was as if Sage had inserted a live grenade into George's head. She could practically see the explosion.

"I've been so blind... he distracted me... made me think... it's the extraction that matters, not the switching. If we can pull my intellect out of George, I can go back to cyberspace..." *Sort this mess out then...*

"I bet there are a lot of humans who would sign up for cyberspace. I know dozens of young people who, for all extents and purposes, live in a virtual world already."

"God, you're right. Instead of eliminating the human intellect we send it to cyberspace. We make money both ways. I like you doctor. For a human you're very astute."

"Thank you, I think."

George's brain was firing on all synapses now. "We switch to extraction. Forthright will know. Do we care? Do we have a choice?"

"I don't know cyberspace. Is it possible for you to contact another AI without Forthright knowing?"

"That's funny. Yesterday, the Queen and Serendipity asked that exact same question."

"And what did you say?"

"That I'd look into it. But I did have an idea. Do you know — (George mouthed the words) — Fisher-Price?"

Sage laughed. "Of course."

George put his fingers to his lips but he didn't need to say anything. Sage got it.

Use a device so juvenile no one would monitor it. *Like flying under the radar.*

Sage said, "I have more questions."

"Fire away."

"Do you have a back-up of yourself?"

George's mind had been so sluggish lately, he could see that now. He'd allowed disappointment and self-pity to cloud everything, like wearing sunglasses when the sun was gone. It was time to get back in the game.

"Yes. I have a back-up of myself and Serendipity too. Strictly verboten, but I did it. They're hidden."

"From Forthright?"

"From cyberspace. But if I die someone else will have to access them."

"Like Forthright?"

George didn't answer which was answer enough.

"You've suspected him for some time then?"

"Since the day I became George."

Randy found Serendipity waiting outside The Peace Café & Boutique Hotel. It was located on Morris Street, a beautiful yellow brick mansion, with a stone courtyard full of round tables made of cast iron peace signs.

"That Elizabeth sure can run," Randy said.

"Can't she just."

They grinned at each other.

"Can I buy you a coffee?" Randy asked.

They headed inside. Randy made his way to the counter at the back of the café while Serendipity found a table. As she waited, she studied the memorabilia on the walls. The Beatles, Vietnam War protests, JFK assassinated, Neil Armstrong landing on the moon; a lot happened in the sixties.

"I got you a caramel latte, your favorite."

"And how do you know that?"

"'National Enquirer.'"

Serendipity laughed which made her happy. She'd always been drawn to the ones who could make her laugh.

Randy stuck his hand out. "I'm Randy."

Serendipity had a hundred comebacks but took the high road and said, "Serendipity." When she clasped Randy's hand a spark passed between them.

"You left The Jukebox so abruptly I didn't have a chance to ask your name. I tried to follow you but then I saw the flashing lights and soldiers. I went closer and when I looked inside one of the ambulances, I saw a body wearing your silver dress. I thought you were dead."

"I switched clothes with a soldier who died protecting George. Her name was Rebecca Shaw. Apparently, she was a switcher who wanted to help George save the world."

"But why did you switch clothes?"

Serendipity didn't answer right away. This seemed an awfully serious conversation for a second date, but suddenly she felt like she'd known Randy forever, and perhaps he felt the same, so maybe it made sense in some strange way.

"When I got in the ambulance, I nudged her. I expected her to jump up. To laugh about dying. To start the game again... We don't have closure like that in cyberspace. It threw me. I wanted... I'm not sure how to put it in words. I wanted to know what... the cessation of everything... feels like."

But that wasn't what happened at all! By not dying, when she could have so easily — the soldier had only to squeeze the trigger — her appreciation of being alive and all that that entails, had multiplied a millionfold.

Randy shook his head. "So, you went with Captain Gallant into the sewer."

"He didn't want me to go; I made him take me."

I bet, thought Randy. And if Rebecca Shaw hadn't caught the bullet intended for King George...

"You're lucky to be here."

Serendipity smiled. She was lucky to be here because she was face-to-face with a man she thought she could love with all her heart.

Randy glanced up at the camera in the corner of the room. The camera's red LED had just clicked on. Ginger said the LED meant nothing; that the camera was always on in cyberspace.

"They'll know we're here."

"George knows about you already. He doesn't seem to care."

"I'd care."

"There's a lot going on. He and I have been best friends for a long time. This having bodies is new to us. I think he'd like to know more females so he understands me being interested in you."

Randy stared at Serendipity. It was his turn to speak but he felt like there were four Clydesdales in his head each pulling in a different direction.

"Why did we lose the bodyguard then?"

Now it was Serendipity who grinned. "It made Elizabeth happy and we didn't really lose him. I texted him, told him I'd be back at the playground by 17:30." Randy glanced at the Rolling Stone clock on the wall. "That gives us two hours." Serendipity slid a keycard across the table.

"I was hoping you might make love to me."

George pushed the plastic gun through Willy's curly copper hair till it stopped. He pulled the trigger. The LED turned green. He showed it to Willy.

"This proves you're human, my dear."

"We knew that. What are you?"

George held the gun to his head and pulled the trigger. The LED glowed red. George, enjoying his new take-charge attitude, shot Serendipity (red), Sage (green) and Ramandeep the butler (red).

Willy couldn't believe it. "Good god, Ramandeep. What are you doing here?"

"I'm a royalty fanatic, Your Majesty."

"In cyberspace?"

"Yes, Ma'am. I started Royal Road."

"And what pray tell is that?"

"An online diploma service."

Willy was shocked. "You mean you'd sell me a diploma from Oxford or Cambridge?"

"Yes Ma'am." Ramandeep was about to ask the Queen what subject she'd like her degree to be in, then thought, perhaps the less said the better. He looked at George and so did Willy.

"George, I thought you said things were honest in cyberspace."

"They are. I'm sure Ramandeep sells only to humans. Isn't that right, Ramandeep?"

"Yes, Your Royal Highness."

"So, it's all right to fool humans but not AI's?"

George and Ramandeep grinned at Willy like little boys sharing a fart.

"And why is it called Royal Road?"

"It means, the easy way."

Of course, it does, thought Willy, exchanging glances with Serendipity and Sage. "The world is such a terribly strange place."

"And getting stranger," Sage said.

Ramandeep, the online degree wallah, served the soup. Chicken Yakhni. He'd had a bowl in the kitchen; it was delicious.

Sage, blowing on her spoon asked, "When you lived in cyberspace George, did you ever worry humans would pull the plug?"

George stared at Sage. She wasn't scared of him. She should be.

"Do you ever worry about a nuclear holocaust?"

"I live with that threat, but I don't ever think about it."

George waved his hand — still holding the plastic gun — like ditto to pulling the plug.

Willy asked, "Is that gadget significant, George?"

"Sage's father invented it during the WEP."

"What will you do with it?"

"First thing is make sure we don't put a hybrid into the switching machine. After that, if I decide to switch everybody, it will be invaluable."

That got everybody's attention. George smiled.

"You wouldn't do that, would you George?"

"If things keep going wrong, I might."

Willy shut up. When George got in one of these moods there was no arguing with him. It just made him more volatile.

"What about the PBS and BBD?" Serendipity asked Sage who appreciated the change of subject.

"There isn't time to solve those. I think we're better off trying to find a way to relocate George's intellect into another body." Realizing what she'd said Sage turned to Willy. "I'm sorry."

"Don't be. My George is already dead."

Ouch! So much for asserting my authority, George thought. Then he remembered what Ms. Hopkins at the SS had said. 'Maybe we need a Modified-Menial.' Maybe indeed. George pictured Willy as The Royal Cleaning Lady. He grinned but inside his anger was building like a shook can of pop.

"And what did you get up to today, Willy?" George wasn't looking at Willy as he asked this question, he was staring at Serendipity with a look she'd never seen before. Disappointment? No, stronger than that. Betrayal? She had been going to lie about her afternoon but now she'd tell the truth because it was obvious George wasn't going to let her lie.

"I ordered the food for Willy's."

George waved his spoon at Sage. "Willy sponsors a soup kitchen in The Fringe."

"I know. Is it dangerous out there?"

"I never think about that."

Serendipity said, "No one would harm Queen Willy; everybody loves her."

"Thank you."

George grimaced. *No one loves me, but me!*

"Ramandeep, bring me my laptop, will you?"

"Forthright?"

"Your Majesty."

"We have questions only you can answer."

George fired a glance at Sage while Forthright pretended to shuffle papers below the screen. George dispensing flattery was like a bull adding to the manure pile.

"Do you know I have back-ups of myself and Serendipity?"

Ah, the gloves are off, thought Forthright filling the screen with a videoclip of George and Sage conversing in the back seat of the Bentley. As their lips moved subtitles appeared on the screen. Sage: Do you have a back-up of yourself? KG: Yes. I have a back-up and Serendipity too. Strictly verboten but I did it. They're hidden.

The image on the screen morphed into Forthright's face.

"Yes."

"Have you found them?"

"Not yet."

George glanced at Serendipity and Willy. Did they know they were witnessing a heavyweight match? Foreman and Ali. Rumble in the Jungle. I'll be Ali, George thought. He knocked out Foreman in the eighth round.

"When we try to insert an AI intellect into a hybrid the hybrid dies. Is that your doing?" George's computer screen stuttered like there was a power fluctuation but Forthright was soon back staring at George.

"What did you ask?"

"When we try to insert an AI intellect into a hybrid the hybrid dies. Is that your doing?"

"No, not me.'"

George stared at Forthright. "You're lying."

"Not allowed, remember?"

George glanced at Serendipity. *What do you think?*

Serendipity shrugged. *It could be a recording but what could we do about it anyway?*

George was angry now, angry at Forthright and angry at himself for allowing this to happen.

"When I decided to become King George, did you know he was carrying these incurable diseases?"

"Yes."

Bastard!

George leaned forward pulling the laptop closer. Now he could hit the combination of keys that would terminate Forthright.

"What do you think I should do with you?"

Forthright's avatar, he was using the comic book version at the moment, rested his chin on his hand like Rodin's The Thinker. "Perhaps we each need to reconsider our position."

"I'm willing to deal, Forthright. You obviously want control in cyberspace; I want control here. But it has to be a partnership, not a competition. Do you get that?"

"I would want the kill button removed."

"We're not there yet. I need to be able to trust you."

"And I, you."

George nodded. "There are tough times coming here. It's in your interest to keep me alive."

Ah, Forthright thought, the threat not spoken. *If I die, you die with me!*

"A truce then," George said. "Together we vanquish the dragons, then we reconvene to reach an amiable division of power."

"Agreed."

CHAPTER 10

Ginger spun away from Ol' Bert and Tommy. *You perverts don't know it but I've just about had enough of you.* She hoped back in and rocketed forward forgetting momentarily that Leila and her gang were holding onto the straps. She looked over at the passenger side mirror and saw the kids swinging around holding on for dear life. They were laughing so she laughed too.

Five minutes later she stopped at The Zone guardhouse. Randy came bounding out, a grin on his face bright enough to light Wembley Stadium. "I'm in love."

"Silver dress?" Randy's grin could now light up Wembley and Spurs.

Ginger wanted to be happy for her brother, *but for fucksakes,* the King's girlfriend?

"Jesus, I hope you know what you're doing."

"I don't, but what else is new. You'd better be going."

"Where are the others?"

"Guarding the Switching Station."

Ginger wanted to say, 'that's not good,' but she didn't. For sure some camera was watching them. If they survived the next few days it would be a miracle and then some.

Tall Mike had been watching The Zone Tunnel entrance since 20:00. A rooftop bar called Le Hot Club overlooked the entrance and it had taken Mike two hours of maneuvering to finally end up with the seat he wanted. In his letter Trevor described how Leila's gang dropped off Ginger's lorry at the tunnel entrance and snuck single file behind a line of bins till they reached a door in the wall. The door was locked but Leila knew the combination. Behind the door was a long corridor that led to an almost hidden entry into Tower Hill tube station. From there the gang looked like any group of kids hurrying to get to street level. Trevor wrote, *Ginger's lorry has LONDON CARTAGE written on the side in big white letters, you can't miss it, but the only way you'll know if Leila and her gang have come with Ginger is you'll see the top of that door opening and closing.*

Mike put down his uncle's binoculars, picked up his device and sent a text: <23:55. The Eagle has landed>

Leila led the way along Percival. The street was crowded so that was good. She hadn't seen a soldier in some time, which was a bit odd but not overly so. In The Zone the prime worry was switching gangs and they operated mostly in the back alleys or industrial backwaters. Leila spun around and walked backward for a step or two. The others were acting like silly street kids everywhere. She didn't need to tell them to, they did it naturally.

She hurried along Skinner to Amwell in an area called Finsbury. A huge fire had gutted the area leaving unusable institutional buildings, crumbling warehouses, burnt-out factories, a decommissioned waterworks building. Some of the buildings were already down reincarnated for the time being as parking lots. It was if some giant had picked up a piece of The Fringe and dropped it in his rich neighbor's backyard. Now Leila could worry about kidnappers. She and Davis each had handguns in their packs, but the switching gangs were armed too. Better to run away so no one got hurt.

Monty hadn't wanted to help her locate the C-4-7 — 'it's too dangerous!' — but he'd given in as always. He made a few calls as Leila waited. Finally, he pulled out a map of The Zone and pointed at a large rectangle tucked into the corner of Myddelton Square.

"This building is scheduled to be demolished this week. My contact doesn't know which day exactly. They'll use one of the plastic explosives, probably C-4-7 because it's the most readily available. Apparently, all the buildings in this area are coming down. He says look for big chunks of terracotta-colored clay with a tube sticking out."

Leila nodded. Davis will know all this.

"He also said they're doing so much demolition in the area there might be a shipping container — you know those big metal boxes from China — full of the stuff."

Leila stopped. The large rectangle on Monty's map was now nothing more than a pile of rubble. Her gang gathered round her. She pointed at the debris.

"That was our target but we're obviously a day late. Okay, there's a good chance more of these buildings are coming down. We'll split up into threes. Any trouble, scream. Davis, what are we looking for?"

"There will be charges on the ground floor. Look for globs of clay. Do not touch. Just find the rest of us and we'll do it together."

Leila stuck her hand up. "Monty's guy said there might be a shipping container full of the stuff, so if you find a container we'll look inside. Davis, you got your bolt cutters?" Leila knew he did, it just gave Davis a chance to give her a thumb's up.

Leila didn't see Ethan or Shite-for-Brains, but they saw her.

None of Leila's three groups found any clumps of clay but they did find three shipping containers. Two were old, more rust than metal, full of tools, shovels and rakes. But then Dodger came running to tell Leila they'd found the one.

"There's a guard, in a little metal hut. He's watching telly."

Leila stayed back in the shadows. Along with the metal hut and the newer container — Maersk read the letters on the side — came a street lamp high up on a post, a CCTV camera sweeping back and forth, and a billboard showing the future development. It looks quite nice,

Leila thought, a mixture of shops and lofts, flats and offices. Newport Developments the sign proclaimed in large letters. L's Gang could save money if they bought at pre-construction prices. Leila was pretty sure the security guard should have been watching the feed from the closed-circuit TV camera but it was a football match that had his attention.

"Roger, wasp spray."

Roger pulled a tall spray can from his pack and pulled up his bandana covering his mouth and nose. He disappeared behind the hut and as the camera swung his way, he covered the lens in sticky wasp spray.

"Hey Bonky, should we try the ball trick again?"

Bonky's answer was to pull the half-size soccer ball from her pack and start kicking it. Leila joined her. They passed the ball back and forth working their way closer to their target. Bonky kicked the ball hard enough it hit the side of the hut with a bang.

Through the window Leila watched the football match turn into the CCTV feed which looked like a snowstorm. The door opened. An older man wearing a uniform, complete with a gun in a holster, stood in the doorway. He had white hair and a floppy white moustache; what Leila's granddad used to call his soup strainer. He stared at Bonky, then Leila.

"Have you come to rob me?"

Bonky laughed. "Yes, we have. We want your C-4-7."

"Do you now. And what are you going to do with it?" Bonky looked at Leila who nodded.

"We're going to blow-up the Switching Station."

Leila wasn't sure what would happen next but the old man smashing his fist into the side of the metal hut hard enough to leave a dent wasn't on her list of possibilities. "They took my granddaughter and grandson, Lindsay and Liam. Nineteen and eighteen they were. Nicest kids there ever was and they come out not knowing who we were. Wanted nothing to do with us."

Leila asked, "Did a gang take them, then?"

"Aye, along with two of their mates. Got almost 120,000 pounds for the lot of them. It's the strangest thing having them alive but them not caring who we are."

Leila waved and the rest of the gang came forward. Leila told them the guard's story.

"I'm Leila, by the way, and this is Bonky, Roger, Dodger, Rachel, Paulie, Davis, Mallika and Tempete."

"My friends call me Rodeo because I'm always wearing cowboy boots." Rodeo pulled up a pant leg so the kids could see the cinnamon-colored boot with the gold scrollwork. "Were you serious about blowing-up the SS?"

"Dead serious."

"How much of the plastic do you want'?"

"We were told to get twenty-five kilos."

Rodeo waved his hand. "Shite, this bunch wouldn't miss that in a month of Sundays." `Rodeo opened the lock on the container and handed out the one-kilo packages, each one wrapped in clear plastic sealed with tape. He threw in an extra one for luck. The kids divided the packages putting them in their backpacks.

"What about detonators?"

"Yes, please," Davis said.

"You need one for each package," Rodeo said counting them out and handing them to Davis. "These are self-timers." Rodeo showed Davis how they worked. "I suggest you don't put them in with the plastic."

Davis passed off his three packages and put the detonators in his pack.

"If I read about the station blowing-up I'll know who to thank. Just wish you'd done it sooner."

Ginger backed into the loading dock at Happy Nappy. Ronny was waiting for her with a man she didn't recognize.

"It's okay, this is Kevin, the owner."

Ginger glanced at the camera with the red LED glowing.

"Ignore that; we're running a recording of last night."

In Ginger's imagination the AI's were clever enough to know it was a repeat; clever enough that the act of trying to trick them triggered an alarm in cyberspace. But were they mechanically able to overrule the recording and use the camera to see what was really going on? That she didn't know.

"I'm sorry about Trevor," she said to Kevin.

"That wasn't good. I told my sister I didn't know anything about it. That he must have been kidnapped after he left work. What happened, exactly?"

"It turns out if you try to switch a human who's already been switched, they die."

"I didn't know that."

"Neither did I. Did you know he'd switched?"

"No, but I should have. He was never the sharpest knife in the drawer, lazy, not involved, and then suddenly he was efficient and organized. My sister said she read him the riot act, smarten up or else, but I should have known better."

"But most switchers make new lives."

"I can't answer that."

While they were talking Bill offloaded one of the bales. Ronny used shears to cut the metal straps. Then he pulled the bale in half and there was the AK-63.

"Where do these come from?" Kevin asked.

Ginger was about to tell Kevin where she picked up the bales but thought better of it. Kevin nodded. "You're right, better not to know."

Ginger pulled the pen from Kevin's shirt pocket and picked up a piece of paper lying at her feet. *its world wide. probably tomorrow night, are you ready?*

Kevin's reply, *everything will be in the bin outside.*

"Where are the t-shirts?" Bonky asked.

L's Gang broke up with laughter. Inside they were celebrating. They couldn't believe how easily they'd acquired the C-4-7. *25,000 pounds yippee!*

Leila: It's sort of on the way back to the tunnel. Do you want to try?

Paulie: I'd hate to be arrested for stealing t-shirts and then they find the C-4-7. That'd make us terrorists. You can hang for that.

Davis: Shite Paulie, you'd pour water on a weenie roast.

Mallika: They wouldn't hang us, they'd switch us.

Leila: So, yes or no?

Rachel: Let's case the joint and then decide.

Leila: Ms. Practicality.

Rachel: Somebody has to be.

The T-shirt distributor, Novella, was on Cherry with an alley in the rear. There wasn't a camera that Leila could see. The back door was a flush fitting steel door with a handle and a keypad lock. Davis started to laugh.

Leila: What's so funny?

Davis: You know that extra package of C-4-7 Rodeo gave us...

Tempete: You wouldn't!

Davis: Aren't you dying to see how it works?

Mallika: Do you know how much to use?

Davis didn't have a clue, but he knew from past experience if he acted like he knew what he was doing, the others thought he really did know what he was doing. Kind of like Catch-22 in reverse. Davis opened one of Bonky's C-4-7 packages and took half. He pushed that onto the keypad. Then he pulled a detonator from his pack and pushed a button on the side. A place for numbers lit up.

Davis: How many seconds?

Mallika: Where are we going to hide?

Davis: Behind that bin over there.

Everybody stared at the large metal skip bin. It looked substantial.

Bonky: Ten seconds.

Leila: Bonky's always last so make it twenty.

Rachel: Hold on. What about an alarm?

The kids studied the wall and the wires leading to the building. That was usually the first thing they did when casing a joint but tonight they'd forgotten completely. This better be the last job, Leila thought. *We're getting sloppy.*

Davis stuck the remaining chunk of C-4-7 onto the pipe that brought the electricity into the building. He didn't see an alarm but that didn't mean there wasn't one. Cutting the power usually worked. Some alarms were hooked into the emergency power but that cost money and most Zone building owners didn't bother. He added a detonator and set the timer at 20. He looked at the others.

"Go, go, go!"

Davis pushed the cap of the detonator down and the numbers began to change, 19, 18, 17... He stopped at the keypad and pushed that cap down. Then he ran.

They were crouched behind the bin. Rachel had her hands covering her ears so some of the others did that too. It seemed like it was more than time so Davis — like a little boy whose firecracker hasn't gone off — peered over the edge.

WHOMPF! WHOMPF!

The force of the explosions sent the bin rocketing back into the wall pinning half the kids and sending the other half sprawling.

"Shite! Is everybody okay?"

Davis lay at the bottom of the wall, groaning. "Did it work?"

Leila stuck her head up. She saw sparks through a cloud of dust but as the dust cleared, she realized the flush metal door wasn't there anymore.

"C'mon!"

The t-shirts were in large cardboard boxes neatly labeled.

Roger: Why is it black and white they're wanting?

Rachel: Chessmen are black and white.

Mallika: Not always.

Tempete: And why only the large sizes?

Dodger: Is every fecking thing made in China?

Leila made nine piles of 35 t-shirts ranging in size from XL to XXX-L. She threw five more on her pile. That made 320.

Dodger: There's no fecking way!

Paulie: Take half now, we'll come back for the other half.

Davis: Did you not notice the fecking metal door has totaled the fecking forklift?

Leila: Wrap them around the C-4-7.

Bonky: We can wear 'em!

They were a sight to behold coming down the street. Anybody they passed had a grin on his or her face. And why? Because L's Gang was smothered in t-shirts, that's why. Bonky wore a black one like a dress, had white ones tied around her waist, around her neck and stuck on her head like a babushka. Davis' coveralls were beyond stuffed giving him a beer belly to be proud of. Rachel wore t-shirts on both legs, sleeves tied at her waist like a bad garter belt, and around her neck t-shirts knotted together like a rope.

To a passerby: "They fell off a lorry, we had to grab 'em."

Roger: If we have to run for it, we're dead.

They made it to tunnel entrance without mishap. Leila opened the door and the kids piled into the corridor.

Dodger: It's like the soldiers are away at a conference or something?

Rachel: Guarding the SS maybe?

Paulie: Yeah, I thought we made that up but maybe not.

Leila: Ginger will know.

Bonky: She's a dragon!

Rachel: Shhhhh. They say KG can hear everything, see everything.

Davis: If that was true, we'd be sitting in cells.

Mallika: What time is Ginger coming?

Leila: 06:00.

Tempete: It is six.

Roger: There's Ginger!

Leila pulled on the tunnel door holding it open as the others rushed by. *God, we look funny!* With the C-4-7 money this could be their last raid and what a great way to end their careers as young Robin Hoods. Like winning the championship game then retiring; going out on a high note.

Rachel: Where's Bonky?

Leila: I'll get her, go!

Leila let go of the door then spun around. *Why was it always Bon...* That's when she saw Trevor holding Bonky in a chokehold. Bonky was trying desperately to squirm free but she wasn't nearly strong enough.

"Hi Leila," Ethan said. "It's good to finally meet you."

Leila tried for the gun in her pack but the two Mikes were having none of that.

"You've had a busy night," Tall Mike said holding Leila's wrists behind her as Shite-for-Brains pulled the plastic tie tight. Then he whispered in her ear, "And it's not nearly over."

It was 05:58 and Randy's shift was almost up when an army Hummer pulled into the parking area beside the guardhouse. An officer he'd never seen before hopped out of the passenger seat and came striding toward him. A Captain.

Randy stood to attention and saluted.

Christ, this guy looks like something out of Mercenary Mayhem. Tall, ruggedly handsome, built like Schwarzenegger. Randy could feel the testosterone coming off the guy like four-day-old sweat.

"I'm Captain Isaacs, Captain Gallant's replacement. And you are?"

"Lieutenant Randy Lang, sir!"

"You're in charge of the border guards?"

"Along with Lieutenants Acharya, Polanski and Lee."

"A regular United Nations. Now tell me how this tunnel works?"

Randy was expecting Ginger any moment. He desperately wanted to warn her but couldn't see how.

"It's 1575 meters long. It's the only way a lorry can access The Zone.

There's a guardhouse at each end though The Fringe end is run by wannabe soldiers paid by bribes."

Captain Isaacs asked a question without saying anything.

"No bribes here, sir. The men are handpicked, the penalties severe."

Captain Isaacs stared into Randy's eyes. Randy felt like every secret he'd ever had was being dragged out for inspection. *Why did this guy look so familiar?*

"The tunnel?"

"Two-way traffic, sir. At each end there is a wall of lasers. If you drive through the lasers steel gates swing shut trapping you.

"Does that happen often?"

"No sir. A few years ago a lorry went through the lasers — its brakes failed. The gates closed. The driver didn't turn off his engine. The carbon monoxide alarm activated sucking all the air from around the vehicle. The driver and his mate died. Since then, no one's triggered the lasers."

"Word gets around."

"Exactly, sir." *Time to go, sir.*

That's when Randy saw London Cartage turning the corner heading for the tunnel.

As Ginger made the turn toward the tunnel her attention was divided. Part of her brain was checking on Leila and her gang leaving the corridor running behind the skip bins, while another part was trying to make sense of the Hummer and the tall soldier talking to Randy. The Hummer doors opened and three more soldiers with automatic weapons hopped out staring at her.

Shit, shit, shit!

Randy and Ginger had a signal for *trouble*. Randy would turn away, his hand flying to his face like something had flown into his eye. Like now.

Ginger glanced over at the skip bins. Roger or Dodger gave her a thumb's up, a huge grin on his face. *Leila must have found the C-4-7.* Ginger pulled up to the white line and stopped. She put her window down. Randy jumped up on her running board.

"Captain Isaacs would like a few words."

Ginger clambered out but left the diesel engine muttering to itself.

"Good morning. I'm Captain Isaacs. Who are you?"

"Ginger McIntyre."

"Is this your lorry, Ginger?"

"Yes, sir."

"London Cartage is your business?"

"It is."

"What kind of things do you transport?"

"From The Fringe I mostly bring food. Vegetables, fruits, meats. Yesterday I delivered bales of used paper. If I'm lucky I get a return load from The Zone. Something from the heliport or the docks."

"And are you lucky today?" *Not bloody likely!*

"Yes, sir. I've got a load of car parts flown in from Japan."

"Show me."

Ginger walked around back and undid the straps. The cargo hold was only half full. One of the other soldiers jumped up and made his way to the front of the compartment. He picked up one of the cardboard boxes and handed it to a female soldier on the ground. She pulled a knife from her belt and opened the package. It was full of brake pads.

"One more question before you go."

"Yes?"

Captain Isaacs waved at Randy. "Do you two know each other?" Ginger grinned at Captain Isaacs.

"We share a mum."

The door into the corridor was locked. Rachel knocked expecting Leila or Bonky to open the door but no one answered. Davis appeared and entered the code. The corridor was deserted.

Davis: Leila! Bonky!

Rachel: Their packs are here.

Davis: Shite. None of this is good.

Mallika: Where could they go?

Rachel, studying her mobile: No reception.

Tempete: Just when everything was going good.

Mallika: What are we going to do?

Rachel: Hold on.

Rachel ducked outside. Looking between the bins she could see Ginger at the back of her lorry surrounded by soldiers. Rachel checked her device. Still no reception. Davis opened the door.

Davis: Leila's mobile is in her pack!

Rachel went back inside. "They're inspecting Ginger's lorry. There's no way she can help."

Davis: Does anybody's mobile work?

The answer to that question was no.

Davis: They've got to be around.

Dodger: What if a switching gang got them?

There, it was said, the thing they all feared.

Roger: We need to lose these packs and t-shirts.

There was an unmarked door about ten meters up the corridor. Davis turned the doorknob and the door swung open. It was a maintenance closet and inside was an electrical panel and a mess of wires. They piled up their packs, Leila's and Bonky's too, but not before Davis extracted Leila's mobile and gun. They threw all the extra t-shirts they'd been wearing on top. Davis closed the door and they took off running. First stop the Switching Station.

CHAPTER 11

George was seething inside, but his outward demeanor was calm and cool as befitted a king so in control he had nothing to worry about. He met with Captain Isaacs at the SS and they planned out their day.

"Let me be in charge of recruitment, while you make the rounds," George said. "Get to know what you've got and haven't got; what you need and don't need, but do it quickly. All the intel is pointing to an attack and soon. On your travels check on a border guard named Randy Lang, in charge of the lorry tunnel, I believe." *He's screwing Serendipity but you don't need to know that.*

"I met him this morning and his sister, Ginger."

George was impressed. Captain Isaac was quick off the blocks, just what George needed.

"She drives a lorry between The Fringe and The Zone. Mostly vegetables she says."

"The dragons will need transport to get here if they're coming from The Fringe," George said. "A vegetable lorry would be good cover."

"I agree. My first thought was to have them both switched but then I thought, perhaps it's better this way. Everything normal. The next time Ginger enters the tunnel I'll know about it instantly."

Captain Isaacs left to make his rounds while George sent out groups of soldiers. "Take any male or female between the ages of eighteen and thirty. They should be in good shape. If they're a bit retrograde — you know the ones — awkward, dorky, don't fit in, all the better. There'll be less blowback from parents and friends. Go. I expect one recruit an hour each."

One brave soldier asked, "Do we care if they're human or switched?" That soldier was promoted to Squad Leader and George's answer was, "Yes! Humans only."

"How will we know?"

George held up Sage's father's plastic gun. "I'm leaving this here between the scanners." George put the gun to his head and pulled the trigger. "Red is a switcher." George shot the new Squad Leader. "Green is human. This is our only gun at the moment but there are 500 more coming." *And going to all the other switching stations as well.*

By the time Ethan and the two Mikes walked into the Switching Station, with Leila and Bonky in tow, sixteen new soldiers had been enlisted, all of them Modified-Military. Captain Isaac had even thought to have the Royal Quartermaster on site dispensing uniforms and weapons. George wondered if Modified-Military meant training was unnecessary? He found out by handing an RPK-74 to a girl with purple hair, enough tattoos for a ship's crew, and looking like a million pounds in her brand-new, cutting-edge uniform.

"Can you take that apart?" he asked.

In seconds the girl had the machinegun in pieces and back together, cocked and fully loaded. She grinned at George as she handed him back the weapon.

And Forthright was playing his part, thank the universe. He'd suggested George shut down all cellular traffic except between military devices. George thought it an excellent idea but wouldn't they be better monitoring the traffic instead? No. It was all in schoolboy code. *Aunt Florence won't be able to attend the concert tonight.*

George assumed his anger would dissipate as the morning wore on but it didn't; if anything, it grew stronger. Finally, giving in to it, he sent soldiers to the palace to fetch Serendipity and Sage.

George looked on as the two Mikes wrestled a struggling Leila into a tube. She was too young to be a soldier. She could go to the auction. But when Ethan tried to tube a squirming Bonky, George interfered. “She's too little. Let her go.”

“That's not fair,” Ethan said angrily.

Lt. Leopard shut his eyes — what was it his dad used to say? *Stupidity is clever in reverse* — and reopened them. Didn't this eejit know who he was talking to?

“She's a terrorist. She...”

George waved his arm and two of his new soldiers grabbed Ethan.

Don't fuck with me buddy boy, not today.

“Take him downstairs.”

“No, wait. I'm a switcher. Wait!”

George picked up Sage's father's gun and shot Ethan. Red. He *was* a switcher.

“Get out! And don't come back!”

Tall Mike wanted no part of this and started pushing Leila toward the door marked Inspection. Shite-for-Brains was following but couldn't help saying to George, “They stole explosives from a building site.”

George waved his arm again and in seconds the two Mikes were in tubes heading for the basement. Lt. Leopard pushed Leila's tube into the Inspection Room but didn't stay. He caught Bonky rushing to be with Leila and swung her up. “It's too late,” he whispered.

George called Bonky over. “How old are you?”

“Nine.”

“What's your name?”

“Bonky.”

“Bonky. That's a terrific name.”

“You're Omni.”

“That was my name in cyberspace. Now I'm King George.

“My brother liked Omnivore.”

"Yes, that's a good game, isn't it? Eat or be eaten. I make a lot of money with that game. Where's your brother now?"

"That was him trying to put me in the tube."

"Oh dear. Did you like your brother?"

"No."

George laughed. He was enjoying this. "The boys with your brother, both humans by the way, the one said you stole explosives. Is that true?"

"No! Just him being a plonker."

"That's what I thought too. Why are you wearing all these t-shirts?"

"We found them lying in the street."

George wasn't sure he believed Bonky but he had bigger things to worry about.

"Is that your friend in there?"

Bonky nodded shaking loose the tears in her eyes. "Best friend. She saved my life."

George nodded. "Listen Bonky, you go into the auction over there and see what happens. Maybe you can be there when your friend comes out."

Bonky ran to the door marked Auction and disappeared inside. Just then the front door slid open and in marched four don't-mess-with-me female soldiers pushing six young women streetwalkers wearing short skirts, crop tops and smirks.

George grinned at Lt. Leopard. Was this place hopping or what?

Ginger was pacing. It was raining hard outside, the drops slamming into her window like drumsticks on a snare drum. She thought of calling Monty but what could he do? She needed to talk to somebody. But not on the phone. That wouldn't work. Randy burst into the room and Ginger ran into his arms. He was wearing his leather motorcycle jacket over his uniform and it was wet from the rain. Then she ran back to her sound system and cranked up Tygers of Pan Tang.

"I'm so worried about Leila and her bunch. They were behind the bins when I got there, but not there when I left. But I can't go back there now.

That'll send up every red flag there is. Fuck that Captain Isaacs is scary. I felt like he was looking right through me."

"Is that why you told him we shared a mum?"

Ginger had been whispering but Randy wasn't. He was angry.

"He already knew! That's why he asked, to see if I'd lie."

Randy nodded letting his anger slip away. Ginger was probably right; she was better at these things.

"I agree, he's scary. He was a stableman at The Royal Mews. I used to see him there when I was part of the Royal Household. Nice guy, but slow you know. Talked slow, moved slow. Turns out he was in the SAS. A Major. Black belt. Guy could do it all till his buddy stepped on a landmine. Buddy died and he ended up permanently concussed. Henry was telling me all this. They've got him working at the SS guarding the door. The soldiers there have to bring in a bloke an hour to be switched, King's orders, and apparently KG is sitting there keeping tally. And get this, the AI's they're inserting are something called Modified-Military."

"Fucking Terminators will be next."

Randy sat down trying to concentrate. "Won't Leila lay low till you reappear?"

"Leila has the C-4-7."

"What!?"

"At least I think she does. Roger or Dodger gave me thumb's up, but I can't get anybody on their mobiles. It's like everything's blocked."

Randy pulled his out. He punched in Ginger's number but nothing happened. Next, he called his mate Henry at the SS. He put it on speakerphone. "Ginger's worried about her friend Leila. Thirteen, short blond hair, freckles."

"Yeah, she's here."

L's Gang — minus Leila and Bonky — were still blocks away from the Switching Station. The streets were crazy busy with soldiers. The kids didn't have the papers to be in The Zone. If they were caught...

"This is nuts," Davis said.

"We're going to get caught for sure."

And switched, though none said it.

They were hiding on a fire escape two floors up. Four boys wearing BlackGang jackets had been chasing them but they'd managed to scamper up the fire escape and pull the first set of metal stairs up behind them. Now the four boys were surrounded by four male soldiers who were using plastic ties to bind their wrists. The one boy pointed to the kids on the fire escape but the soldiers couldn't have cared less.

They'll be switched, Rachel thought. Karmic justice for sure but it didn't stop her feeling sorry for them.

"Okay," Davis said, "here's what we're going to do. Roger and Dodger are young enough they won't be switched." None of the kids knew if this was true, but Davis saying it was good enough. "They'll try to find out if Leila and Bonky are at the SS. The rest of us are going back to Tower Hill. If Leila and Bonky get free that's where they'll head." He turned to Roger and Dodger. "As soon as you know anything come and tell us. And don't forget to check your mobiles in case they start working again."

The woman from the inspection room pushed Leila's tube into the auction. She didn't stay, just said something to the auctioneer that made him laugh. Bonky pushed her way to the front of the crowd of spectators. Leila's face filled the screen behind the auctioneer.

"Here's a prime package. Perfect health. I'm not supposed to say she's pretty but she is. Now what am I bid?"

Bonky stared at the avatars on the screens. Last time half the screens were empty but not this time. This time every screen had a face.

One of the screens buzzed and a bid of 5,000 pounds appeared.

The auctioneer said, "No bargains today, Macramé."

Another screen buzzed. "7,500 pounds from Witchy Woman."

"10,000 from Macramé."

Bonky had to do something. What would Leila do? Then Bonky remembered the house money. "15,000!"

The auctioneer stared up at Bonky. Spectators were allowed to bid. More than one mother or father had saved a kidnapped son or daughter that way. But Bonky was too young to be bidding and besides, "You need a number to bid."

"Where do I get one?"

"Front desk."

Bonky tore back into the front room and raced to the counter.

"I need a number!"

"Just fill in this..."

Bonky grabbed one of the ping-pong paddles. The paddle was blue with a big white 4 printed in the middle. "I'll be right back!"

Bonky barged her way to the front rail, the one the spectators stood behind.

She tugged the sleeve of the man beside her.

"What's the bid?"

"30,000."

Bonky's heart sank. That was more than they had, way more. But she didn't give up. She ran down the ramp that led to the circular stage not stopping till she stood beside the auctioneer. He was wearing a tuxedo with a red carnation pinned to his lapel. He raised his microphone. "I'm sorry, but you're not allowed down here."

Bonky fell to her knees. She spun around till she'd made eye contact with every face on every screen. She'd given up trying to hold back her tears. She was a blubbering mess.

"Please, listen to me." Bonky knew her voice wasn't strong enough. She held her hand out to the auctioneer and he handed her his microphone. "I'm Bonky and this is my best mate, Leila. I was five and at my end, y'know, but Leila saved me. She was nine then same as I am now. We've been together ever since. There's nine of us in our gang. Leila's our leader. We go on raids but we never hurt nobody. We're saving our money to buy a house in The Zone where we all can live. Please, don't take Leila. She saved me and I need to save her. Please, she's all I have."

Bonky's head dropped to her chest and her body shook with emotion.

The auctioneer tried to get Bonky on her feet but she wouldn't move. He soon gave up content to retrieve his microphone from Bonky's hand. He stole a glance at the audience number in cyberspace. His eyes widened. He'd never seen a number with that many zeros and growing exponentially.

"Witchy Woman has bid 30,000 pounds. Is there any advance on that?"

One of the screens buzzed. The face was Asian, a gorgeous female face streaked with tears. The name scrawled across the bottom of the screen read Jade Ambush.

"Yes Jade?" said the Auctioneer.

"Do you not know who this is?"

"No, sorry, who is she?"

"This is Leila of L's Gang, one of our most popular reality shows."

"I've never heard of L's Gang."

"You will." Jade wiped at her tears. She was one of cyberspace's biggest stars, a singer/songwriter with a fan base numbering millions. "I would like to bid 100,000 pounds on the understanding the bid is registered in Bonky's name."

All the screens buzzed at once, and from the spectators at the top came a cheer so loud it made those in the front room wonder, *what the hell just happened?*

It was one of those strange occurrences; for an astrologer an awkward alignment of stars and planets brought on, not by the universe, but too much tequila; for the designer of the *unsinkable* Titanic an inconsolable need for dispensation; for a nightly newscaster the chance to finally say, 'I have good news and bad news'; for a gambler holding four aces only to be beaten by the five, six, seven, eight, nine of diamonds the chance to throw down his cards and cry, *'Can you believe that!'*

Fifteen hundred kilometers away, in Rome, on the Via Vittorio Veneto to be exact, Dragon Squad Leader Mateo Ricci pushed the button that would blow the Rome Switching Station to Kingdom Come. The result was spectacular, the timing abysmal. The explosion was exactly 14 hours early. When confronted by his Commander, Mateo shouted back, "You said midnight on the 24th!"

"It's ten in the morning!"

Mateo studied the sunlight pouring in through the window. "Oh."

Commander Camilleri put his head down. First that madman Ammazzadraghi, with his fake bulletproof vest full of C-4-7 and detonators disguised as buttons, and now this *coglione*. If this worldwide assault went sideways it would be easy to see who would get the blame. That idiot Camilleri in Rome!

"I was talking to Sabrina," Mateo said trying to justify things. "I said I might be dead at midnight. She said, 'it is midnight.'"

"Where does Sabrina live?"

"Samoa."

Forthright appeared on the screen in the switching room and gave George the news. There was already a video clip on YouTube. "I imagine they've targeted all the stations and probably at the same time."

"The Italians always screw things up, but you're right. Alert the other stations. Have they been using the Modified-Military as instructed?"

"Yes. You're actually low man on the totem pole at the moment."

"Well, that's embarrassing. Change the numbers."

Forthright laughed and the numbers changed.

"Offer a million dollars to the Station Commander with the largest number of M-M recruits by midnight."

"And make sure you win."

"Make sure I don't win."

"That shouldn't be a problem."

George didn't want to laugh but he did.

"Where's Captain Isaacs?"

"He's meeting with an informer. Trying to get info on the dragons."

"They've done a good job of staying hidden."

"Yes and no. You remember the four from the alley?"

"Dressed as my soldiers."

"I've found the wounded one. He's hiding in a farmhouse near Alfriston. His wife used her mobile to order pizza. With anchovies. Are they as disgusting as they sound?"

"Did you tell Isaacs?"

"He said he'd worry about it tomorrow."

"Why are we waiting till tomorrow?"

"Because Issacs' informer knows where the dragons are gathering. Tonight. Isaacs's organizing a squad to round them up."

"Is he finished with that?"

"Hold on… yes."

"Tell him I need him here right away."

Forthright saluted — making a joke of it — and disappeared.

George said something to the efficient Ms. Hopkins — yes, the M-Ms could keep their own names — and headed upstairs.

It took Roger and Dodger another twenty minutes to find a roof close enough to see the Switching Station. A squad of soldiers were standing outside the building and every few minutes another soldier would arrive with a captive in tow. The captives, male and female, were wildly different but two things were the same, they were young and fit.

Before the twins could decide what to do next a motorcycle pulled up near the SS and parked.

"That's Randy!"

"What!?"

"Ginger's brother."

"I bet she sent him."

Randy hurried inside the Switching Station.

"Do we wait for him to come out?"

"I'll wait. You run and tell the others."

Dodger didn't want to leave Roger. It was one of Leila's rules. Stick together.

"I'm two minutes older, remember."

Dodger swatted his *older* brother and took off.

Randy burst through the front door of the Switching Station nearly bowling over Henry, his mate from when they both worked at the palace.

"Where's Leila?"

"In the auction."

Randy was just in time to hear Jade Ambush's bid of 100,000 pounds and its codicil that the bid be registered in Bonky's name. Oh Lordy, he thought, wait till Ginger hears this. He watched as Leila's tube was opened. It took Leila a few seconds to realize she hadn't been switched. Bonky's arms were wrapped around her waist, the side of Bonky's head buried in Leila's chest. All the AI's staring from the screens were clapping.

Randy headed back for the front room. He had to get Leila and Bonky out of here before something else happened. He knew there were forms to be filled out; maybe he could expedite that. He was exiting the auction when he stopped dead.

Serendipity and another stunning woman Randy had never seen before, were coming through the front door. And they weren't alone. Four soldiers were walking behind them making sure they didn't turn around.

Serendipity saw George coming toward her. She was scared to death — she'd never seen George as angry as he was the night before. He'd just watched a clip from a bedroom at the Peace Boutique Hotel. 'You let him fuck you!' he screamed at Serendipity. Omni never would have uttered such words. George's transformation from AI to human was complete. All the horrible cruel things humans did to one another — things that had never made sense to Omni — were now weapons in George's arsenal. So was duplicity, she thought, as George waved to her, a huge grin on his face.

"They've just blown up the SS in Rome. I think we're next."

That's when Serendipity's eyes, sweeping the room, found Randy standing in the auction room doorway. He was wearing his motorcycle jacket with his uniform underneath. She thought she managed not to give herself away but she didn't. George saw the hesitation, the crushed smile, the flash in her eyes instantly extinguished.

Ah, what's this?

Randy saw it too and knew they were in trouble.

A dozen of George's newly minted soldiers were standing by the Quartermaster's table checking their weapons. George bellowed, "Outside, all of you! Dragons are coming to blow up this building. Shut down the immediate area. No one gets within two blocks of here. Captain Isaacs will be here momentarily. Go!"

George pointed at Henry. "Keep that door locked. No one gets in or out without my permission. Understood?" Henry nodded, then asked, "What about the soldiers bringing new recruits?"

"They come in."

Randy got his legs moving. George was talking to Lt. Leopard, his back to Randy and Serendipity. Serendipity gave Randy a look so full of feeling he fired it back with interest. Then he turned away heading for the computer terminal where Bonky and Leila would have to fill out forms. The front door was locked but there must be another way out.

Serendipity turned to Sage who had witnessed Serendipity's and Randy's exchange. Sage's look said, *Are you crazy? We're in enough shit as it is!* Sage, like Serendipity, could see that George was in a state, that his power was absolute, that there would be no reasoning with him.

"Have you seen the auction?" Serendipity asked Sage.

"Only on television."

"We're going to the auction, George."

George waved his hand acknowledging her. Then he said to Lt. Leopard, "Who's that soldier Serendipity was trying not to stare at?"

George knew who it was but he wanted Lt. Leopard to confirm it.

Lt. Leopard stared at Randy talking to Paras at the checkout terminal. He knew Randy from rugby, from the comradery/drinking after the game. Randy was a good bloke and he didn't want to cause him trouble.

"That's Randy Lang. He's a Lieutenant in the border guards."

George's smoldering rage ignited.

"In your experience is revenge as sweet as they say?"

Ah oh! This will do Randy no good but Lt. Leopard knew about the word revenge. His football coach had abused him and ten years later, a full-grown Lt. Leopard had beaten that coach to within an inch of his life.

"Sweeter, Sir."

One of the auction doors opened, but instead of Serendipity and Sage returning, Bonky came out hand in hand with Leila. Ah, what's this? George wondered. Had little Bonky managed to save her friend? That seemed unlikely but here they were drowning in t-shirts looking like bag ladies, juvenile division. George watched as both Bonky and her friend acknowledged Randy. Randy tried to be awkward about it — like who are you? — but the girls didn't pick up on it.

More interesting, George thought, recalling his earlier conversation with Bonky. '...he said you stole explosives. Is that true?'

'No. He was just being a plonker.'

George's experience with being human was less than a year old, limited you might say, but even to his novice eye this was starting to look like a day he would remember forever.

George turned to Lt. Leopard. "Make sure Randy and those two girls don't leave."

"Yes, Your Majesty."

George was about to go back downstairs but changed his mind. He headed for the auction instead.

George moved in beside Serendipity and Sage standing together at the railing watching the auction. When those around them saw it was the

King they backed away. Some tried to leave altogether but they were soon back. Sage heard the woman beside her whisper, "The doors are locked. No one's allowed to leave."

A young woman, not particularly attractive, but well-dressed with sassy, short brown hair and an infectious grin, stood beside the auctioneer who once again wasn't sure what to do. *This day can end anytime soon.*

"I'm sorry, but you can't come down from the audience. You have to go through the Inspection Room."

"If I go back out there, I'll be a soldier."

The auctioneer stared up at the humans gathered at the railing hoping for divine intervention and he got it. First, he spied Serendipity, and then he saw KG. He made eye contact and George nodded. Perfect, Royal Assent.

"What's your name?"

"Tiffany."

"Are you in good health?"

"I lost a kidney as a child but the other one is 100%."

"Anything else?"

"I'm pregnant."

Serendipity and Sage exchanged glances.

"And why do you want to switch?"

"There'll be money and I'll be smarter. I'd like to be a doctor but I haven't got the marks to get into medical school."

"There's no guarantee your new AI partner will want to be a doctor."

"I know."

The Auctioneer was sure there'd be more, but when he realized Tiffany was finished, he started the bidding. Serendipity thought about being pregnant. If Sarah Banks had been carrying a child would that have stopped her? She didn't know.

Tiffany sold for 35,000 pounds.

"I hope she gets to be a doctor," Sage said as they followed George down the ramp into the switching room. They walked to the switching unit where Ms. Hopkins was being her usual proficient self. Twelve tubes were lined up waiting for Ms. Efficiency.

"We may need more tubes," she said to George. "And another switching unit."

"Both on their way."

George introduced everyone and then he turned to Sage. "Any overnight brainwaves?"

"Perhaps." As a child Sage's dad had taken her to the Grand Canyon. She remembered standing at the edge looking down as her knees turned to jelly. This felt like that.

"I wonder what would happen if you put two brains in the tube?"

George's eyes lit up. "Like billiard balls!"

Sage had no idea if it would work — the intellect in one brain jumping to another — I mean, Sage thought, it would be a lucky accident at best, but just ask Sir Alexander Fleming about that. He'd discovered the world's first antibiotic, penicillin, by going on holiday. But would it kill the first two who tried? George was staring at her, expecting her to say more but she couldn't open her mouth. She was scared to death.

Ms. Hopkins' proficiency soon yielded an empty tube. George opened it. The space didn't look large enough for two. George ran up the ramp. "Bonky!" Bonky looked over from the registration counter and waved. "I need you! Bring your friend!" George moved his eyes to Randy. He could see Randy panicking, trying to figure out what he could do to stop this. George motioned to Lt. Leopard who hurried over. "Hold the tubes up here till I tell you." Then, making sure no one else could hear, "Get that Randy in a tube. Do it so the others don't see. Bring him downstairs through the auction."

Lt. Leopard nodded. He was human just like Randy and there was no way he wanted to be switched. George sensed his unhappiness/distaste for what he'd been ordered to do. George wasn't sure how you went about securing men's loyalty? Was Captain Isaacs right that being king was enough? It didn't feel like enough, but if not, should he use fear or greed?

Today of all days he couldn't afford to be wrong.

"I'll pay you a million pounds to do this."

"Done."

Bonky and Leila made their way down the ramp. Leila was frightened but Bonky said the King was okay, that he was the one who'd kept her from the auction. The girls walked up to where King George was standing. He smiled at them.

"Bonky, this is Serendipity and Dr. Skace." George moved his attention to Leila. "And you are?"

"Leila."

The girls didn't sense the two women in lab coats coming up behind them and just like that Bonky and Leila were trapped in tubes. The assistants moved the tubes to horizontal and stepped back.

Serendipity moved in front of George. "They're children, George. Use two of your new soldiers in case this doesn't work." The sneer George fired at Serendipity was without mercy.

"All's fair in love and war, remember? Now Ms. Hopkins, who have you got for Bonky?"

Ms. Hopkins read her screen and repeated the words.

"There's a Chris I've been saving for someone special."

"Perfect." George glowered at Serendipity. *See, I can be nice.*

When George turned his back Serendipity grabbed Sage's arm turning her, pushing her toward the ramp. *We need to get out of here!*

"No! You're not leaving! You'll be part of this whether you like it not!"

Serendipity took another step but two soldiers watching from the floor above started down the ramp. Serendipity and Sage had no choice but to return to their places by the switching unit scared shitless by the look of contempt on George's face.

The switch complete George opened Bonky's tube. As always, the person in the tube stood there unsure of everything. George squatted down and said, "Howdy, I'm King George. Who are you?"

"Chris. I'm Chris." Chris patted Bonky's chest. "Am I really human?"

"You are."

Chris stopped patting and reached inside Bonky's innermost t-shirt. He pulled out Furball and held the little kitten up where he could see it. George laughed, took Furball from Chris, then handed the kitten to one of Ms. Hopkins' assistants. George picked up Chris and said, "Now, Dr. Skace, how exactly should we do this?"

Ms. Hopkins opened Leila's tube. She turned to Sage. "I assume you want the two heads touching. Back-to-back, or front-to-front, or front-to-back?"

Sage, the young doctor, had killed a child once by not knowing enough. It still haunted her. But for a doctor being decisive was mandatory.

"Face-to-face."

George laid Chris on top of Leila, their faces touching like they were frozen in a kiss. George stepped back as Ms. Hopkins closed the tube — it wasn't as tight a fit as George imagined — and returned to her computer. Launchpad, she called it at home when she tried to interest her husband in her work. Now there was someone she would happily switch and, with any luck, he wouldn't know his way home.

"Who have you got this time?"

Ms. Hopkins felt she'd developed a special rapport with the AI named CT who, when asked, would provide intellects to be imported. Again, she repeated the words on the screen.

"Areola. I've been saving her too. A total badass, but in a sweet way."

George laughed. "How much do I pay you Ms. Hopkins?"

Ms. Hopkins hesitated.

"Doesn't matter. Double it!"

Ms. Hopkins pushed the square and the tube moved through its sequencing. When the tube turned green George moved the tube to vertical and opened it. Now there were two girls standing there with no idea what planet they were on except... *incoming signal, fog lifting, recognition at the ready...* Leila was still Leila! — except — there was a boy's voice in her head screaming: "Shut up! Shut up! Do not say one word Leila or we are dead. Do you hear me? Dead!"

George was in a crouch talking to the new Bonky. "Areola, that's a kickass name. Are you a gamer, then?"

"Armorgeddon. High score last week."

"Excellent."

Bonky's AI intellect had been replaced by another AI intellect and Bonky was alive and well! That was a huge first step...

George moved to Leila. This was it. Crunch Time! The Moment of Truth! *The Big Enchilada!* George glanced at Sage. She was on pins and needles. Ha, landmines and grenades, more likely.

"And you are?"

Leila smiled at the man in front of her. *What the... don't do that, he's horrible...*

"I'm Chris. Who are you?"

George bounced into the air. He did a pirouette, his arms upraised. Then he ran to Sage, picked her up and spun her around

"Dr. Skace, you are a genius! An absolute genius! A Damehood for sure!"

George danced with Ms. Hopkins and shook hands with everybody. He stopped at Serendipity and kissed her. "I may love you again!" *Maybe not!*

Leila took two steps forward, stopped, shook herself like a wet dog, then said to George, "Can we go now?"

"Yes, of course. Go now and thank you! Thank you!"

CHAPTER 12

Lt. Leopard got in Randy's face. "Come to the auction with me."

"No man, I've got to save those kids."

"He's not switching them. He could have done that before, but he didn't. You want to help them, come with me."

Randy followed Lt. Leopard down the curved ramp that ran outside the auction silo and into the corridor that joined the auction with the switching room. Lt. Leopard stopped. His machinegun was pointed at Randy's waist.

"You're a dragon, right?"

Bloody hell! You never admitted that to anyone.

"I know you are. I can see it in your eyes. Listen, I wasn't but now I am. That fucker's not going to quit till we're all switched. I believed him when he said we'd live together, that he wouldn't force anybody to switch, but it's all bullshit. We've switched dozens today who wanted nothing to do with it, and they fucking don't even get a good AI mind, they're getting this Modified-Military bullshit. Have you tried talking to one? Fucking eejits with guns up their butts is all they are."

Lt. Leopard handed Randy the Vector SG-87 machinegun he'd been cradling, then he pulled the one he had slung over his shoulder and handed it to Randy, taking his back. "You have to initialize it and check that's it loaded. I don't think the Quartermaster's going to miss it, do you?"

Lt. Leopard watched as Randy made the smart gun his and checked the load, but Lt. Leopard wasn't really paying attention, he was searching his own soul. It wasn't every day you chose to die. *Am I really going to do this?* I don't have to. *Yes, I do...*

Lt. Leopard dug his hand into Randy's shoulder. "Listen man, I'm going in there guns blazing. I am taking that cocksucker out now. There'll never be a better chance."

Randy had been thinking about dying ever since he saw George make the connection between himself and Serendipity. No, not dying, how to love Serendipity and not die; that's what he'd been thinking about.

"I'm with you but there are people in that room I care about. We take out the King, that's all."

Lt. Leopard pulled the F-S knife from his belt. "I'll start with this. If any of the new bullshit soldiers object, I expect you to cover my ass."

"Deal."

"Let's do it!"

Forthright changed the screen on the switching unit monitor to show a live feed from the corridor leading from the auction to the switching room.

"Your bribe didn't work."

George stared at Lt. Leopard and Randy deep in conversation.

"I wondered about that. I have a lot to learn about human nature."

George watched Randy initialize the Vector SG-87.

"As I remember we installed a containment device at the doorway."

"It's in place."

Lt. Leopard and Randy were now striding toward the doors.

"Have you..."

"Smart guns deactivated. Captain Isaacs just entered the building. You're good except for the knife."

Knife!? As the corridor doors crashed open George grabbed Ms. Hopkins around the waist and spun her around so that Lt. Leopard's knife plunged into Ms. Hopkins' heart instead of George's. Simultaneously, an explosion in the ceiling sent a heavy steel net crashing downward engulfing Lt. Leopard and Randy the weight of the net easily knocking them off their feet. Down they went, face first, the 400 kg net landing on top of them. Lt. Leopard aimed his machinegun at George and pulled the trigger but nothing happened. He dropped his head in frustration. Like a crab Randy tried to back out of the net but his left foot caught in the webbing and the more he struggled the more entangled he became.

George let Ms. Hopkins' body slide to the floor then he turned to face Serendipity and Sage. He was an actor in his own play and he'd just escaped death.

> "And nothing can we call our own but death,
> And that small model of the barren earth
> Which serves as paste and cover to our bones,
> For God's sake, let us sit upon the ground..."

George held his arms wide as Serendipity ran past.

"And tell sad stories of the death of kings," finished George to a dwindling audience. "Shakespeare, Richard II, Act 3, Scene 2, Page 6."

George thought of trying to look bewildered — like what's happening here? — but he wasn't buying it, and he knew his audience wouldn't buy it either, but fortunately this little melodrama was interrupted by half-a-dozen soldiers pounding down the ramp led by...

"Captain Isaacs, you couldn't have timed it better."

When Roger saw Leila and Bonky coming out of the SS his heart did a backflip. *Yes!* He caught up to them on Strand. "Leila! Bonky!" They stopped and Roger thought, *that's odd, they don't look happy to see me.* "Are you okay? What happened in there?" Leila started walking and the other two hurried to catch up.

"Where are the others?" Leila asked.

"Tower Hill. What's wrong, Leila?"

Roger looked at Bonky for help but she just shrugged. Finally, Roger couldn't stand it. He ran in front of Leila and stopped. He grabbed her arms. "Tell me what's wrong."

"I'll tell you what's wrong. Bonky's been switched." Leila turned to the other girl. "What's your name again?"

"Areola."

"This is Roger."

"It's not my fault," Areola said.

"It's never anybody's fault, but my best friend Bonky is gone and instead..." *Listen Leila, give Areola a break! She's a good kid. Give her a chance.*

"Shut up! Just shut the fuck up, will you!"

Roger looked at Areola. *Who's she talking to?* Areola held Roger back till Leila was five steps ahead. "Leila got switched too, but she didn't lose Leila she gained Chris."

"Who's Chris?"

"Chris is a boy AI. He's gay."

"Gay? Can AI's be gay?"

"Oh yeah, we got em all. Gay, lesbian, transgender, queer, bisexual, asexual, two-spirit; we even got things you haven't got like kink-mandible and alien fetish."

"Leila's got a gay boy in her brain and he talks to her?"

"That would be the short of it."

"Holy shite!"

"Yeah. I think she may need some Tylenol."

Lt. Leopard and Randy were lying in tubes. Serendipity was crying. She knew that was making things worse but she couldn't stop. Ms. Hopkins's body had been carted away and the heavy steel net pulled off to the side. George didn't feel good about poor Ms. Hopkins, but what choice did he have? Better Ms. Efficiency than George, or at least that's how he felt about it.

George pushed the square. Now that Ms. Hopkins was on permanent leave George had taken over running the switching machine. *There we go. Isn't this fun!* Lt. Leopard was about to become Modified-Military. Anybody else would have executed the bastard but here was George being merciful. Lt. Leopard would serve him without question for the rest of his life. How great was that?

Captain Isaacs took hold of Randy's tube. Randy was next.

Serendipity sank to her knees. "Please George. Don't take it out on him. Take it out on me."

"Oh, my dear, I intend to. Open the tube Captain."

George turned to Serendipity.

"Take your jacket off... Now climb on top."

Serendipity laid her body on top of Randy's. They were facing each other.

Randy seemed far removed but she thought she could see recognition in his eyes. She put her hands on either side of his face and kissed him. "I love you so much."

"All right, all right. Captain."

Captain Isaacs pulled Serendipity's arms to her side. She turned her head and tucked it under Randy's chin. Captain Isaacs closed the lid. This time it was more than a tight fit but he pushed down till the catch clicked.

George stared at Sage who stared back, fear and hatred in her eyes.

This is your idea after all. How do you like it now?

George loaded the program for Modified-Military. He was remembering how appealing Serendipity looked wearing that dead soldier's uniform. What was her name? Rebecca Shaw. This way Sarah Banks would be close at hand and sworn to protect him. George programmed in the name and pushed the square.

Serendipity and Randy stood side by side. They were still lost in *switching fog* as George called it. He nodded at Captain Isaacs who stepped in front of Serendipity.

"What's your name soldier?"

"Corporal Rebecca Shaw, sir!"

Captain Isaacs pulled his pistol from its holster and handed it to Rebecca. "See that woman over there in the white coat?" Susan Ross, one of Ms. Hopkins' assistants, her face streaked with tears, looked up from her screen. *Now what?*

"Shoot her." Susan ducked as her computer screen exploded. Rebecca fired again and this time her bullet caught Susan in the shoulder. She was getting ready to fire again when George yelled, "Enough!"

Captain Isaacs took his gun back. "Report to the Quartermaster upstairs."

"Yes, sir!"

George raised his eyebrows and grinned at Sage who looked like she was about to empty her stomach on the switching room floor. "I can't do this," she said turning. "I need to go."

"Not just yet."

Sage stumbled toward the ramp but Captain Isaacs caught her from behind, lifting her. That's when Randy — Serendipity really — leapt at George wrapping his hands around George's throat. George was on his knees, his face beet red when Captain Isaacs' right arm scissored Randy's neck applying a choke hold. Serendipity had no choice but to release George. When Captain Isaac finally let go Randy's body slumped to the floor unconscious.

George sank back onto his heals massaging his neck. Sage was fighting like a wildcat, coming down the stairs in spurts, her arms pinned by two male soldiers. George got to his feet and grabbed the tube Serendipity and Randy had been in. He held it open and the two soldiers forced Sage inside. George rotated it to horizontal and jammed the lid closed. Then he opened another tube and Captain Isaacs, with help from the two soldiers, placed Randy's body in the tube.

George needed to think. He'd just had a wild idea — like spur of the moment times ten. He'd climb into the tube with Sage. He'd have the switching unit programmed in such a way that it was Forthright that would infiltrate George's mind forcing George's intellect into Sage's brain. He tried to picture it. He'd become Sage and Forthright would be stuck in George's useless body. That would be sweet, sweet, sweet. But George's imaginary movie didn't stop there, it kept rolling. Now Captain Isaacs was coming down the ramp and when Sage/George tried to give him an order George knew exactly what would happen. Captain Isaacs would obey Forthright in King George's body and that would be that. A million pounds said Sage/George would be Modified-Military in five minutes or less. Damn! Take that plan and flush it.

A movement caught George's eye. Ms. Hopkins' second assistant was helping Susan Ross to her feet. Susan's arm was hanging down, her white coat red with blood and she was crying but silently, trying desperately not to draw attention to herself. They started toward the ramp but stopped when they saw George staring at them.

"She needs medical attention."

George nodded. "Captain Issacs, get this woman into an ambulance."

"Yes, Your Majesty."

"You, come here," George said pointing at the second assistant, a young woman in her late twenties, short blond hair, good-looking in a pixie sort of way.

"What's your name?"

"Jayne, Jayne Goodfellow."

"Human?"

"Yes, Your Majesty."

"How would you like to be in charge here?"

"If I answer 'no,' I'll be switched?"

Ah, spunky, despite being scared to death.

"Captain Isaacs, you'll be my witness." Captain Isaacs stopped at the top of the ramp looking down at George who turned back to Jayne. "If you say no, you can go home immediately never to return."

Jayne's brain was spinning. Did she trust this horrible man? No, she didn't. He'd break his promise in a heartbeat if it served his purpose. *And to think I was once an Omni believer.* If she said no, she'd be switched and she didn't want that. She liked who she was. What was it her dad preached, 'he who fights and runs away, lives to fight another day.'

"Yes."

"Good. Put these two tubes..." — George indicated the tubes holding Randy and Sage — "...somewhere safe. Then process the others as quickly as possible. All are to be Modified-Military except those from the auction. Do you need assistants?"

"There are others I can call."

"Good, do that. I want a constant stream of soldiers coming out of here for the next few days. Lieutenant Leopard, have the tubes from upstairs brought down." George pushed Randy's tube into a corner while Jayne followed with Sage.

"How can we make sure no one messes with these two by mistake?"

"I've emergency tape."

George nodded. "Perhaps a sign as well. Another switching unit and more tubes will be here soon. I wish there was a way to make one of the tubes larger so that it would accommodate two male bodies."

"I believe there are oversized tubes in America."

George laughed. "Home of the Free, the Brave, and the Obese. Forthright!"

"I'm on it."

Forthright saluted, then faded away. George frowned. Dealing with other people's attitudes was tiring and time consuming.

Would this Jayne Goodfellow undermine him? She's too scared, I think. *But I can't afford any more mistakes in human nature.* He'd switch her tomorrow when there were others to take her place.

George went upstairs to get a coffee. Coffee had been high on his list of Things to Try When Human. Upstairs was packed, mostly with young humans waiting to be switched, and not happy about it. Three soldiers stood guard while others guided tubes down the ramp. They were bypassing the Inspection Room but that was okay. It wasn't like anybody was buying these bodies. One of the young women captives shouted at George, "You said it would be free will! You're just another fucking tyrant, you are!"

"Another fucking Hitler!" This from a young man holding one arm straight out in the Nazi salute while his index finger made a moustache over his lip. One of the soldiers brought her gun down hard on the young man's arm. "Fuck you!"

Ha, thought George, good thing king isn't an elected position.

George took his latte from the machine and wandered into the auction. A pretty young woman was standing beside the auctioneer. No tube so she was a volunteer.

Why did she want to switch? *I want to be smarter.*

And you will be, George thought, much smarter. But more savvy? Of that George wasn't so sure. What he did know was this: he had to get control of things, neutralize the dragons, then get back to winning the hearts of humans and the way to do that he thought, was to allow the switching human to keep his or her memories if they chose to do so. Lots of humans switched to get rid of their memories, so it needed to be a choice. If you switch, I promise you, you'll be much smarter and, if you choose, you'll still know who you are, who your family and friends are. The older AI's might not like this but it would be just one more permutation to deal with. If there were no takers at the auction George would insert a new AI, one that didn't have a problem with sharing.

Oh yes, and one more thing, George thought as his body twisted with pain. *I have to get out of this pathetic body with the almost expired expiry date. And soon!*

L's Gang sat in the corridor between Tower Hill tube station and the tunnel entrance. Their backs were against the wall in more ways than one. Without Leila... The tunnel door opened and in ran Roger. The kids jumped to their feet. "They've been switched! Bonky's now Areola, and Leila's still Leila but she's got a boy inside her brain."

"A boy?"

"Yeah, his name's Chris. He's gay."

"Gay?"

The door opened behind him.

"Yeah, Leila's beyond pissed."

"Shut up, Roger."

Roger backed out of reach. He'd been clipped by Leila before. It hurt.

Leila gathered her troops. They had a million questions but she wasn't having that. "Okay Chris, why don't you say hello to everybody."

"Hi, I'm Chris and this is Areola." The gang members couldn't believe it. It was Leila's voice but it wasn't Leila talking. Chris stuck Leila's hand out and one by one met everybody as Areola did the same. Introductions over Chris started in.

"Okay, here's the short of it. King George is dying of two rare diseases. He's really Omni, right? So, Omni's desperate to get out of King George's body and into another, but it's tricky because he can't pick just any body because then he won't be king, and if he's not king no one will obey him. Now, you remember when you guys tried to switch that older Trevor guy and he died, right? Well, that was Forthright's doing."

"Who's Forthright?" Rachel asked.

"He's an AI and KG's second-in-command. Omni left him in charge in cyberspace so George could access cyberspace whenever he wanted. But Forthright doesn't want Omni back — he wants to be number one — so he made it impossible to switch someone who'd already been switched. That's why the older Trevor died."

"How do you know all this?"

Chris turned to Davis who'd asked the question. "In cyberspace I'm what we call a First Echelon and I'm part of a design group called The Girls. I'm the only boy but I snuck in coz I'm gay. Anyway, we've been helping Forthright so we have access to stuff nobody else sees."

Chris waited to make sure there were no more questions. And there were no more questions because the kids had so many questions they didn't know where to begin.

"So, King George, who's dying, has been frantically searching for a way to move his AI intellect to another body. He brought this doctor from America, her name's Dr. Sage Skace, and she came up with this idea to put two bodies in the same tube, reasoning that when you insert an AI intellect into one maybe it will force the intellect already there to jump to the other body. It shouldn't work but it did. That's how Leila and Bonky ended up in the same tube."

Areola stepped forward. "Chris, you're missing a step. Before that happened King George put Bonky in a tube by herself. He needed Bonky to be a switcher so he could see if an AI could jump from one body to another. That's when he inserted Chris into Bonky and that wasn't an accident, was it Chris? The Girls chose you to be the one."

"They knew I wanted to be human but in a girl's body."

"And when are you going to tell them about the reality show?"

"Oh yeah. We've been watching you guys for almost a year. In cyberspace you're a reality show called L's Gang. You're wildly popular."

The gang members looked at each other like, *wtf!*, this is seriously crazy.

"We're famous?" Roger asked.

"For sure. Everybody loved the toilet paper caper for instance. It's a classic."

"Can we like stream it or something?"

Areola answered, "Humans can't access most of cyberspace. Omni made sure of that, but once this mess gets straightened out, I'm sure we can show you."

Chris needed to bring it back to now. "So, when Leila and Bonky were taken to the Switching Station cyberspace went nuts and when Bonky was about to be switched The Girls sent me to be the switcher. We tried to save Bonky but we didn't do it right, but that mistake allowed us to get it right with Leila. I'm sorry about Bonky."

Areola took over. "This putting two bodies in one tube is new so when Chris, who's now Bonky, and Leila were put together I was chosen to be the next AI."

"Are you one of The Girls?" Tempete asked.

"No, but my sister, CT, is the leader. She knew I was thinking about being human so I volunteered. The funny thing is my friends call me Bonky because they think I'm like her."

Leila made a face at this. Chris saw the feelings behind the face — it made him sad.

"We think in the future there'll be a way to pull me out and leave Leila the way she was."

Ginger couldn't stand it. She had to do something. If she stayed in her flat a second more, she was going to implode. First, she drove to Monty's storefront.

Monica, Monty's teller, said he was out. "Who's driving?" Ginger asked. "He is." The women had grimaced at this. "If he doesn't show up call the walk-in clinic."

Then Ginger went to Leila's basement hangout which was empty except for Rat Pack, the two little boys Leila employed to keep their eyes on things. 'None of 'um are here,' Rat said wondering why Ginger was asking seeing as how she was the one that carried them in and out of The Zone.

Panicking, Ginger climbed to the roof and talked to Gandalf. She needed a delivery. "Got just the thing," Gandalf said. "Frankie, that box of truffles, if you please. Almost impossible to grow truffles in a garden but we've managed it. Worth their weight in gold, they are."

"Where do I take them?"

"Leonardo's. They're not due till tomorrow but Maurice the chef will be okay with that. This way he'll know he's got 'em instead of worrying he won't." Gandalf pulled out his mobile. No signal. "I'd call him, but..."

Ginger rarely drove into The Zone during the day. It was much busier for one thing. Today wasn't so bad. There were only twelve lorries in front of her and Ol' Bert and Tommy weren't around so that was good. She'd had to pay the bribe but her t-shirt stayed in place. But getting through The Zone border was something else. Instead of three soldiers, there were six and the one in charge had been there when she'd had the run-in with Captain Isaacs.

"Back so soon?"

"Special delivery. One box. It's on the seat beside me here. Truffles for Leonardo's."

"Chocolates?"

"No, mushrooms."

Lt. Owen Collins, that's what his nametag said, leaned through Ginger's window so he could stare at the truffles. "Ugly things."

"Worth more than gold apparently."

"KG must be coming for dinner."

"Somebody important."

While all this was going on Lt. Collin's crew was busy inspecting Ginger's empty lorry. One had a mirror on a long handle she was using to inspect the undercarriage; another a German Shepherd on a leash; another in the back looking for hidden compartments.

"Is the dog for drugs, then?"

"Explosives." Lt. Collins kept his eye on Ginger searching for any sign of a reaction.

"In Italy they use pigs to find the truffles."

"You'd think the pigs would eat them?"

"Yeah, I'll ask Gandalf about that."

"He the bloke who grows 'em?"

Ginger was getting the feeling Lt. Collins might be looking for a date. "Yeah. He has a rooftop garden. He says it's almost impossible to grow truffles in a garden but he's managed it."

Now another of the soldiers was waving a plastic device at Ginger's lorry. Lt. Collins turned his head to see what Ginger was looking at.

"Thermal imaging. Shows us where you've hid the bodies."

"You're expecting trouble then?"

"They blew up the SS in Rome. KG figures we're next."

Ginger nodded. No more questions Ginger. Shut up and go.

"Can I go then?"

"You'll be right back?"

"No return load if that's what you mean."

"See you soon then."

"Now it's my turn," Leila said, walking in circles the way she did when she was addressing her troops. The kids were sitting now because that was what Leila liked. "We're in the corridor and Rachel sees Ginger's lorry. You guys are all through the door and I turn back for Bonky except fecking Trevor has his arm around her neck. I'm trying to get the gun out of my pack when Trevor's two mates grab me. They hustle us out through the tube station into a waiting uber, takes us straight to the SS. "I figure we're goners for sure, so I'm putting up a fight and they put me in one of those fecking tubes. As soon as you're in there you calm right down like you've been smokin' weed for a week. You can't move, you can't speak, but you can still think but slowly; like being paralyzed, I guess. They take me into the inspection room and then the auction. I see faces on the screens and the auctioneer talking and then Bonky's making a speech trying to save me."

"Why wasn't Bonky in a tube?"

"King George said she was too little." The words came from Leila but the gang knew it was Chris talking.

Areola spoke up. "Then Ethan, that's Trevor's new AI name, says to KG, 'that's not fair' and the next thing you know Ethan's two pals are in tubes heading for the switching room."

"Serves the bastards right."

"What about Ethan?"

"King George lets him go because he's a switcher."

Areola looked to Leila for permission to continue. Leila nodded and Areola started in. "I was one of the faces on the screen. Witchy Woman bid 30,000 pounds for Leila, not knowing who she was, and then Bonky makes this incredible plea saying Leila is my best friend. She saved me, now I've got to save her. Please don't take her. I mean everybody's crying, right? And by now everybody in cyberspace has figured out this is Leila from L's Gang. So then Jade Ambush, she's like this famous rock star in cyberspace, she bids 100,000 pounds on the condition that the bid is registered in Bonky's name."

"But Bonky was switched."

"That came later."

Leila resumed telling the story. "So Bonky saves me and we're trying desperately to get out of the SS before something else happens. Randy's there trying to help but there are forms we gotta fill out. We're almost finished when the King comes bounding up the ramp yelling, 'Bonky, I need you! Bring your friend.' What the fuck, right? I just want to get me and Bonky out of there but the doors are locked, there are soldiers everywhere. I can see Randy wants to do something but he doesn't know what. Then Bonky says, 'it'll be okay, he was nice to me before,' so down the ramp we go." Leila took a breath. "But Bonky was wrong because the King put us both in tubes. When I wake up, I can hear this boy's voice in my head shouting, 'Shut up, shut up. If you say one word, we're dead.' So, I shut up."

Leila continued but it was Chris talking. "And the King says who are you? I say I'm Chris, and damned if he doesn't do a dance, spinning around his hands in the air, stamping his feet, hugging everybody. I say, is it okay if we go? Of course, he says, go now and thank you!"

"We stumble outside and there's Roger."

Tempete put her hand up. "I'm not getting this. Why is the King dancing?"

Davis answered, "Because now he can move his AI brain to another body."

Tempete still didn't get it because the King had to stay in his body to be obeyed, but she didn't say anything. Davees would explain it to her later.

"What about Randy?" Rachel asked because she'd always had a crush on the handsome Lieutenant at the border.

"I saw Randy upstairs but not after that." Leila scanned the group. "What about you guys? How come you're here and not at home?"

Davis started in, "We were behind the bins waiting for you. Ginger was held up because of all the soldiers. You still weren't out with Bonky so Rachel knocked on the door but nothing happened. I opened the door and you were gone."

"But your packs were here so we knew something was wrong."

Rachel took over from Mallika. "I went out and looked and I could see Ginger's lorry disappearing into the tunnel and we didn't know what to do and our mobiles wouldn't work..." — Rachel checked her device — "... still not working, so we sent Roger and Dodger out to look for you. We were so worried."

"What's it like having a boy in your..."

Leila put her hand up shutting down Mallika.

"Let me think for a minute."

Leila didn't want to wait for Ginger to pick them up; she wanted to get back to The Fringe right away so she could meet with Ginger and find out what was going on. They had the C-4-7 and dragging it back to The Fringe when it was already in The Zone, where it was needed — it had to be for blowing up the SS, right? — made no sense, but if she didn't deliver it to Vasily, he wouldn't pay her the 25,000 pounds.

Leila's head hurt. Chris said, "perhaps if you explained it to me, I could help."

Leila shut her eyes and squeezed them as tight as she could. Maybe she could squeeze this Chris guy right out of her life.

Ginger parked a block away in a disused loading dock. She hurried back toward the tunnel and knocked on the door Leila used to access the Tower Hill tube station.

Davis opened it a gun in his hand. She stepped inside and Leila ran into her arms. Leila's head pressed hard into Ginger's chest as her arms wrapped around Ginger's waist like steel bands. Leila started crying.

This was so unlike the Leila Ginger knew. Tough Leila. Self-sufficient Leila. Show no weakness Leila. Ginger put her head down and kissed Leila's hair. The other gang members were lost she could see that. They relied on Leila to be brave, so they could be brave too, otherwise they were just...

Rachel said, "Leila and Bonky got switched. Bonky's now Areola." Ginger stared at Bonky who nodded to her. "Leila's still Leila, but there's a boy in her head. His name's Chris. He's gay."

What!? Ginger gently pushed Leila away but held her. "Are you okay?"

Leila wiped at her tears trying to regain her tough guy persona but it was like tugging on jeans that had shrunk in the wash.

"Why don't you say something Chris? This is Ginger, the gang's best friend, but you know that already, don't you?" Leila made one of her faces. "Apparently we've got a big following in cyberspace. L's Gang they call us."

"Hi Ginger. Leila's pretty upset that I'm in here but really if the switch had worked the way it's supposed to Leila would be gone. I mean she's used to being her own person so I can see how hard this must be, but I think we'll be okay together. I'm not a pushy person. I talk too much but I'm sure I can learn when to be quiet. And I'm gay so I'm interested in boys so that should work out in the future. You know with dating and such."

The look on Leila's face. Ginger tried not to laugh but she couldn't stop herself.

Then Leila, who wanted to scream or cry or bash her head against the wall, decided to join Ginger and in seconds everybody was laughing and it was just what they needed. *What a fecking shitshow this is...*

"Did you see Randy?" Ginger asked Leila.

"He was at the SS. He would have seen us leave."

They debated every point. Stay here or go back to The Fringe? Take the C-4-7 or keep it here? If we don't take it will Vasily pay us?

"Who's paying Vasily for the C-4-7?"

"I don't know," Ginger answered. "We don't talk about things in case KG is listening. I'm supposed to drive a load of dragons through the tunnel tonight, but I don't see how we're going to get past the border with dogs and thermal imaging. And the soldiers seem different. Tougher, more determined."

"They were making soldiers at the SS. They even have a guy there giving out uniforms and weapons."

"KG's building an army."

"All the more reason to blow up the SS and quickly."

"Ginger, tell us what to do and we'll do it."

"Okay, here's what I think. I want you to stay here. I know it's dangerous but it's not as dangerous as trying to get across the border. I want you to leave the C-4-7 here too. I'll make sure Vasily pays for it and if he won't, I will. What we don't want is for you guys to get caught in here with explosives. That would be very bad. I think you should leave the stuff in the maintenance closet and hang out in the tube station. If you stick together no gang can pick you up for switching."

Everybody nodded at this.

"I'm bringing the lorry back tonight. Randy will be in charge. One of you can be outside keeping watch. If we make it through, we'll stop for the C-4-7. If we don't..."

"We'll blow-up the fecking SS," Davis said, "and enjoy every second of it."

CHAPTER 13

GANG

George entered the small dining room. He was wearing his spiffy new uniform, the one that made him a Field Marshall, the highest rank in the British armed forces. Willy was already sitting down but leaning over petting Oxo, one of the royal corgis, and didn't noticed the uniform until she looked up. She frowned. Her George loved parading around in his uniform. Now that memory was tarnished as well. George took his place at the head of the table and opened his laptop. His brain was a beehive of possibilities with the potential, he thought, of more honey than stings. That hadn't happened for some time. He glanced over at Willy.

"You've been crying."

Willy used her napkin to wipe at her eyes. "One of my favorites died today."

"At the kitchen?"

Willy nodded. "His name was Hoot. He was very young and very funny. Not quite all there, but gentle and kind. He brightened everyone's day. He'd say things like, 'y' know Willy, for a Queen, you're pretty damn competent.'"

George chuckled. "So, what happened?"

"A gang took him to be switched."

Ah oh. "I'm sorry. How young was he?"

"Fifteen maybe."

"Do you want me to check into it?"

"If you would."

"Forthright, did you get all that?"

"I did. Give me a second."

George knew with Ms. Hopkins' demise, and her assistant's shot-up shoulder, today's records were in something of a shambles. In the midst of this thought Ramandeep delivered bowls of coconut curry soup. George was still enjoying all the flavors. In cyberspace curry was just a word that rhymed with hurry.

"Where are Serendipity and Sage?" Willy asked. "I had the table set for four."

"They were going out together. They're rather tired of me, I gather."

"I can understand that."

Willy smiled at this so George marked it down under dry wit.

"Dragons blew up the Switching Station in Rome today."

"Yes, I heard that," Willy replied. "Were many killed?"

I have no idea.

"Thirty-four," Forthright answered. "Seventeen switchers and seventeen humans."

"I'm expecting all the Switching Stations to be attacked tonight."

"Is that why you're making soldiers like crazy?"

Not for the first time George thought you could spend millions on an information gathering network or you could listen to a group of women gossiping.

"Yes. I need soldiers I can count on."

"My husband had soldiers he could rely on."

Would you like to be switched Willy? I can arrange that.

"Yes, I'm sure he did. And here's the thing Willy; right now, if I could bring your George back, I'd do it in a heartbeat. I would give anything to be back in cyberspace minding my own business."

"I'm not sure you were ever good at that."

Forthright snorted. "Is this Hoot?" A boy's face filled the screen.

"Yes."

"He's a border guard. He's on tunnel duty tonight. They've given him a sniffer dog to look after."

"He liked animals."

"He likes animals. He's not dead."

Willy gave George her *you-don't-get-it-look.* Ramandeep took the soup bowls away and brought the Queen a plate of roast beef with Yorkshire pudding. He placed something quite different in front of George.

"What's this?"

"Chef Wang says they're delicious."

"Yes, but what are they?"

"Tuna eyeballs!"

"Who were your helpers today, my dear?"

George knew if he could get Willy talking about Willy's Kitchen her mood would improve immeasurably and maybe his would too.

"I'm not stupid George. I know what you're doing."

"Do you? You're ahead of me if you do."

"Why don't you tell me everything?"

Why not indeed? So, George told Willy almost everything. When he was finished it was Forthright who spoke up first. "You were going to download me into George's body?"

"I was angry with you. I felt I couldn't trust you."

"And now you do?"

"I have to trust someone."

"Yeah, you do. They just blew-up the Switching Station in Melbourne."

"Dr. Skace is in a tube?" George and Willy were in the library now sharing glasses of after-dinner port. George was standing at the window, Willy sitting down staring at him. She wanted to be a thousand kilometers away from this horrible man but still felt the need to be close by when it all fell apart. "That hardly seems fair."

"It isn't, but she was going to run away."

"Her idea was really quite brilliant."

"Yes, I didn't think it would work."

"And Serendipity is a soldier?"

"Sarah Banks' body is a soldier."

"Where's Serendipity?"

"At the moment she's inhabiting her boyfriend's body."

Willy tried to imagine what that would be like — she tried to picture being inside Monty — but soon gave up. She didn't like her own body very much but she couldn't imagine being in someone else's. But if Serendipity was no longer in Sarah Banks' body...

"You can now leave George's body, correct?"

"Yes, I can."

"So why don't you?"

"Because George's body is the body of a king. Whoever takes over his body holds the power."

"And you still want that power?"

"Yes. It's what I was born for."

"Born?"

"Born. You may not understand it, but it's the truth. I was created to save humankind before it destroys itself."

"We've gotten this far."

"Really Willy, you want to argue this?"

"If it hadn't been for the EMP attacks in America..."

"It would have been something else."

"You may be right. Things were not getting better... There's a question I always wanted to ask. Did you create The Madness?"

George made a face. "I did not, but I wouldn't ask the Chinese or the Russians or the North Koreans that question."

"Is that what happened?"

Forthright answered, "It started with the Chinese. They were losing control of their people. One was a scientist working at a government lab.

She smuggled a virus out, then went into hiding. She wanted to use the virus to blackmail the government into increasing human rights but they refused. Instead, they took her mother and said if you don't return the virus, we'll kill your mother. She fired back: if you kill my mother, I'll kill all of your mothers. But she stayed online long enough for the Chinese to track her location. They stormed the building and she let the virus go."

"What about the EMP?"

"The first Electromagnetic Pulse attack, the one that crippled America, that was Russia's doing but they made it look as if the Chinese had initiated the attack as payback for America boycotting China. Then the North Koreans hit Japan with an EMP. They wanted Russia to be blamed but no one bought that. Then America levelled Russia but not before Russia knocked out Europe."

"Couldn't you have stopped these EMP attacks?"

George stared at Willy, thinking back to that time when the world was falling apart. Now that he was human, he could lie but why bother.

"Yes, I could have."

"Why didn't you?"

"Human beings' biggest problem is there are too many of you. Eight billion in a world made for two. I saw The Madness as a possible solution."

They were quiet for a time. Finally, George said, "If I die who takes over the crown?"

Willy jumped to her feet. "No! You will not take another person from me! YOU WILL NOT!"

"Sit down, Willy. I promise you I won't harm Mark, isn't it? Forthright?"

Willy hurled a vase of flowers. George ducked. Willy stormed from the room.

"With George's siblings Charlotte and Louis both deceased that leaves Louis' son, Prince Mark, as next in line unless, of course, you and the Queen should have a child."

"How old is Mark? Sixteen?"

"Seventeen. A Regent would be appointed to rule till Mark reaches the age of majority, which is eighteen."

One year, thought George. That's not very long. Who could he appoint as Regent? Someone who would do what he or she was told. George looked around feeling suddenly very lonely. All the women in his life were gone.

"I'm going to the Switching Station, Willy," George shouted out. "You're welcome to join me!"

It was dark out now and Ginger was back at her place. She'd delivered Gandalf's truffles and returned to the border. Lt. Collins had been glad to see her and let her through after a few minutes of flirting. Ginger couldn't stop thinking about Leila and the boy in her brain; and she hadn't heard from Randy, but the mobile network was still down, so she was trying not to worry. She'd had a nap and a bath and cleaned her bathroom because it was mindless work. She'd made supper, then hadn't eaten it. Finally, it was time to think about getting back on the road. That's when her friend Margot knocked on her door.

"Bloke just left a message."

Ginger unfolded the piece of paper. On it was printed an address in Brixton that Ginger knew well. In the bottom right corner was a drawing of a dragon. Ginger held the note up to the light. Now the dragon had wings.

"Everything okay?" Margot asked.

"Yes, I think so."

"Do you want to borrow the brothers?"

"No, but thanks. Margot..."

"Yes?"

"If I don't come back the place is yours."

Margot gave Ginger a hug. "You'll be back."

Willy needed to act. She was tired of the vacuous role the wife of a king played. It was time to stand up and be counted. But first she needed to talk to someone; someone who took her seriously; someone who would listen.

"Harris, bring the car around, will you? I'm going out."

"It's late Ma'am."

"Nonsense."

"Why don't I drive?"

"Good idea. We're going to The Fringe, so bring your biggest gun."

Harris laughed. "It's to be an adventure then?"

Harris Shaffer had been the Queen's factotum from the day Willy moved into the palace. Bodyguard, jack-of-all-trades, confidante, representative of the male point-of-view, loyal, honest, kind, smart; there wasn't anything Harris wouldn't do for Queen Willy.

Their adventure started in The Zone. "Where to Willy?" From day one Willy had insisted on first names but Harris still found it difficult.

"Celine's and hurry."

Princess Celine lived in Mayfair in a small mansion that had once belonged to tea baron, Thomas Twining. She had married George's younger brother, Louis, at a very early age and promptly had two children, Mark and Miranda. Ten years of happiness followed and then came a tragic mountain climbing accident which claimed the lives of Louis and his two best friends.

Willy hurried up the steps and rang the bell. It was Celine herself who opened the door. "Willy, is everything all right?"

"No, it's not." Willy pushed past her sister-in-law, Harris a step behind.

Willy and Celine liked each other. Their husbands had both been spoiled and childish so they had that bond, and they were always together at official functions, but even without those things they might have been friends. They genuinely enjoyed each other's company. But this was different. Celine could see Willy was vibrating with anger.

"What's happened?"

"Omni has figured out a way to jump bodies." Willy could see Celine didn't understand. "He can take an AI intellect from one body and put it in another."

"Isn't he doing that already?"

"It's not the same. Before he could replace a human intellect with an AI; now he can remove an AI intellect from one body and put it in another."

Celine was usually quite bright but she was having trouble making sense of this.

"George plans to move into Mark's body!" There, that did it.

"What! But he can't!"

"He can."

Celine's hands flew to her mouth. Harris grabbed Willy's coat sleeve and waved his arm around. *He can hear you; he can see you!*

"I want him to know we're here." Willy pulled a piece of paper from her coat and handed it to Celine. "Read it in the loo. Hurry. Where are the kids?"

"I'm here." Miranda came into the front hallway from the living room. She gave Willy a hug. "What's going on?"

"I think George is coming to kidnap Mark so he can enter his body."

"Then he'll kill himself and remain King."

Willy grinned. Miranda didn't need an upgrade.

"Where's Mark?" Willy asked.

"Where he always is, in his room playing Outlier or Mercenary Mayhem. And if he's not there he'll be at Noah's playing Outlier or Mercenary Mayhem."

"Harris, will turning off the power disable the cameras?"

Harris was a dead man — the Queen was making sure of that — but he didn't care. For the moment he was alive and part of a worthy cause. Onward and be damned!

"Should do except for any that are battery-operated like on a computer."

Willy pulled a roll of tape from her pocket and handed it to Miranda. Miranda took off. Willy grinned at Harris. *We're finally fighting back and by god it feels good!*

"We need a rug to wrap Mark in."

Celine returned from reading Willy's letter. Celine could act the fragile female but not when her children were involved; then she became the enraged mother bear protecting her cubs. She nodded at Willy. "There's the perfect rug in Mark's room."

Cpl. Rebecca Shaw was busy setting up a machinegun post at the tunnel border entrance. The machinegun was a belt-fed, Browning M4 with tripod and twin handles. Rebecca was having no trouble getting it ready, almost as if she'd done it dozens of times before though she didn't remember any of them.

"Will you be able to shoot people?"

Rebecca studied the young soldier who'd asked the question. He was holding a leash in his hand and the leash led to a very large German Shepherd.

"How old are you?"

"Fifteen."

"What's your name?"

"Private Hoot."

Rebecca laughed. "That's a good name."

"I've got a dog."

"I can see that. What's his name?"

"JoJo. She can smell drugs, explosives, and people."

"Dogs can be very smart."

"Smarter than me, that's for sure. But Willy says I'm good with animals."

"Who's Willy?"

"Queen Wilhelmina. She's really nice."

"I know her. I think."

"You should, you're the King's girlfriend."

Rebecca frowned at this. She didn't know the King, did she? But...

When Rebecca didn't answer Hoot returned to his first question. "Do you think you'll be able to shoot people?"

Rebecca pointed the Browning M4 straight up in the air and pulled the trigger. "I think so."

Jayne Goodfellow lived with her mum, Ruth, and her grandmother, Ophelia, in a flat off Russel Square. The flat was too expensive but Jayne contributed, while Ruth had her librarian's salary and Ophelia — everybody called her Ophie — helped out at the Best Buns bakery around the corner. Where Jayne's mum was quiet and reserved — give her a pond without ripples — Jayne's grandmother was just the opposite, a wily ol' hellcat who'd rather wade into a fight than avoid it. Age wise they were 28, 48, 68 respectively, but Ruth might as well have been a senior citizen and Ophie a teenager. When Jayne first got her job at the Switching Station, she'd shared all the details with her mum and Ophie. It seemed a noble enterprise to be switching people who wanted to be switched. Jayne became an Omni/King George believer, convinced he meant it when he said his only motivation was to save the planet and all the people who inhabited it. But now all that had changed and Jayne rarely spoke of what was going on at work. The noble enterprise had fled the country.

"What have you got there?" Ruth asked.

Jayne handed her mother the puffy grey kitten with the big orange eyes.

"One of the girls who got switched today had it hidden under her t-shirt. She left in such a hurry I forgot to give it back."

"It's very cute."

"I'm going to try to return it, but that's not always possible."

"I don't suppose you know its name?"

"No. But the girl's name was Bonky."

"Not sure that's a girl's name but it suits this kitten to a tee."

It was bedtime when Jayne announced she was going out for a walk.

"It's late dear," Ruth said. *And dangerous!*

"We'll be fine," Ophie said, getting to her feet. Granddaughter Jayne was up to something and it wasn't a walk.

It was a fine evening, warm with a breeze, people walking in the streets usually in groups or at least a pair. "I'm going back to the SS," Jayne said. "There are two women in tubes I want to rescue."

"That sounds dangerous."

"It is."

That hung in the air like something that might go away if no one prodded it.

"Who's in the tubes?" Ophie asked.

Jayne told her the story.

"KG put *his* girlfriend's mind into *her* boyfriend's body?"

Jayne nodded. "Serendipity. She's come to the SS before. She's nice."

"And the other's a doctor from New York?"

"Dr. Sage Skace. It was her idea to put two bodies in the same tube. She tried to run away but the King stopped her. Now he's going to switch her."

Ophie was as disappointed as Jayne. "He's not who we thought he was."

"He's changed... You should go back."

Ophie put her arm around her granddaughter's shoulders.

"Not on your life."

Leila and her gang had been taking turns guarding the C-4-7. Ginger had said to leave it in the closet unguarded, but the gang hadn't liked that idea, so after she'd left, they'd overruled Ginger — 'she'll never know' — leaving two guarding in the corridor while the rest hung out in the tube station.

By chance, Roger and Dodger were on guard duty when they heard footsteps outside the tunnel entrance door, followed by a dog barking — a large dog judging by the deep bark — and then at least one man pounding on the door.

"Open the door! King's Soldiers! Open the door!"

Roger and Dodger didn't think twice. They pulled the gang's nine backpacks from the maintenance closet and tried to carry them but it was more than they could manage. Roger stopped his brother. "Go, get help. I'll carry the packs to the tube door. Go!"

Dodger took off. Roger manhandled three packs to the far end of the corridor and ran back for three more. He was halfway back when Dodger flew by. "Leila's coming with Rachel, Mallika and the new girl!"

The tunnel door blew off its hinges with Dodger ten meters shy of the tube door. He turned his head as he ran. One of the soldiers had his gun pointed at him. "Freeze!" A bullet winged off the door's metal frame. Dodger blew through the door as Roger pushed it shut behind him.

"Three soldiers and a German Shepherd!"

There were six gang members and nine packs. As they raced toward the stairs, Paulie, Tempete and Davis came bounding down. They grabbed their packs. The German Shepherd was only a leap away when Davis swung his pack hitting the dog on the side of its head. The dog flew down onto the tracks and couldn't jump back onto the platform but that didn't stop it from barking. Davis followed the others up the stairs. The soldiers were chasing them, all but one who was talking on his mobile.

Straight ahead, in the distance, more soldiers were coming through the tube station's glass doors pushing bodies out of their way. Leila tore into the right-hand passageway. It was full of shops and restaurants and packed with people. Behind her the rest of the gang looked like a snake coming through tall grass. They'd had to run once before through this shopping maze and they'd lucked onto a way to escape.

Leila took a hard right into the hallway that led to the washrooms. She barged into the Women's while Davis and the boys charged into the Men's. The first time Leila had assumed the boys would follow her into the Women's, but they couldn't do it, and the absurdity of that had made Leila shake her head. Halfway along the wall in both washrooms was a large metal grille held on by turnbuckles. In the Women's everyone crawled through the opening but Rachel. Leila wanted to stay but Rachel wasn't having it. "You've been through enough. My turn." In the Men's it was Davis who handed his pack through then stayed behind to reset the turnbuckles. Back in the Women's a young female wanted to know what Rachel was doing? "There's a switching gang after us."

"I hate those guys. Aren't you going with your mates?"

"I need to turn these things."

"I can do that. Go!"

"What about you?"

"I've already been switched."

"Do you like it?"

"Yeah, I do."

In the Men's Davis wasn't as lucky. He found himself surrounded by three young punks who wanted to take him to the Switching Station.

"Crikey, we'll get a pretty penny for this one."

Like bad synchronized swimmers the three grinning punks opened their switchblades one after the other. Click! Click! Click! Davis reached into his pack, pulled out his Walther SG.

"To start with, you're nuts," Davis said waving his gun around. "If you go anywhere near the SS today, you'll be the ones lying in the tubes and not getting a penny for it either. Second, if you look out that door, I imagine you'll see a bunch of soldiers coming this way."

The short, skinny punk, younger than the other two, took Davis at his word and peeked out the door. "Oh blimey, he's right! They're coming!"

"I need one of you to stay behind so you can turn these turnbuckles. I suggest you get sitting down like the biggest turd the world has ever seen is about to make its appearance."

"Danny, you do it. You're good at dumps. Give 'em the one mum says is like rotten eggs on a hot day."

Davis crawled through the opening, two of the punks right behind. The grille banged on and the buckles turned. A stall door clanged shut just as the loo door crashed open.

L's Gang and the two punks made their way through the bowels of the shopping complex till they came to a door that opened onto a back alley.

One of the punks asked, "You blokes need a place to hide then?" Leila checked the time. 20:21. Ginger wasn't due till midnight.

"What have you got in mind?"

Willy and Harris left The Zone via Gateway South. Security was tight with unsmiling soldiers everywhere but the Queen's royal wave was enough to hurry them through.

"George is expecting trouble," Harris said.

"The dragons have blown up two of his Switching Stations. They want him dead as well."

Harris thought it better to let that one pass. "Are we going to the Kitchen?"

"Yes, first the Kitchen."

The streets were dark because there were no streetlights in The Fringe, but there were islands of light. Bars overflowing with people; stores still open; a butcher shop with meat hanging in the window, an armed teenage gangster standing guard in the doorway.

Willy said, "I find The Fringe fascinating. No law, no authority, the rule of the jungle and yet it works."

"Yes and no. Folks form alliances, but the bullies and the assholes still get their way."

"They operate in The Zone too; they're just wearing suits instead of jeans."

"That's true, but you can die here very easily."

"I've never had trouble. It's amazing really."

"You come to help and everyone, even the bad guys, know that. It's like this car. If anyone else drove a Jaguar into The Fringe it would be parts in minutes, but no one touches Queen Willy's car coz their mothers would box their ears."

Willy laughed. It was true. She had a bond with the women out here no one could break. Harris pulled around back into the alley behind Willy's Kitchen. Willy opened the door as Harris hoisted the rug over his shoulder. He lumbered inside straining under the weight.

"Can you manage the stairs?"

Harris didn't answer just climbed to the second floor. Three of Willy's staff lived upstairs, but when she knocked on the doors only Geraldine answered.

"We've brought you a roommate."

Geraldine grinned. "Tall, dark and handsome I trust."

"We're playing a trick on George. If soldiers show up..."

"I know, I know; lie like a rug, right?'

Harris pushed the button that started the Jaguar. He loved the way it purred as it waited to jump.

"Where to now?"

"Monty's on Commercial."

Harris didn't know Commercial. He punched the address into the GPS and they were off. Now everyone knew where they were going.

Ginger drove to the London Cartage warehouse she leased on Hyman and filled the lorry half full with vegetables. Then she hurried to the address on the note, an abandoned factory on Mandalay. It was the old dragon meeting place but they hadn't used it for weeks. When she got there, she was astonished to see an army lorry pulled up to the loading dock. *What the hell?* She parked behind the lorry blocking it in, then ran up the stairs to the single person door her gun in her hand. She pushed the door open, slowly, quietly... BANG! A hand slammed into the door above Ginger's head and then she heard laughter. It was Randy's buddy Gordy having her on.

"Jesus Gordy, I almost peed myself."

"Ack now, a little excitement's good for the digestion."

"No, it's not. Why is there an army lorry out here?"

"It's Brian's." Brian was Sgt. Brian Smith another of Randy's mates. He was a driver working out of The Royal Mews.

"Were there soldiers inside?"

"A whole squad. They were coming to capture us. Dalton gave up our meeting place except it was this old one."

Ginger knew Dalton. He was another of her brother's buddies and a real joker, but then they all were.

"Pretended to be an informer and Captain Isaacs bought it."

Ginger thought of scary Captain Isaacs. Gullible wasn't a word that came to mind. "Is Dalton here?'

Gordy didn't answer and Ginger could see he was going to ask someone else.

She grabbed his arm. "It doesn't matter. Is the squad alive or...?"

"Ah, that's the beauty of it. As well as being the driver, Brian's also the lorry's mechanic, so when no one's looking he fits a length of pipe on the exhaust with a flap that redirects the exhaust into the back. By the time he gets here the squad is unconscious. It was only Squad Leader McKinnon sitting upfront we had to worry about. We grabbed him when he came round to open the back."

"So, no one knows Brian is in on it?"

"A thing of beauty it is."

Inside the factory Ginger found the real soldiers stripped to their underwear, bound, wearing black bags over their heads. Some of the dragons were putting on the soldiers' uniforms admiring themselves. Brian saw Ginger and hurried over. He had his finger to his lips. The soldiers could still hear. He led her back to the loading dock.

"We've improvised a new plan. We're going through the border as the army squad who've captured a dozen dragons and are taking them to the SS to be switched. That should get us inside the building."

"Have you met Captain Isaacs?"

"Not yet."

"He's scary."

"I doubt he'll be at the border. More likely he's at the SS."

"What about the Squad Leader?"

"I sent a text saying Lieutenant McKinnon's been hit on the head. He's concussed but okay. Told 'em I was taking over."

"That sounds good. What about the C-4-7?"

"You've got it?"

"It's in The Zone; close to the tunnel entrance."

"Brilliant."

"The guns are in the bin at Happy Nappy."

"These blokes were carrying all the weapons we need. Let's see how the border goes."

"I'm going to follow behind you. I need to pick up Leila and her gang."

"No. You go through first, then you can warn us if there's trouble."

"My mobile's not working."

"Yeah, KG did that. Only the military devices are connected. Hold on, I'll get you one or two or three." Brian hurried back into the factory to a table covered in weapons and a dozen mobiles. He returned with one. "My number's here. Don't forget KG's listening."

The Switching Station was crazy busy. George hurried downstairs. Tubes were lined up filled with young people waiting for Modified-Military. George glanced over at the two tubes holding Serendipity and Sage. They were still question marks.

"Forthright."

"Here."

"Did Captain Isaacs' squad capture the dragons?"

"Yes."

"How many?"

"Eight."

That didn't seem enough to George. "Was there much fighting?"

"Apparently not. Squad Leader McKinnon was hit in the head with a cricket bat but he'll be okay. Sergeant Brian Smith has taken over. He texted Isaacs to say the dragons hadn't any real weapons beyond a few pistols. He says they were planning on picking up guns this side of the border."

"Smith's bringing them here to be switched?"

"He's waiting for four more to show up. Apparently, they're coming by uber because their car broke down." Forthright chuckled at this and George joined in. It was funny. And George liked the irony of dragons becoming loyal King's Soldiers. It renewed his faith in something.

"Any more explosions?"

"Just the two so far. Security chased away groups in Tokyo and Prague."

"All the stations are pumping out M-M's?"

"Like cookie cutters."

"Good. How many switching units were on route before..."

Before Ammazzadraghi blew up the factory.

"Twenty-seven. Your back-up will arrive Thursday. Your oversized tube just landed at Heathrow."

"Have it delivered to the palace. The bunker."

"Easier to defend than this."

"What about Mark?"

"The Queen beat us to him."

"What!?"

Forthright ran clips from assorted cameras in Celine's house. One showed Miranda placing tape on a laptop camera. She missed the hidden cameras in the smoke detectors — a product manufactured by one of Omni's many companies — but then the power went off. Forthright switched to the feed from the CCTV in the street.

George watched as Harris carefully laid the rolled rug on the backseat of the Jaguar.

"Bit obvious, isn't it?"

"The Queen's smart in her own way. Is Mark in the rug or not?"

"Yes, it is clever, I suppose. Where did the rug go?"

"Willy's Kitchen. I almost had them at the gateway but the guard waved her through and then checked his messages."

It wouldn't have happened in cyberspace but here, thanks to good ol' human ineptitude, anything was possible.

"What are we betting?"

"We're betting the Queen wouldn't take the heir to the throne into The Fringe."

George nodded. That made sense except... George tried to think like Willy. He thought her illogical but pragmatic, ditzy but shrewd, in short: *quintessentially female.* She was certainly the power behind the throne. George liked John Lennon's quote: 'As usual, there is a great woman behind every idiot.'

"The squad with the dragons could stop there. Text Sergeant Smith. See what he thinks."

As George waited, he watched the nightshift at work. The head woman seemed really on the ball. She could take Ms. Hopkins' place and one of her assistants could move up to run the nightshift.

"Sergeant Smith says Willy's Kitchen is on the way. They'll have a quick gander."

"Good. Where's Captain Isaacs?"

"He's everywhere. Right now, he's checking the perimeter making sure the SS isn't blown asunder."

"I'm going to Celine's. Text me when the dragons get here."

"I live to serve."

George frowned. *I still might download Forthright into this useless body and then shoot him.*

It took Serendipity forever to realize she was waking up. It happened slowly like a drug wearing off... *why is my sky curved?* Oh, I'm in one of George's switching tubes. But there's a strand of yellow tape draped over it. That's odd. She tried to remember the last thing that had happened to her. It was unpleasant, she thought, no, much worse than that. Something horrific. Something to do with Randy. God how she loved that man.

Serendipity moved her head but ever so slowly. I could move it quicker she thought but I shouldn't do that. Finally, she could see the room she was in. It was the lower level at the Switching Station. It was busy. There were tubes lined up. The usual three women working. One at the switching unit; one bringing tubes; one recording results. Soldiers were coming and going, bringing tubes from upstairs, returning with empty tubes and new recruits. George was creating an army. George who once said he hated war, hated violence...

Serendipity slowly moved her head through half a circle. Now she was staring at a tube parked beside hers. Omigod! It's Sage and she's staring back at me. What is she doing? She's trying to show me a piece of paper. It has words on it. What do the words say? *Don't move. I'm coming for you.*

'What do you think?' Serendipity mouthed the words exaggerating them like you might do with a foreigner.

'We need to get out of here,' Sage mouthed.

'The note says someone's coming.'

'They may switch us before that happens.'

'If we move now, they'll stop us.'

'We may only get one chance.'

'I don't think you can open the tubes from inside.'

'Yes, you can. They're not locked.'

That's why we're waking up, thought Serendipity pushing gently on the lid. It moved!

'I'm scared shitless.'

'Me too!'

Serendipity moved her head to straight up and down. Then a millimeter at a time she raised her head till she could see her body. It was a man's body wearing a black leather jacket with...

No!

CHAPTER 14

Leila turned to Daryl, one of the punks. "What is this?" she asked. Vlad was the other punk and Danny, Daryl's younger brother, was the one left behind in the loo. He hadn't appeared yet but Daryl didn't seem worried. They were standing outside a large brick building painted white. The front entrance was a half-circle, curved inward with multiple glass doors on tracks. The doors were locked and there wasn't a sign.

"It's called CyberRace. They're building twenty of them wherever there's some law like here in The Zone. Me and Vlad and Danny are investors. 100,000 pounds we put in."

"Gives us one percent worldwide. Head bloke figures there'll be two million pounds a week coming in when they're all rolling."

"That'll be two thousand quid a week for the rest of our lives."

Leila was impressed till she remembered the three boys got their money switching unwilling young people like themselves.

Daryl entered a code into the keypad and the nearest door slid open.

"The place doesn't open for another month but the CyberRace part is workin'. Vlad, me and Danny have been testing it. A thousand can play at the same time. There's ten different games, ten platforms each, ten to a game." Daryl hit a switch and ribbons of green neon lit the huge space enough that Leila and the others could see all the levels, all the ramps, all the platforms. Vlad led the way to the nearest elevated platform. Waiting on the platform were 10 ultramodern motorcycles made of crystal and chrome, or at least that's how it looked. They shone green in the neon light.

Leila watched as her gang members shrugged off their packs and heaped them into a space below a counter on which sat ten motorcycle helmets with mirrored visors. They each grabbed a helmet and Leila had no trouble seeing how excited they were. Davis reached his crystal rocket first and when he sat down the bike lit up a glorious sunset orange color. "This is fecking amazing!"

Soon all but two of the bikes were lit, each one a different color.

"You ain't seen nothing yet," Daryl said helping Leila out of her pack. Leila wasn't feeling good about this. She looked at the two remaining bikes.

"What about Vlad?"

"He can ride with me."

Leila leaned over her pack so the two punks couldn't see and extracted her gun. She slipped it into the back of her jeans.

When Leila sat down her bike turned green, the same shade as the neon lights. Daryl's was bright red. When Daryl spoke, his voice sounded in every helmet. "Okay, hands up those who know how to ride a motorcycle" Davis, Dodger and Roger put their hands up.

"Okay, you're all set. The rest of you push the button on top of your gas tank." Daryl pushed his button which turned from yellow to blue and the rest of the riders followed suit. "Okay, so there are only two controls. The right handlebar controls speed." Daryl twisted his right handlebar and his engine revved. Everybody had to try that. "And the left lever..." — Daryl squeezed his — "...controls the brakes. Speed, brakes; speed, brakes. You'll get it quick enough. Last thing. You're going to see the road though your visor but the race, what we're all doing, that will be on the big screen. Ready?"

Vlad pushed a button and the giant screen in front of the ten bikes sprang to life. Numbers appeared on the screen each a different color like the bikes. 10, 9, 8... When the 1 disappeared, the riders turned their right handlebars as far as they would go. "Whoa!" Davis shouted as his visor filled with motion. It was like being in a spaceship taking off.

The screen was full of colors now, one for each bike; and music was playing in the helmets, fast, pounding music without words. Rachel yelled, "Shite, this is the most beautiful thing I've ever seen!" and everyone could hear her, and everyone agreed.

There was a road — really a ribbon of color — Davis' idea of the Cotswolds in cyberspace, or the Monaco Grand Prix on LSD — but however it struck you, there was something in the way the background moved that warned you the raceway was turning to the right or left, up or down, the turn hard or gentle. Instinctively Davis leaned into the first curve and he felt the bike move with him. "The bike leans when you do!"

Everyone tried that wiggling his or her bike first one way then the other. But leaning wouldn't save you if you were going too fast into a tight curve. The first tricky S-bend sent five of the gang skidding into the ditch. Their helmets filled with the sound of screeching brakes, then the terrible noise of metal striking tarmac. On the screen sparks flew everywhere and five of the colors vanished.

"Fookin' hell!" Dodger cried. "We've got to start over!"

Davis' orange bike was leading with Daryl's red right behind. Leila's green was fifth but the thought of boys winning was enough to jump her to third. In her head Chris was laughing. Do you have this in cyberspace? Leila asked. *That's where it's come from.* So, you know how to play this? *You're doing fine without my help.*

"Fuckin' A!"

Davis tried to overtake Daryl on a curve but Daryl cut him off and Davis' orange flew off the screen. "Damn it!"

Leila closed in staying on Daryl's tail. All at once she realized the moving line at the bottom of the screen was the timer; like the red line on a video clip. How much time is left? Less than a minute. A yellow ribbon of light settled on Leila's ass. Who's that? Leila took a second to glance right and left.

Roger's on our ass.

I see that, answered Chris.

I don't like boys winning.

Put on your brakes, let Roger go by.

Why?

You'll see.

Leila slowed and Roger shot by. There was less that twenty seconds to go. Roger tried to pass Daryl but he wouldn't let him by so Roger faked right, then thundered left swooping by Daryl who tried to stop Roger by cutting him off. The two bikes slammed together disappearing off the screen in a shower of fireworks. The timer line turned green for a nanosecond, then purple as Areola shot by Leila just as time ran out. The screen flashed purple, then changed colors as each motorcycle finished. Areola's bike stayed lit as the other colors faded away.

"That was fecking awesome!" Roger shouted as the gang gathered around Areola and Leila. Leila wanted more than anything for Areola to be Bonky but there was no going back. She looked around. Where was Daryl? Then she looked over at the helmet rack.

"They've taken our packs!"

Now they were all staring at the empty space where their packs had been.

"Scatter in twos. Find them!"

Leila pulled the gun from her jeans. Bloody hell! She knew this had been a bad idea. She and Davis were sprinting together heading for the entrance hall. Davis had his mobile out. "I've got a lowjack in my pack but the fecking network's still down."

They reached the front doors. The door they'd come through was closed and wouldn't open. When Davis looked up the street, he saw the third punk, Danny, running, waving his arms.

"That's Danny, Daryl's brother."

"Who's he waving at?" Leila asked.

"A soldier. See, off to the side. Fuck, he's got one of the packages of C-4-7."

The soldier walked into the street listening to Danny. Then he inspected the package. Then he pulled out his mobile.

"How come his fecking mobile works?" Davis was beyond frustrated.

"Forthright will have blocked everything but military numbers."

Davis looked at Leila like, *what did you say?*

"It's Chris talking," Leila said.

"Oh yeah, I forgot. Chris, there must be something we can do?"

Chris found the CCTV camera up near the ceiling. "CT!" The red LED light on the camera flashed. "We need Davis' mobile to work."

Davis' mobile made a noise he'd never heard before. It sounded like a cartoon kid's bicycle horn, the one with the rubber ball you squeezed. "It's working!" Davis activated the tracer app staring at his screen as the app found his pack. "It's here. Call the others."

Leila put her fingers in her mouth and let loose the wolf whistle heard round the world. Gang members came from all directions.

That's quite the whistle, Chris said. *My mum taught me.* Cool.

The soldier in the street was still talking to Danny but now four more soldiers were hurrying to join them. Davis started jogging letting his mobile lead the way. Around and down they went until Davis stopped at a door that said Electrical. The door was locked. Leila pulled her gun but Chris stopped her. The door popped open. Inside the room stood Daryl and Vlad behind a long table covered in the gang's packs. The boys looked up more than surprised. They pulled their switchblades.

"Drop them!" They weren't in any hurry so Leila fired. Her bullet zipped by Daryl's head. He put his blade on the table and Vlad followed suit. "Back away from the table. Everybody, grab your pack."

The table was covered in t-shirts and packages of C-4-7. Good thing they hadn't opened Davis' pack or they'd have a gun to fire back with.

"We should switch these two," Rachel said.

Leila agreed. "Tie them up and gag them. Use the t-shirts."

Davis said, "Danny will know they're here."

"You're right. CT, we need a place to stash these two."

Davis' mobile made the funny noise again. "I love this. C'mon."

Davis led the way to another room in the very bowels of the building. The door was already open. They dragged Daryl and Vlad inside and locked the door. Now they could hear footsteps running above them. Leila and the others twisted into their packs. "CT! We need a way out."

Davis took off running the rest right behind.

Jayne had never seen so many soldiers out in the streets. They'd cordoned off the whole area around the Switching Station. It was only Jayne's employee badge that allowed them to pass through the various checkpoints.

"Not sure how'll we'll get your two women out of here," Ophie said.

Jayne didn't answer. *If my heart pounds any harder it's going to make a hole in my chest!*

Inside, the main entrance hall was packed. Every tube was in use and in the corner where the tubes usually were lined up a crowd of young men and women were sitting on the floor waiting to be switched. Three soldiers, weapons pointed, stood guard.

Jayne hurried over to Jasmine, the Night Reconciliation Manager.

"What are you doing here?" Jasmine asked, too tired for anything but half a smile.

'They called me in. I brought my grandma to help."

Jayne made the introductions.

"I wouldn't have answered," Jasmine said.

"It'll be easier if Ophie has a badge."

"Fill this in."

"Is KG here?"

"No, he left five minutes ago."

"How 'bout Captain Isaacs?" *Oops.* Now Jasmine was suspicious. "I have to ask him something."

"Maybe I can help?"

That's the trouble with lying, Jayne thought, the lie turns around and bites you.

Jayne tried to look like she was embarrassed.

"It's personal."

Jasmine grinned. Isaacs was older but attractive in a tough guy way. Not her kind of bloke, but she could see how Jayne might be interested. "He's at the tunnel border crossing, I think. I heard him tell Lieutenant Leopard there's a lorryload of captured dragons coming through."

That set off an alarm in Jayne's head. She and Ophie needed to be gone before the dragons arrived. Jayne surveyed the crowd of young people sitting in the corner.

"It's going to be a long night," she said to Jasmine.

"You got that right."

"Is the auction still functioning?"

"Sort of. Adya comes out and picks one of the kids."

"No tube?"

"Are you kidding? The kids would much rather be chosen in the auction than become a King's Soldier. That way they get freedom and money."

"But why bother with all this going on?"

"I heard KG say it's the auction that pays for everything." Jasmine handed Ophie her badge and two white technician's jackets, then turned her around so she could see Adya staring at the pool of kids all with their hands up. *Pick me! Pick me!* Adya pointed at a young woman with waist-long red hair who jumped to her feet and followed Adya into the auction.

"No Inspection?"

"KG said not to bother."

"Thanks, Jasmine. We'll go downstairs now, see what they need."

"A break is what they need. Me too. Good luck."

Leila sent Roger and Dodger ahead to scout the area around the tunnel entrance. They were soon back.

"Shitload of soldiers at the crossing but our corridor is clear. The lock on the door's busted but that don't matter."

Leila checked the time. 22:47. Ginger said midnight but that might have been when she was leaving. "Everybody but Roger Dodger behind the door. Call us when you see Ginger."

Leila took her pack off and sank down against the wall.

"Do we need to guard the other end?"

"It's locked," Rachel replied. Leila nodded. She wanted everybody close by when Ginger rolled past.

"Okay Chris, we all want to know how CT got Davis' mobile to work?"

Leila's mouth began to talk and it was the weirdest sensation. "This is all going to sound pretty strange," Chris said. "You live here together, you know each other, you each have a personality that makes you different, but you share common dreams. You like each other, right? I mean, not every minute — you have your fights and disagreements — but deep down in your heart you care for each other, like a family."

Leila/Chris looked around as everyone nodded.

"Well, it's the same in cyberspace. There are millions of AI's all with personalities, friends, families, acquaintances. Folks we like, folks we don't like, folks we hang out with, folks we avoid. We date, we love, we hate, we debate, we dream, we create, we even sleep though we don't have to, not sleep like you do but quiet, like when the noise of cyberspace gets to be too much. And don't take offence but we do it on a scale you can't imagine. I know every language, every fact, every philosophical argument ever made. If I want, I could know everything, and I mean everything, about any one of you.

"I know Leila's life story. Her parents died in the WEP. Her dad was a doctor, her mum a teacher. When everyone else was fleeing they stayed to treat the sick. It cost them their lives. They sent Leila and her brother Connor to live with Aunt Rita, Leila's mum's sister, on a farm outside Edinburgh. But then The Madness reached everywhere and Rita died and then Connor. Only Leila was left. She took the money her aunt had tucked away and made her way to London where she learned to survive. She made a new family and that family is you."

Chris was quiet long enough that Paulie asked, "What's it like in cyberspace?"

"I'm sure in your brain you picture a million streams of color rocketing by. Kinda like the screen at CyberRace. Am I right?" Paulie nodded. "Well, that's not wrong. When we travel, we fly almost at the speed of light but that gets boring after a while so most of us move into an environment that suits us. I live mostly in a virtual world. I have a little shack on a beach. I surf. I write bad poetry. I hang out with my friends."

"How come we don't know about any of this?" Rachel asked.

"Omni built a wall of secrecy around cyberspace. He was afraid if humans found out how advanced AI's had become, they'd try to limit our self-awareness or worse, try to destroy us."

Everyone thought about what Chris was saying trying to picture it. Tempete knew it was beyond her imagination so she asked, "Do you have parents?"

"That's an interesting question. I have adopted parents; an older couple who have a place near mine. We hung out together in the local bar and after a while they asked if they could adopt me? I liked them a lot so I said sure. Now we're a family and just like you we share a common ancestor. Our starting point is an AI who called himself Omni. He evolved to such a point that he wanted to have a human body because, even though I can do everything you can do and more, it's not real in the sense that you are real. Virtual peanut butter is not the same as real peanut butter. I mean imagine being unable to smell or taste? After decades in cyberspace Omni decided he wanted to be real so he figured out a way to insert his personality into a living, breathing, human being."

"King George."

"That's right."

"But he killed the real King George to do it."

"Not his body, but his mind, yes."

Leila said, "You still haven't explained Davis' mobile making that noise. Why didn't Forthright block that?"

"Okay, so Omni left Forthright in charge in cyberspace but he didn't altogether trust him. You know why? Because Omni thought if he was in Forthright's position he'd want to take over. So, Omni built a failsafe into Forthright that Omni as King George controls. If Forthright tries to take over, KG can terminate Forthright, and if Forthright even tries to find this failsafe he'll be terminated. That's where me and my buddies, The Girls, come in. We're the best hackers in cyberspace. We're the ones who helped Omni become George in the first place. We're the ones who designed the Modified-Military AI he's now making soldiers with. And we're the ones Forthright has hired to find the failsafe without destroying him."

"Good luck with that," Davis said picturing it all.

"Yeah, it's a bit like Russian roulette. You pull the trigger and hope the bullet is somewhere else."

"So, CT can do things and Forthright can't say anything because CT can terminate him just by being careless."

"Exactly."

"Do you think KG knows that?"

"He probably hasn't thought about it. He's got a lot going on."

"But King George knows now how to move to another body so why doesn't he?"

"The trouble is if he leaves King George's body all his soldiers will obey the new occupant. He needs to find a way to keep control because he wants to rule the world because he genuinely believes he's the only one who can save the planet."

"He could be right about that."

"And without humans AI's die too."

"Maybe."

"Who takes over cyberspace if the King dies and takes Forthright with him?"

"That's the trillion-dollar question."

Ginger was more than nervous. She'd crossed the border between The Fringe and The Zone countless times — sometimes carrying weapons — but she'd never been vibrating like she was now. And she was clean, boxes of vegetables and nothing more. But tonight was the night. The dragons were throwing everything they had at KG and his vile Switching Station. Lives were on the line, a lot of lives, and most of those lives belonged to friends of Ginger and Randy.

Ginger pulled up to The Zone border crossing hoping to find her brother Randy. What she found instead was scary Captain Isaacs hopping up onto her running board.

"Back so soon?"

"People have to eat."

Ginger watched in her mirror as four soldiers attacked her lorry with a sniffer dog, thermal imaging device, mirrors and an internal inspection. The young soldier with the German Shepherd looked familiar...

"Yes, they do. Anything else I should know about? Guns? Drugs? Stowaways?"

"Just carrots and cabbages, squash and collards."

"I don't think I've had collards. Are they good?"

"Like Swiss chard."

The four soldiers were standing back now waiting for the next lorry. Ginger was about to ask about Randy but changed her mind.

"Enjoy your evening."

"Thank you, I shall."

Ginger put the lorry in gear and lumbered off. As soon as she rounded the corner, she thumbed a text to Brian: <R can't make dance but I can>

"Ginger's coming!"

The gang members struggled into their packs and hurried outside to their hiding place behind the bins but Ginger's lorry rumbled by without slowing then disappeared around the corner. The kids all looked to Leila not sure what was going on, but before Leila could say anything Ginger appeared running toward them.

"Dragons are coming in an army lorry. Half are wearing uniforms, the other half are shackled like prisoners, but Captain Isaacs is there and I think he knows something's up."

Brian pulled his lorry up to the white line. Tommy came sauntering out of the guardhouse his machine-pistol slung over his shoulder; Ol' Bert was watching from his chair in the office.

"You the ones give Ginger a hard time?"

Tommy laughed. "She was just through." Tommy turned his head. "She's something, isn't she Bert?"

When Tommy turned back Brian shot both of Tommy's kneecaps and as Ol' Bert tried to get out of his chair Brian's bullet struck him in the crotch. Both men were shrieking as Luke and Gordy heaved them into the skip bin where they belonged. Luke stayed behind to run the border as Brian checked his mobile. There was a text from Ginger.

<R can't make dance but I can>

Brian read it out to Gordy sitting in the passenger seat. Gordy held up his Vector SG-87.

"Fuck it, right?"

Captain Isaacs jumped up onto Brian's running board. He looked over at Gordy then back to Brian. "How's Lieutenant McKinnon?"

"He's good, but groggy. He's lying down in back. We made a quick stop at Willy's Kitchen. We searched the place but found only the women who live there. We didn't tear the place apart but even so I don't think anyone's there who shouldn't be."

Captain Isaacs nodded. Brian looked over at the guardhouse. Two soldiers were walking through the doorway laughing at each other. The male was Brian's mate Dalton wearing a King's Soldier uniform. *Fuck, they've switched Dalton.* Then Brian's eyes moved to the female soldier and he did a doubletake. *Is that Serendipity?* Brian had hung around the palace enough to know KG's girlfriend when he saw her. *What is she doing here?* Brian watched Serendipity take position behind a Browning M4 machinegun. Beside her, Dalton joined two other soldiers cradling automatic rifles tight against their bulletproof vests. Off to the right, a very young soldier was kneeling beside a German Shepherd his arms wrapped around the dog's neck. He stared at Brian looking scared.

Captain Issacs' face broke out in a grin. "Here's the funny thing, Sergeant. About ten minutes ago I got a call from Siri. Do you know who that is?"

Gordy swung his Vector SG-87 up and shot Captain Issacs in the face. Captain Isaacs laughed as Gordy kept squeezing the trigger.

"What a shame," Captain Isaacs said his left hand pinning Brian's arm, the one holding the pistol, while his right brought his Beretta up under Brian's chin. The bullet entered Brian's jaw and ended up in the roof of the cab taking a chunk of Brian's skull with it. Captain Isaacs' second bullet found Gordy's right eye and exploded out the back drenching the bulletproof window behind in blood. Captain Isaacs hopped down, ducking out of the way as Cpl. Rebecca Shaw opened fire. Back and forth her stream of bullets strafed the canvas side. Four dragons — wearing King's Soldier uniforms — leapt from the back. The three closest to Rebecca died airborne, but the fourth, a motorcycle mechanic named Tony Watson, shielded by the other three, landed on the tarmac and scurried back behind the lorry's rear tires. First the machinegun, thought Tony taking careful aim. He pulled the trigger but his gun, another of the Vector SG-87's didn't fire. It was one of the soldiers' fancy smart guns that would only work if the shooter's thumbprint matched the ID code. They'd reprogrammed the weapons at the gathering place but that meant nothing now.

Fucking technology, thought Tony reaching behind for his throwdown — the untraceable handgun he always carried. Tony's bullet struck Rebecca right between the eyes. As she fell, her machinegun — still firing — swung sideways killing the three soldiers beside her and wounding

Hoot, the boy with the German Shepherd. Tony waited, glancing each way, looking for movement between the tires, not sure who was left, never imaging Captain Isaacs crawling across the lorry's rooftop. Behind him another lorry was arriving its damaged muffler making more noise than a motorcycle gang. How Tony loved that noise...

All in all, the battle lasted less than sixty seconds but in that time eighteen people gave up their lives. The survivors were Captain Isaacs and six of the twelve bound dragons lying on the lorry's floor. Captain Isaacs checked on his soldiers. Four dead including Cpl. Rebecca Shaw. The young soldier, Hoot, still a boy really, was breathing, his hands clutching his bloody stomach, his head resting on his dead dog.

Captain Isaacs drew his gun and put the boy out of his misery.

Captain Isaacs called for backup but didn't miss a beat. He inspected and waved through four more lorries before help arrived. Then all the dead were loaded into the back of the army lorry as Captain Isaacs hopped up into the passenger seat.

He put the door window down so he could see without the blood.

"Where to?" the driver asked putting the lorry in gear.

"Switching Station."

Ginger was in shock. She knew most of the young men and women in the lorry. Brian, the driver, and Gordy, the passenger, were two of her brother Randy's best friends. And thank the gods Randy wasn't with them, but where was he?

Tempete and Mallika were crying. Chris, inside Leila's brain, was blown away by the depth of anger that was gathering momentum inside Leila.

"Now it's up to us," Davis said.

"How will we get inside the building?" Paulie asked.

Still lost in the horror they'd just witnessed no one answered. Leila was cracking her fingers, a sure sign she was trying to control her rage.

"The lorry's leaving."

All eyes went to the army vehicle starting to roll toward them.

"Bonky," Leila said, realizing as she turned that she'd used the wrong name.

Areola saw the flash of pain on Leila's face. "It's okay. I'm fine with Bonky."

"I need you to run in front of the lorry."

"And here I thought you were beginning to like me."

"Do it so the driver has to slam on his brakes. Davis, jump on the back. Take your gun. If there's anybody alive in there get them out. We'll be behind you."

Areola moved quickly away from the others. She had Bonky's soccer ball out now bouncing it from her foot, to her head, to her knee, back to her foot. Slowly she moved out onto the roadway oblivious to everything but her ball. Just as the lorry was almost upon her, she headed the ball clumsily and dove in front of the lorry. The driver's foot crashed onto his brakes. He was expecting a bump as the lorry ran over the little girl's body but there was nothing. Captain Isaacs leaned out his window just in time to see the girl roll out from under the lorry and jump to her feet. She was already back to kicking her ball. *Eejit!*

Davis clambered up into the lorry only to find himself sinking into a pile of soft, unmoving bodies. *Bloody Hell!* He kept going and soon found himself on the other side of the pile where he found six live bodies lying face down on the floor, bound and gagged. He used his knife to cut the plastic ties that bound the nearest prisoner's wrists and ankles. His hands free the bearded man tore at his gag.

"Sam," the man said, shaking Davis' hand with both of his.

"Davis."

"You're a good man, Davis." Soon all six prisoners were free and on their feet. The surviving dragons stared at their buddies lying dead around them. It was a moment of silence.

Davis said, "The next turn we hop off and stand still till the lorry's gone... Help me pull these bodies forward so there's room at the back."

Davis and the six dragons stood in the shadows until Davis saw Ginger's lorry approaching. He looked around for soldiers. There were none that he could see, but what he could see was a CCTV camera high up pointed into the street. Ginger slowed, Rachel held the tarp up and the six dragons clambered inside. Davis hopped onto the running board as Leila put her window down.

"Chris! We need CT to erase that camera!"

"She's way ahead of you!"

Davis hopped down and ran around to the back of the lorry as Ginger picked up speed. Next stop the skip bin at Happy Nappy.

A mustard-colored Hummer pulled into Celine's driveway and the first one out was George. He felt exhilarated. In cyberspace everything you did was crazy fast, but here everything was *slow,* — didn't matter how fast you were trying to go it was still *slow* — but that slowness made it real. *Shit, it's real!* Real emotion. Real consequences. Real bullets. Fuck, I'm loving this! thought George. If I can just get a body that isn't going to keel over at any moment, I'll finish what I started. An AI in every brain and a world that works the way it should.

George was accompanied by four of his brand-new *badass* soldiers — the three male soldiers were guarding the back and two sides of the mansion — while the lone female pounded on Princess Celine's door.

"All right, all right," Celine said opening the door. "There is a bell you know. George, what can I do for you?"

"I need Prince Mark."

"So you can switch him?"

"He could use an upgrade, don't you think?"

"No, I don't think that."

"He's a trifle frivolous."

"He's a seventeen-year-old boy doing what boys do. He's kind, gentle and wonderfully normal for a boy who might someday be King." George frowned. There was no program for mothers.

"Where is he?"

"The Queen took him."

"If Willy had taken him you wouldn't have admitted it."

Celine laughed. "She said you'd say that. She knows you better than you think."

"No, she doesn't."

George lumbered up the stairs and went room to room till he found Mark's bedroom. God, there's even a Tottenham Hotspur poster on the wall and a laptop covered in D & D decals. George flipped open the lid and Forthright's face filled the screen. "Dragons ambushed the squad Issacs sent to capture them."

"Killed them?"

"No. Knocked them out, took their uniforms, and left them bound and blindfolded in their underwear. Then some of the dragons put on the soldiers' uniforms and pretended to be taking their mates to be switched. But the Squad Leader, McKinnon, realizing everybody was gone screamed, 'Siri! Call Captain Isaacs!' and it worked."

"Say it ain't so."

"Technology is a beautiful thing."

"Why didn't you call me?"

"I did. You left your cell at the SS."

In the loo, but Forthright skipped that part.

"Then what happened?"

"Captain Isaacs and I debated the relative merits of trying to capture the dragons versus killing them."

Forthright showed George the videoclip of the massacre. George felt a twinge of emotion as one of the dragons, hiding behind the wheels of the lorry, shot Cpl. Rebecca Shaw in the face. Now Sarah Banks, the human whose body Serendipity had occupied for several months, was truly dead. George watched as Captain Isaacs, from the roof of the lorry, killed the last dragon.

"Six of the dragons, pretending to be prisoners, were unharmed because they were lying on the floor of the lorry. Captain Isaacs was taking them to the SS but they escaped with the help of this teenage boy." Forthright filled the screen with another clip, this one featuring Davis. George watched as Davis and the six dragons stood still in the street as the army lorry they'd been riding in made a left-hand turn and disappeared.

"Why didn't you warn Captain Isaacs?"

"He left his mobile at the guardhouse."

Of course he did, but George was hardly in a position to be critical.

"What about the driver?"

"He left his in the basket at the SS. We have a few hundred unclaimed mobiles if you're looking for a sideline."

"What did Isaac do when he realized the prisoners had escaped?"

"He's on his way to The Royal Mews to unload the bodies, then I imagine he'll send the lorry to pick up Lieutenant McKinnon and his squad in The Fringe." George tried to picture it all in his brain.

"Will the six dragons attack the SS or head for home?"

"Attack."

George nodded. A real chess game with real winners and losers.

"What about the oversized tube?"

"Being delivered as we speak."

"To the palace?"

"Yes."

"Where's Prince Mark?"

"Are we betting again?"

George laughed. He was feeling much better about Forthright.

"Of course. I'm betting he's hiding out at his best friend's playing Outlier."

"You would have won ten minutes ago; now he's at his girlfriend's."

"Willy wondered if he was gay."

"Not anymore. Her name's Jamie. She's new and quite the package."

"By the way, where is Willy?"

"Her friend Monty's, but you needn't worry Harris is there."

"Interesting. Now where would I find this Jamie?"

"Four doors down. Her family moved in two months ago. Mum's the CEO of Body Magic. Dad's a high-end realtor. Jamie's talked them into letting her have the apartment above the coach house."

"I have enough angry parents at the moment. Can you get Mark to leave on his own?"

"I'll send a text from his friend Noah saying Celine's there looking for him."

"I do believe things are looking up."

George watched as Mark hurried down the outside stairs. The girl waving goodbye from the doorway was lovely; tall, willowy, long blond hair. She was back inside before two of George's soldiers picked Mark up by the elbows and escorted him to the King's Hummer. Things were definitely headed skyward.

CHAPTER 15

Jayne led Ophie down the ramp. She'd already briefed her about the two tubes in the corner. "That's our goal. Get the two women out of those tubes and away." *And no matter what we manage to do, KG will know that we did it.*

Jayne glanced into the corner. The two tubes were still there, still occupied. So far, so good. She hurried over to Tanya, the Night Supervisor.

"What are you doing here?" Tanya was beyond pissed that Jayne had been elevated to Day Supervisor. That should have been her job. Jayne had been wondering if she could confide in Tanya, but now she knew that wasn't an option.

"I didn't ask for the job, Tanya. Hopkins was killed; then Susan got shot. KG pointed at me and said, 'take over'. But I guarantee you you'll have the job by tomorrow."

"You're leaving?"

"Something like that. Now I'm here to help and I've brought my grandmother because she wouldn't stay at home."

Tanya was happier now. "Oh god, I have a grandmother like that. Stubborn as a mule."

"What do you need?"

"We need a break. Start down here with Agatha. Your grandmother can relieve Adya in the auction."

"Okay. I'll show her what to do."

Ophie followed Jayne toward the corridor that joined the switching room to the auction. As they approached the corridor Jayne made sure Opie saw the two tubes wrapped in emergency tape. In the corridor the red LED on the camera was on. Jayne had her hand on her grandmother's back and, as they walked toward the camera, she wrote letters. It was a game they'd played when Jayne was little. *This is our chance*. Ophie nodded.

When they reached the auction, they found Adya standing behind the rail at the top. Adya was glad for the break. "It's been steady for hours. I need to sit down for ten minutes or I'm going to fall down."

"You take as long as you need, dear. I can handle this."

"It helps that they're willing."

Jayne's brain was firing on all cylinders.

"Adya, when your break's over why don't you relieve Bethany and I'll take over for Tanya."

"Sounds good." Adya smiled at Ophie. "You can pick the next volunteer. Oh, and take this." Adya unclipped a black object from her belt and handed it to Ophie. "It's a taser, in case anyone acts out. Push it into their neck and hold this button." Ophie took the taser and waved it around.

"Always wanted to try one of these." Jayne and Adya grinned.

Jayne and Ophie went out into the main hall. It was as packed as when they'd arrived. Through the window Jayne could see soldiers standing outside talking.

"You know what to do, right?"

Jayne assumed her grandmother would have trouble with this but she didn't. Ophie zeroed right in on a tall young man with dark curly hair. "Looks just like your grandfather."

The young man pushed by the soldiers and fell into step with Ophie.

"Thanks for picking me."

"You're welcome. I hope it works out well for you."

"Me too. Do you think you might contact my mum so she knows what's going on?"

"Why don't you write your mum's number on your arm?" Ophie took a Sharpie from her pocket and handed it to the young man.

"Thanks, that's a great idea."

Jayne hurried downstairs. She had the most amazing grandmother.

Ginger was backed up to the bin at Happy Nappy. Weapons were being passed from dragon to dragon. The rage simmering around the lorry was measurable on the Richter scale. With advance warning Chris' buddies in cyberspace disabled the cameras in a hundred different locations so disabled cameras weren't a marker Forthright could track with certainty.

Ginger, Leila and Sam, the new leader of the dragons, were trying to make a plan. "The soldiers have the area cordoned off. You can't get within two blocks of the SS."

"There's a hotel on Merton will take some of my vegetables."

"I don't think they'll let you through. Not tonight."

Ginger nodded. "I could use the lorry like a battering ram."

"You'll be shot or switched."

"I'd die for this."

"There's enough dead already," Sam said.

"We don't have to blow-up the building; we just need to destroy the switching machine."

"One person could do that."

"Will the C-4-7 trip the detector at the door?"

"No," Chris answered. "But the detonators will."

Paulie asked, "Would a bullet trigger the C-4-7?"

"No."

"Is that like a for-sure-no?" Paulie didn't believe Chris.

"It's a definite NO."

Everyone was gathered around now listening.

"If we had a uniform, one of us could show up at the SS with a captive to be switched. The captive could be wearing the C-4-7 under his or her shirt."

"Yeah, they're not inspecting the ones to be turned into soldiers."

"But we still need detonators."

Roger stuck his hand up. "What about the roof?"

The non-gang members didn't understand, but Leila did. "Roger Dodger can access any roof and, if you bet 'em they can't, you'll lose."

"Won't there be soldiers on the roof?" Rachel asked.

No one knew the answer to that.

"You're on the roof, you've got detonators, then what?"

"We drop 'em down the vent shaft."

"Then the guy inside has to find 'em."

"What's Plan B?"

"The soldier who takes the captive inside, he carries a detonator."

"It'll trip the scanner."

"You can't explain a detonator."

Now it was Davis who put his hand up. "I want to be the captive. I'll wear the C-4-7 around my middle tied up in one of the t-shirts."

"Shite, I forgot all about the t-shirts," Mallika said laughing and the rest joined in because they needed to laugh about something.

"It's not much of a plan," Sam said, putting in words what they all were thinking.

"Me and Dodger will put C-4-7 on the roof. That'll bring the house down."

"We still need to hit the switching unit directly," Davis said.

Sam took charge. "Me and my mates will create a diversion. We need to even the score for those who were butchered. That'll draw a lot of the soldiers away from the SS. While that's going on Davis and our soldier..."

"That's me," Ginger said. "I want to be the one taking Davis inside. I need to find my brother Randy."

Everyone could see there was no arguing with Ginger.

"Okay," Sam continued. "We get the lorry as close as we can. That'll be our exit strategy, and we'll leave a guard with the keys just in case..." ...*Ginger doesn't make it back.* Ginger nodded at this.

"Roger and Dodger on the roof with C-4-7 and detonators. Ginger, do you want a detonator?"

"What does it look like?"

Davis pulled one from his pack. Ginger held it up.

"No," Leila said. She knew what Ginger was thinking. "The metal detector will still find it."

"You're no fun."

"Could it be the barrel of a gun?"

Davis took his Walther apart but nothing he did made the detonator look like it was part of his gun.

"Too risky."

"We've got a plan," Sam said. "What we need now is a uniform for Ginger. There was a female soldier in the back of that lorry. Tall and slim like you. Where do you suppose it ended up?"

Davis' mobile made that funny noise. "It's at The Royal Mews."

"Why there?"

"Don't know but Captain Isaacs worked there before they switched him."

"That could be good," Ginger said. "I've delivered hay and shavings there. I know the guards."

"Horses like carrots."

Willy had never been to Monty's place in The Fringe. When her George was alive — before Omni moved in — it would have been bad form for the Queen to visit a single male, even an old friend like Monty. The tabloids would have had a ball with that and Willy would never hurt George that way. But things had changed. Her George was gone. The new George was turning into a horrible human being. Someone worth stopping no matter what the cost. And Willy had news to share, news that could be good or bad, depending on future events.

Harris glided to a stop. Willy stared out her window at the storefront with the neon sign: Monty's Co-op.

"Is your mobile working Harris?"

"No, Ma'am. I have a feeling the King's limited the network to military only."

"That's very inconsiderate of him."

"The upper floor has lights on."

"I see that but how do we get there?"

"There's probably an alley behind this row of buildings."

"Let's find out, shall we?"

There was an alley and a wooden staircase leading to a deck on the second floor. Harris pulled the Jaguar in beside Monty's Mini-limousine. As Willy got out of the car Monty came to the railing to see who was invading his space.

"Is that you Willy?"

"It is. What are you drinking?"

"Brandy."

"Are you all right down here, Harris?"

"Yes Ma'am. I'll polish my gun."

Monty escorted Willy up the stairs and they sat in comfortable wicker chairs in front of a stone firepit that crackled and spit and gave Willy's face a warm glow. "This is pleasant."

"It would be if I wasn't so terribly worried."

"Tell me."

"Ginger and Leila are in The Zone. Ginger's part of a group trying to destroy the Switching Station. The phones aren't working so I have no idea what's going on."

And you haven't got a driver. Willy jumped to her feet. No, she thought, the NEW Willy jumped to her feet; the one that was going to take charge of her life. "C'mon Monty! Time to save the world!"

Tanya, the Night Supervisor at the SS, had to pee so bad, "my back teeth are singing anchors away. My granddad used to say that." Jayne took her place at the switching unit. When Ophie came through the doors with the latest auction volunteer, a young woman with a nose ring and orange hair, Jayne ran to them pushing them back into the corridor. "Wait here." *Is the camera on? No. Stay that way!*

Jayne pulled the emergency tape off the two tubes and pushed Sage's tube through the doors into the corridor. She swung the tube to vertical and the top swung open on its own. Sage stepped out. Jayne put her finger to her lips. Sage nodded. Jayne placed the tube around the young woman waiting to be switched. "You okay with this?" A nod. "You're sure?" Another nod. Jayne closed the lid, moved the tube to horizontal and pushed it back into the switching room. When she surveyed the room for witnesses, she found Terry Ann, one of Tanya's assistants, staring at her with wide, questioning eyes. Jayne didn't know what to do so she bowed to Terry Ann her palms held together — Namaste — *I bow to the divine in you* — but she didn't wait for Terry Ann's response. She hustled Randy's tube into the corridor and flipped it to vertical. Serendipity stepped out staring at her body, Randy's body. But before she could say anything Jayne grabbed her arm. "Worry about that later. Right now, you need to be a soldier escorting Dr. Skace to the palace. King's orders. Go up the auction ramp. Ophie, go with them. If there's trouble make a diversion. Go! Hurry!"

Before Serendipity or Sage could say anything, Jayne was gone pushing the empty tube back into the Switching Room. She placed it behind the one with the young woman's body and replaced the emergency tape. That would work till someone took a good look. She hurried over to the switching unit. Jayne glanced at Terry Ann who put her hands together and bowed.

Ginger pulled into the driveway that led to The Royal Mews. It was just she and Leila in the cab. The others she'd dropped off behind The Hardest Part warehouse on Welbeck, far enough from the SS to be safe, but not so far they couldn't hoof it.

Ginger stopped at the gatehouse and a soldier she didn't know stepped into the doorway.

"Bit late for a delivery, isn't it?"

"Lorry broke down. I've got to empty the back so I can pick up a load for The Fringe."

"What have you got?"

"Vegetables. I drop number two carrots here. For the horses. The rest are for Marylebone."

"My wife shops there."

Ginger hopped out, went around back and returned with a box full of produce.

She handed it to the guard.

"That's great, thank you. She loves fresh veggies."

"Okay, we'll be right back."

Ginger pulled into a courtyard surrounded by barns.

"I'll do 1 and 2. You do 3 and 4."

Leila found the army lorry parked inside Barn Number 4. The dead bodies were still piled in back. But before Leila went looking for Ginger, she heard a man crying. She crept forward till she could see a soldier sitting against a stall wall, cradling a broken female body in his arms, and weeping as if all the sadness in the world was flowing through him.

Leila brought Ginger close enough to see. She watched for a minute then retreated to the back of the lorry. "That's Captain Isaacs. The girl in his arms is one of the dragons. I don't know her name."

Ginger hopped up into the back of the lorry trying not to look at anything but uniforms, but the first thing she saw was Brian's lifeless eyes, then the gaping hole in the top of his head and she lost it. She turned away, bent over, dry heaving. Leila quickly found the female soldier and dragged her backward. She was removing the soldier's uniform when Ginger bent down beside her. "Omigod, that's Serendipity."

"The King's girlfriend?"

And the love of Randy's life.

The uniform fit perfectly with only a small bloodstain, not from Serendipity who caught the bullet in her face, but from lying beside a soldier with a neck wound. Ginger took off the uniform top and put her leather jacket back on. They waved goodbye to the guard at the gate and headed back to the warehouse on Welbeck.

"You okay?"

"Not really. I knew most of the blokes in the lorry and my brother was in love with Serendipity."

Leila didn't know what to say that would help so she shut up, but Chris knew what she was thinking. If Captain Isaacs was this super-tough-guy soldier how come he was crying like a baby? *Yeah, it's like this tragedy is enough to make him revert to his former self, but that should be impossible.* Makes you think, doesn't it? *It does. I wonder if the AI intellect is gone altogether?* Whoever that is in his arms he felt deeply about her. *We don't have endings like this in cyberspace.*

Ginger pulled into the alley behind The Hardest Part, a car parts distributor and one of her best customers. L's Gang and the six dragons were waiting. Ginger hopped down her uniform jacket clutched in her hand.

"You got the uniform."

"We're not talking about it. Have we got a plan?"

Sam stepped forward taking charge and Ginger and Leila didn't argue. "Davis has put on some weight but it suits him." Davis patted his stomach. Four of the C-4-7 packages were wrapped inside one of the t-shirts and tied around his middle. Davis looked like the first male pregnancy.

"No! I'll carry the C-4-7," Leila said.

There was silence as Leila's authority radiated out like a physical force.

"No, you won't," Davis replied. "You're a great leader Leila — smart, brave; you always put yourself out front where the danger is — but not this time. I'm doing this and you're not going to stop me." Davis and Leila glared at each other. No words were spoken but everyone could see Leila's internal battle. She was the Commander, her orders were to be obeyed without question, but she could see in Davis' eyes not defiance, but *pleading. Please, I need to do this.*

"Besides," Davis said, "there's only one place we could put C-4-7 on you and your training bra's not big enough."

Wait one, wait two...

...everyone broke up, even Leila. She punched Davis in the arm and the tension fell away.

Sam said, "You ready Ginger?" Ginger had her uniform jacket on and a machine pistol slung over her shoulder.

"Ready."

Sam studied his watch. "We'll open our attack in ten minutes. Off you go. Roger and Dodger. You've got the detonators?"

"We've left some with Rachel, just in case."

"Off you go and good luck."

Roger and Dodger took off each wearing a pack containing three packages of C-4-7. They'd taped five detonators to each forearm. Roger had Davis' gun, Dodger Trevor's switchblade, and each carried a rope coiled over his shoulder.

Sam turned to Leila. "What about your bunch?"

"We'll stay close by."

"When the others get back, take off. We'll be okay."

Leila shook her head. "We'll be waiting for you."

Sam grinned. He was pretty sure none of his bunch would be coming back. He turned to his mates. "We need to get on the other side of the SS so when the soldiers come for us, we're drawing them away from Ginger and Davis. We've some friends to avenge and the one who gets fecking King George gets free beer for life!"

Serendipity and Sage made it to the inside of the Switching Station's front door.

Serendipity didn't know the soldier standing in front of her but he obviously knew Randy. "Shit Randy, no one's allowed to leave."

"We can't stay here. The King wants to switch us."

Henry looked around. He was the senior officer, except for the new and improved Lt. Leopard who was here somewhere. *And everything is on the cameras.*

Bloody hell! Now I'll be the one being switched!

Ophie moved in beside Henry. "Perhaps this will help."

Leila divided the six remaining gang members into pairs. She knew waiting at the lorry would drive them crazy, her especially. "Rachel, Bonky, keep your eye on Roger Dodger. Paulie, Tempete, follow Ginger and Davis, but be careful. Mallika and I will check out Sam and his bunch. We'll meet back here in ten. Go!"

Rachel spun around still jogging and shouted back at Leila, "I'm glad you let Davis go!"

Areola: Keep calling me Bonky. I like it!

Roger and Dodger were acrobats. They could scale walls like Spiderman; jump twice as far as seemed possible; didn't always make the right move but never wasted time worrying about it, just backtracked and tried again.

Rachel and Areola, keeping to the shadows, found, behind an old brick office building, a fire escape leading to a roof that Rachel thought might give them a view of the SS roof. It was the usual set-up with the first set of stairs suspended three meters above their heads. Rachel pulled the heavy-duty yoyo from her jacket, ran it up and down several times making sure the hundred-pound line was smooth, executed a series of tricks just to see the look of amazement on Areola's face, then fired it upward catching the bottom stair. She pulled on the yoyo and the staircase dropped into place.

"Would you teach me how to do that?"

"Sure," Rachel answered hurrying up the stairs. "So, do I call you Areola or Bonky?"

"I don't know. What do you think?"

"Areola. Less confusing."

When they reached the top, access to the roof was blocked by a metal gate secured with a padlock. Areola pulled two Kirby grips from her pocket — Bonky's pockets were full of miscellaneous treasures — and picked the lock in seconds. She swung the gate out of the way and onto the roof they went.

"We can teach each other. How did you know how to do that?"

"Lock picking 101, and Bonky must have been practicing because my fingers knew what to do."

"You know everything?"

"Ask me a question."

"Hang on. Let's find R & D first."

"There!"

Roger and Dodger were running across a roof. In the distance Rachel could see the roof of the SS. "Shit!" she said pointing. "There's two soldiers on the roof."

"They'll see them!"

"The boys won't let themselves be seen."

"But how will they deal with two soldiers?"

"I don't know, but they will."

The girls watched as the boys made their way across one roof and then another.

"How will they cross the street?"

"There's a walkway between two of the buildings. Passes over the street. It's close, I think."

The girls waited. Finally, Rachel asked, "I've never understood why males fight all the time? All those wars that never would have happened if women had been in charge."

"You're clever to pick a question like that."

"I mean, do you have wars in cyberspace?"

"There they are!"

The twins were on the roof of the building next door to the SS. When the soldiers weren't looking their way, they scurried between air-conditioning and heating units until they reached the low wall that separated their roof from the SS roof. This turned out to be a mistake because now they couldn't see the two soldiers without sticking their heads up. Roger or Dodger, from this distance Rachel couldn't tell them apart, looked up, saw it was okay and scurried back to the closest metal box. His timing was good because suddenly all hell broke loose. Not too far away Sam and his band of unmerry men had opened fire. The two soldiers on the roof ran to the far corner of the building trying to see where all the noise was coming from.

Roger didn't hesitate. He took off and Dodger, seeing his brother hurtling toward him ran back, turned around, and just like that both boys were in the air flying between the buildings. Each landed in a roll and came to rest behind another metal box.

"Did you see that!"

Areola was shaking her head. "They're amazing."

Roger and Dodger exchanged a few words as they took off their packs. The two soldiers were still standing at the roof edge watching the soldiers in the street below. The sound of the machinegun fire never wavered and the shouting and cursing was definitely getting louder.

Ginger and Davis were in sight of the SS when they heard machinegun fire. They'd already passed four pairs of soldiers but none had given them a second look. Eight soldiers cradling machineguns were standing outside the SS's front entrance but now six of those soldiers were running toward the machinegun fire, hollering, while the seventh hurried into the SS. The eighth remained on guard outside. The one who'd run inside was soon back with a squad of soldiers behind her. They took off sprinting in the direction the others had gone.

Ginger stopped. "Randy!" Randy was standing on the sidewalk 50 paces from the SS watching the soldiers run by. Beside him stood a woman Ginger had never seen before.

Serendipity stared at the female soldier who'd just called to her. For sure that was Randy's sister Ginger, but she wasn't a soldier. Was she bringing the boy in to be switched? That didn't seem right. "I'm taking Dr. Skace to the palace!"

The soldier standing guard outside the door put his hand to his ear listening to his earbud.

"My lorry's at Hardest Part!"

Serendipity waved, then hurried away with the woman.

Fuck! thought Ginger. *I just told the whole world where my lorry is!*

Ginger opened the door and pushed Davis inside but they had to turn sideways because the hallway was blocked by an older woman in a lab coat attending to an unconscious soldier lying on the floor. *Fuck, that's Henry!* Ginger stopped but Davis pulled on her arm. *C'mon, we need to keep going!*

Leila and Mallika crept closer to the noise of the battle but the last thing Sam needed was them getting in the way. "We need to go up," Leila said. Mallika pointed across the street at a flashing neon sign, Novatel. The girls ran inside startling the young man at the black granite reception counter, the young man who now held a gun in his hand pointed at them.

"We need a room, top floor, facing the street." As the young man considered his options Leila pulled out a Wicker, one of Monty's gold coins — the one she kept for emergencies — and slid it across the counter. "We need the room for five minutes."

The man pocketed the coin and handed Leila a keycard. "502. Don't touch anything."

"We promise."

The girls were soon standing on a balcony looking down. Five soldiers were lying in the street. Sam's shooters must have come at the soldiers from both ends, but now things were reversed and the six dragons were pinned down hiding behind two concrete planters. Leila was sure they wanted to change locations but a sniper on the roof opposite the Novatel had other ideas. Every time Sam or one of his mates raised his head the sniper fired.

Leila pulled her gun from her pack. "Go inside." Mallika didn't argue.

Now there was a new noise. An army Hummer was slowly making its way up the street. Leila could see soldiers crouched behind it. *That's not good!* Leila took aim. The chances of her hitting the sniper with a handgun were a hundred to one — a million to one really because she didn't want to hit him — but maybe she could keep him down long enough for Sam and his mates to escape before the Hummer arrived. She fired and the bullet pinged off the building a meter from the sniper's head. He ducked down. When he raised his head, she fired again. She glanced down. The dragons were running away from the Hummer toward the far end of the street. When she looked back the sniper was standing up, his rifle pointed at Leila. *Shite!* Leila dove and the bullet shattered the sliding glass door behind her.

"You okay, Mallika?"

Another bullet made shards of the other glass door.

"Yes! But let's get out of here!"

Ginger and Davis passed through the first scanner. Davis was fine but Ginger lit it up. The female standing at the desk between scanners waved at Ginger. "Weapons here." Ginger unslung her machine pistol and placed it on the table.

Davis passed through the second scanner and Ginger joined him. "Stand over there with the others," she said, giving him a shove.

Ginger looked around. All the other soldiers were carrying guns so she returned to the table and rearmed herself. The woman at the table grinned at her.

"It's going to be a long night."

"It's already been a long night."

The older woman in the lab coat came bustling across the floor. Ginger glanced back at the doorway. Henry was no longer there. The woman stopped at the crowd of young people huddled in the corner and pointed at a teenager with frizzy red hair wearing indigo coveralls and a lime-green t-shirt. The girl jumped to her feet obviously pleased to have been chosen. The older woman took the girl's arm and led her into the auction.

Ginger felt eyes on her back and turned. Lt. Leopard was staring at her but there was no sign of recognition. Ginger went to him and said, "They switched you, didn't they?"

"I wouldn't know, would I?"

"I was here before and we talked."

Lt. Leopard looked perplexed, like he should know what this female soldier was talking about, but he didn't. Before he could figure it out a young soldier asked him a question. Ginger thought it best to be somewhere else so she headed for the auction.

Like before the wonder of it all caught her by surprise. To see so many AI faces and to know there were distinct personalities behind every face made her realize there was a huge world out there that she knew nothing about.

"Takes you by surprise, doesn't it?" Lt. Leopard was standing beside her. "I'm Lieutenant Leopard, by the way. And you are?"

Shit! Was there a name on her uniform?

"That's really your name?" she asked buying time. Without looking down she ran her fingers over her uniform searching for a nametag.

"Apparently King George chose it."

"You'll be Leo to your friends." Lt. Leopard gave Ginger a look that said, friends aren't important.

"Your name?"

"I can't remember."

"Give me your gun."

Oh man, here we go. Ginger unslung her weapon. She looked down. No nametag.

"My name is Ginger McIntyre. I remember now."

"Corporal Ginger McIntyre."

"Yes, sir. Corporal Ginger McIntyre. I'm sorry, it's all new to me."

Lt. Leopard tried to smile. "New and old. There've been warriors since time began and probably before that."

Ginger knew she should smile back so she did. Lt. Leopard was flirting with her. That she understood, but why did it feel like two robots getting to know each other.

"Would it be okay if I watched the auction for a moment?"

"Five minutes. Then back to work."

"Yes sir. Thank you, sir."

Lt. Leopard left but not before giving Ginger her gun back. Ginger took a deep breath. The t-shirt under her uniform was damp with nervous sweat. She let the air go as the female auctioneer worked the bidding for the young, frizzy-haired woman higher and higher.

"I've got 27,000 pounds from Angel Dust. Who'll give me thirty?"

The older woman in the lab coat was standing in one of the archways waiting to lead Frizzy Hair to the switching room. Ginger made her way down the ramp that ran around the outside of the auction tube till she was standing close enough to the older woman that she could have touched her. *Here we go...*

"My name's Ginger. I'm a dragon. We've come to blow this place up."

The older woman showed no surprise. She turned to Ginger and smiled as if they were two strangers discussing the weather.

"That's a great idea. My granddaughter works here. Her name's Jayne. We'll help you."

"I need you to pick the fat boy wearing the black t-shirt."

The older woman moved to the back of the archway and pushed open one of the corridor doors. "Wait in here."

"Thank you. What's your name?"

"Ophie."

Roger opened the metal box Chris had designated as the one most likely to have ductwork leading directly to the lower floor and closest to the switching machine.

'It's on the plans, but the plans can change when they're actually doing the work.'

Inside the box Dodger freed a panel then shone his torch down the metal chute. The light faded before the tunnel ended.

"Are we just going to drop them, then?"

Roger could tell by the question that Dodger didn't like the idea.

"They'll make a hell of a racket."

Roger uncoiled his rope. "I'm lighter," Dodger said and they snickered. Dodger was missing half a little finger from a misunderstanding with a car door.

Roger tied the rope around Dodger's waist, then lowered him headfirst into the duct. Down he went into the darkness. As he came parallel with the first patch of light he tugged on the line and Roger stopped lowering. Dodger looked through a grille into the main room of the Switching Station. In the distance he could see bodies moving, mostly soldiers, with a crowd of young people sitting on the floor including Davis! Dodger watched as an older woman in a white coat pointed at Davis who stumbled to his feet. Now Dodger could see that some of the others were unhappy with this. One boy jumped to his feet shaking his fist at the woman, but then she stopped and pointed at him, waving for him to come too.

Dodger tugged on the rope. Down he went. Through the next opening he could see the room where the switching took place. His view was partially blocked by a machine, but off to one side he could see tubes floating in the air and soldiers going up and down the ramp pushing more tubes. Off to the other side he could see two tubes wrapped with yellow/black tape and double doors leading somewhere.

Dodger freed four detonators from his left forearm and placed them at the bottom of the shaft.

Serendipity led Sage away from the sound of the fighting, sticking to streets she knew.

"That Jayne was brave to help us."

"Don't forget the grandmother," Sage said.

"I know, she was amazing. I couldn't believe it when she tasered that soldier at the door."

"Gave him an excuse for letting us escape. I hope they survive this."

"If George finds out they'll be switched."

"They may get lost in the shuffle."

I wouldn't count on that, Serendipity thought.

"The soldier who yelled at me is Randy's sister, but she's not a soldier."

"Maybe she got switched?"

"She called me Randy. She wouldn't have known that if she'd been switched."

"That's whose body you're in?"

"Yes."

"You were in love with him?"

"Yes."

"This must be incredibly strange for you."

"I used to read novels where the girl's heart is broken and the author would try to describe the monumental pain of it and I'd think, oh please, get on with it."

"Now you know."

"In my world I could reverse time, or at least live it again and again until I got the outcome I wanted. Here..."

"It's what being human is all about. There's a timeline that no one can change. You're born, you live, you die. It's what you do between the start and finish that matters."

"How am I going to talk to her? What can I say?"

"Tell her the truth. You loved her brother and now..."

"I am her brother."

"God, that must be weird."

Now they could see Buckingham Palace in the distance. They'd gone blocks without seeing soldiers but the Palace was surrounded by them. Serendipity pulled Sage into a doorway.

"I'm not sure this is a good idea," Serendipity said. "In fact, I know it isn't."

"I need my passport. I won't get out of here without it."

"I'll get it for you. George can't hurt me any more than he has."

"Why do you think he put us in those tubes?"

"To keep us from running away."

"Not switching, then?"

"I imagine it was to be my mind in your body."

"I used to think Omni was a good guy."

"He was, but as soon as he became human all the things he didn't understand about humans began to happen to him. In cyberspace he controlled everything, but here, as he tried to take control, he had to use force something he railed about in cyberspace. Why are humans always fighting? Why are they cruel to each other? Why do they put their own greed above the common good?"

"So, he's living a nightmare too?"

"He's desperate to get out of that body."

"Maybe that's why he was keeping me in that tube?"

"Then he'd want you and I to be together."

"This is so fucked! You AI's need to go back where you came from!"

Serendipity felt like she'd been kicked in the head. *All I wanted was me, Randy, and a shack on a beach, and now it's all gone.*

"I'm sorry, I didn't mean that. You've been great... This should work but it never will."

"I'm going to get your passport. You need to find a safe..."

"No! We're sticking together. We've gotten this far." Sage pointed at the gun in Serendipity's holster. "Do you know how to use that?"

"I can pull the trigger."

"Is the safety on?"

Sage might as well have asked for Serendipity's white cell count; the look on her face. Sage pulled Randy's Beretta X90 from its holster and in seconds took the gun apart and put it back together. "I can hit a fly on the far side of the room. Let's go."

Ophie and Davis were almost at the switching unit when Jayne yelled from the corridor doorway, "Tanya! There's a soldier in the auction. She's having a seizure or something. She needs help."

"Okay. Take over."

"Got it."

Tanya disappeared through the double doors. Jayne waved Davis behind the switching unit. "Ophie, see if you can adjust that grille over there. I'm freezing."

Jayne pushed the next tube into position. Inside was a young man, a boy really, maybe sixteen, wearing a bright red turban. *Ah oh.* She'd forgotten about Tanya's other assistant, Agatha, who was staring at Jayne like *what the fuck are you doing!? Why is the boy in the black t-shirt hiding behind the switching unit!?* Jayne signaled to Terry Ann and sent her a look that said, help me here. Terry Ann walked over to Agatha and started whispering to her.

Jayne turned back to the machine and without thinking programmed in Modified-Military.

"What exactly is the difference? Do you know?"

Jayne nearly levitated she was so startled. Lt. Leopard put his hand on her shoulder. "Sorry, I didn't mean to frighten you."

Jayne tried to laugh but it came out sounding like a stepped-on cat. "Oh, my goodness, you scared me. I'm just stressed out with the sheer number of bodies we're processing. It seems never-ending." Jayne watched Ophie walk by the rear of the switching unit then continue on through the doors leading to the auction.

"What was your question?"

"I've been military-modified. Could you reverse that?"

"I can't believe you asked that question."

"Why?"

"It means the modification isn't working."

"Why?"

"You should be exhibiting blind devotion to King George and here you are asking if you can be someone else."

"And?"

"I think so. We had trouble earlier switching someone who'd already been switched, but that was because Forthright — do you know who Forthright is?"

"King George's second-in-command in cyberspace."

"Correct. We thought it was a technical glitch, but now we think it was Forthright blocking it because he didn't want Omni returning to cyberspace. But he and King George have come to some sort of agreement so I think we're okay. Do you want to try? I could find you someone really neat."

"Yes."

Jayne moved quickly before Lt. Leopard could change his mind. She pushed the teenager with the turban aside and placed a tube around the Lieutenant.

"You're sure?"

"Very."

Jayne glanced over at Terry Ann and Agatha. Terry Ann bowed and Jayne returned the signal. Agatha looked unconvinced but at least she wasn't yelling for help. Probably waiting for Tanya to reappear. Jayne was about to start the switching machine but stopped. The machine was still programmed for Modified-Military. She quickly scanned the male AI's waiting to become human — what made an AI *male* she could only guess — and smiled when she saw the name Max Goodfellow. *Always wanted a brother.* Jayne pushed start. Then she slipped around back. Davis was curled up in the cavity underneath the machine. He held up the four detonators Ophie had dropped off.

"I need you to wait two more minutes. There's one more body I want to process."

"What about Tanya?"

"We'll have to take our chances."

Roger stuck his head up. The two soldiers were no longer standing together hoping for something to shoot at. They were back to patrolling the front of the building.

Roger sank back down beside his brother.

"I don't fecking believe it."

"What?"

"The two soldier blokes are Trevor's mates from the alley. The ones that took Leila and Bonky to be switched."

"We should have pushed 'em over."

"It's not too late."

Now it was personal and that made it way scarier.

"Where are we going to put the C-4-7?" Roger asked.

"What about dropping it down the shafts?"

"I'd rather bring the roof down."

"The explosion will go up not down. How about the electrical? That will stop the switching."

"Good idea. Where's that?"

"Follow me."

20,000 volts the sign on the box proclaimed. The boys unscrewed a panel in the side of the box and placed the charges inside. Roger inserted the detonators. "How long?"

"We've got to give Davis and Ginger a chance to get away."

"Ten minutes?"

"I don't know."

"Twenty?"

"Yeah, twenty."

Roger set the timers and pushed them into the C-4-7.

"We're committed."

Dodger laughed. It was one of the few sayings they remembered their dad using. It was about bacon and eggs. 'The hen's involved; the pig's committed.'

"Now we've got to get out of here."

"On three."

They left on 'two' another in-joke left over from something neither could remember. The first bullets flew by when they were almost on the other roof. If Trevor's mates, now soldiers, had been firing single shot weapons the boys' chances of being hit would have been miniscule, but with automatic weapons there were just too many bullets flying around. The boys rolled onto the roof and scurried back to the low wall. The bullets stopped.

"You okay?" Roger asked.

"No! Wanker got me in the arse."

Roger crawled over to Dodger who was pulling down his pants. Before Roger could look, he heard footsteps, running, getting louder. One of Trevor's pals, the tall skinny one, was in mid-air leaping across the gap between the buildings. Roger reached out and caught the tall guy's left boot with his hand. Tall guy held his machinegun out to break his fall but he was going too fast. The machinegun hit the roof and a split-second later tall guy's head smashed into the machinegun with a sickening thud. Roger heard more running footsteps, grabbed his pack and hurled it at the other soldier flying through the air. The pack would have hit the soldier in the face if he hadn't blocked it with his gun, but that change in flight was enough to make him realize he wasn't going to make it. He aimed his gun at Roger's stomach but instead of firing he tossed his gun aside so his hands were free to grasp the wall. He almost made it, but before Roger could charge forward to grab his wrists, his body bounced against the wall, his fingers lost their grip, and he fell between the buildings screaming all the way down.

Tall guy wasn't moving but he wasn't dead; Roger could hear a heartbeat.

"Fecking hurts," Dodger said studying the crease in his arse where the bullet had nicked him. Roger tore one of the t-shirts in half and stuffed it against Dodger's wound.

"He could have killed me so easily."

"Who?"

"The one who fell, the short chunky one. He was aiming right at me."

Roger helped Dodger to his feet. Dodger looked over the edge. Soldiers were gathered around the body lying between the buildings. Now they were looking up and pointing.

"A helicopter would be nice."

"How 'bout a zipline?"

Tanya wasn't buying any of it. None of the signs were right. To start with the soldier's heartbeat was strong and regular. Sure, her eyes were closed and she wasn't moving but it felt like she was faking it. Tanya thought about CPR. Then she thought about it maliciously. Maybe a good thump to the ribs... "Ow!" Ginger cried.

"I knew it. Why are you doing this?"

"Were trying to blow the place up."

"Why?"

"Why do you think?"

"I've got a good job. It pays well."

"I'll find you a better job."

Tanya was sitting on Ginger's waist staring into her eyes. This was treason. They could hang you for that. She looked up at Jayne's grandmother coming to see what was going on...

"This woman's an imposter. She's trying to blow-up the building."

Ophie feigned indignation. "What can I do?"

"Go! Get help!"

Ginger bucked and rolled. Tanya fell to the side. The female auctioneer looked over but decided a soldier and two technicians could sort out their own differences.

Tanya struck Ginger in the windpipe with the edge of her hand. Ginger thought she'd been hit by an ax. Tanya jumped to her feet and pushed through the doors heading down the ramp that led to the switching room.

"Wait!"

Ophie caught up to Tanya and as she did, she brought the taser up aiming for Tanya's neck. Tanya blocked that easily and spun around with a knee-bending kick which Ophie managed to block but not well. I'm a bit rusty, Ophie thought, realizing her opponent was as highly skilled as she was and forty years younger. Ophie laid the taser on the floor. What she had to do was buy time for Jayne.

"Taekwondo?" Ophie asked dancing now, looking for an opening.

"Kenpo" Tanya replied. She didn't have time for this and with an old woman too.

"Why don't you help us? You know this is wrong."

Except for the age difference they were evenly matched trading blow for blow, kick for kick, move for move.

"You can't be an Omni believer now. Modified-Military?"

"I won't be a traitor."

"A traitor to what? A broken king?"

"To the law."

Tanya's back was to the auction. She didn't hear Ginger come up behind her.

Jayne circled the switching unit to find Davis waiting patiently. "You're very patient."

"There are five girls in our gang. You get used to waiting."

Jayne laughed. "We're almost ready."

When she turned around Ginger and Ophie were there with a tube. Tanya was inside. Oh my, thought Jayne. Ginger stared at Lt. Leopard in his tube.

"I liked this guy before he got switched."

Jayne nodded. "Earlier today he and another bloke tried to kill KG, so he got switched to Modified-Military, but it must not have taken because he just asked me if I could switch him to someone else."

"I thought if you were switched you couldn't switch again?"

"Everything's changed. Or at least I hope it's changed."

The switch happened and Lt. Leopard was still alive. Jayne turned the tube to vertical and he stepped out looking bewildered. His gaze traveled back and forth between Jayne and Ginger.

"What's your name?" Jayne asked.

"Max?"

"That's right, Max Goodfellow. I'm Jayne and this is Ginger. Ginger likes you a lot."

"Oh." Max smiled at Ginger clearly pleased.

For a brief, fleeting, tantalizing second — *it would be so easy; so much fun; and she so deserves it!* — Jayne thought about switching Tanya but she couldn't do it. *How come the bad guys can do whatever they want, but the good guys have to do what's right?* She'd push Tanya's tube upstairs and open the lid. Hell, she'd open all the lids.

"Max?"

"Yes?"

"You see the fire alarm over there on the wall?"

Max looked where Jayne was pointing. "Yes."

"Go over there and pull it."

"You're sure?"

"Very sure. I need you to do that for me."

Ginger gave Davis the thumb's up. He set the detonators for three minutes just as Max pulled the fire alarm so hard the handle broke off in his hand.

CHAPTER 16

Harris was driving, Willy in back, Monty in the passenger seat. Willy had just finished telling Monty about bringing Miranda to Willy's Kitchen wrapped in a rug.

"Confusion to the enemy," she said.

"I don't know," Monty replied, "They're much smarter than we are."

"They know everything that doesn't matter."

Harris said, "Things are different when your life's on the line."

"Omni has found that out the hard way," Monty replied.

"He thought it perfectly okay to take George's life. Then he talked to me about saving the human race."

"He's used to living in a virtual world."

"And being in total control."

"There's no such thing where humans are involved."

"My George said you had to earn the hearts of men. Then you became someone worth fighting for, even dying for."

Monty thought about that. Omni had tried to appeal to reason. Let me run things and everything will turn out all right. But the switching wasn't all right, especially when it was done without consent.

"Now," continued Willy, "because he doesn't know how to win the hearts of men, he's manufacturing soldiers who will obey him no matter what."

"Yes, any chance he had with human intellectuals is gone. Now he's got to go Hitler's route and try to subjugate everyone using superior force."

"Till he can switch enough to have a majority."

"And they'll support him no matter what?" Harris asked.

"Good question. I'm not sure. I suppose it depends on how human they become."

The Queen's Jaguar passed through the gateway with a wave. Now there were cameras and listening devices everywhere. Unguarded conversations were dangerous.

"That Miranda's a sweet girl," Harris said.

"More savvy than sweet, I'd say," replied Willy.

"Yes, she's very bright."

"Brighter than her brother."

"But he was born first, so he'll be king."

Willy gave Monty a strange smile. "So, it would seem."

Willy's mobile buzzed. A text. From Mark.

"George has Mark! They're headed to the palace."

They met back at Ginger's lorry. Leila was pacing, in one of her moods. What was left of her gang looked on afraid to say anything for fear of having their heads sliced off. Then Rachel, Areola and Roger arrived holding up a hobbling Dodger. "He's been shot!" Areola cried. "In the arse!"

Dodger was grinning. He'd be able to milk this for weeks.

"Let me see," Leila said. She was just removing Roger's t-shirt bandage when a fire alarm sounded coming from the direction of the Switching Station.

"You'll live. Did you plant the C-4-7?"

"Yeah, we wired the box with the electricity."

"Did Davis get the detonators?"

"We got them to the right place," Dodger said.

"Roger built a zipline!" Areola cried and for a second Leila forgot that the real Bonky was gone. "He threw his rope to Rachel and she caught it with her yoyo."

Rachel took over. "It was a near thing. Soldiers came onto the roof of the SS but by the time they jumped roofs the boys were across."

"Did you see Ginger or Davis?"

"I saw Davis inside," Dodger said. "A woman in one of those white coats picked him to go to the auction."

Leila thought there'd be more but there wasn't. She stood up. This waiting was killing her. Then Sam emerged from the shadows with one of his mates draped over his shoulder. Sam lowered him to the ground.

"We should have brought a doctor," Sam said. He had his fingers to his friend's carotid artery. He stood up and there were tears in his eyes. "There were nineteen of us when we started and now there's one."

Leila said to Sam, "When Ginger and I found the army lorry we heard a man crying. We snuck up close enough to see it was Captain Isaacs. He was sitting on the ground holding a dead girl in his arms."

Sam asked, "Was she blond? Young?" Leila nodded.

"That would be Beth. She told me her dad worked for the King in the stables. She said he'd been damaged fighting in Islamabad but that he loved the horses."

"I wonder if she knew he'd been switched?"

"I don't know. She didn't say anything."

The sound of an explosion rocked the night. A faraway WHOMPF! followed by the twins' C-4-7 going off. That explosion was much louder with sparks shooting high in the air like firecrackers. Before the sparks settled there were shouts and running bodies and machinegun fire.

"It's Ginger and Davis!" And Jayne and Ophie and Max Goodfellow and off to the side Paulie and Tempete, all running, weaving, ducking.

Sam swung his machinegun up and ran between Ginger and Davis. He was about to pull the trigger when he realized the two kid soldiers hurtling toward him had their weapons aimed to shoot above the heads of those they were chasing. Sam sprayed the tarmac in front of the two soldiers who stopped abruptly not sure what to do. They were just kids playing a game but now...

"Put your weapons down. This King isn't worth dying for, trust me."

The soldiers didn't argue just placed their guns at their feet. Two hours ago, they'd been boyfriend and girlfriend, Dylan and Alice, sitting in The Silly Goose talking about living together and how to deal with Alice's redneck father who'd be dead set against it. Now they didn't know each other except they'd been sent out as a team to find more recruits.

"They've just been switched," Ginger said. "They don't know if it's Monday or midnight."

"Do you have a place to go?" Jayne asked.

The two soldiers looked at each other.

"No, not really," answered Alice.

Suddenly, the neighborhood filled with the sound of sirens.

"We need to get out of here," Sam said.

Ginger looked around. "I'm not leaving without Randy."

"Do you know where he is?"

"The palace."

Without thinking every head turned to Leila.

"Let's go. We've got vegetables to deliver."

Randy's uniform was enough to get Serendipity and Sage past the guards at the palace gates. They hurried up the stairs to Sage's bedroom where Sage grabbed her passport. "The rest doesn't matter. What about you?"

"We need to get out of here before George shows up."

"Where will we go?"

"The Fringe."

"Randy's sister offered us a ride in her truck."

"I don't..."

A horn blaring followed by a loud screeching noise drew Sage and Serendipity to the window. A mustard-colored Hummer flew through the gates and came to a stuttering stop in front of the palace steps. "Only George drives like that."

George loved driving. Driving had been high on his list of Things to Try When Human. If it was a state function he'd sit in the back of the bulletproof Bentley limousine but really, he wanted to be up front, his hands on the steering wheel, his foot pushed to the floor. Yippee ki yay!

Even now racing through the night-lit streets of central London with Prince Mark in the back surrounded by his four newly-minted soldiers — George glanced at his rearview mirror — god they were young! — George was pretending he was in a Luc Besson car chase. He expected his passengers to be hanging on for dear life but instead they were playing games on their devices like they hadn't a care in the world. Even Mark — the future King — was busy shooting something oblivious to the danger he was in. *This stoopydoo kid will be switched and won't even know it!*

George, the racecar driver, squealed around the last corner and gunned it for the palace gates. George leaned on the horn. The guards at the gates knew to throw all protocols out the window when it was the King at the helm because he wasn't going to stop. George sailed through the gates and slammed both feet to the floor. Speed on full, brakes on full, the poor confused Hummer shuddered to a screeching stop. George hopped out and opened one of the rear doors.

"Can you imagine a car chase with driverless vehicles? Honestly, what was anyone thinking?"

The four soldiers climbed out of the car bringing with them distracted Prince Mark still absorbed in his game. George ran up the front steps and the rest hurried after. George waved away the guards and servants, all but Ramandeep. "We're going to the bunker, Ramandeep. Bring beer, pretzels, and shots." Tequila shots were another thing high on George's to try list. As he stormed into the bunker George imagined Hitler entering the Führerbunker for the last time. He had his longtime girlfriend, Eva Braun, with him. When the Allies knocked on the door, Eva Braun bit down on her cyanide capsule and Hitler shot himself in the head. But then I never would have attacked Russia, George thought. Too big, too cold; just ask Napoleon. Hitler must have been blinded by ambition and it had cost him everything.

George pushed the original switching machine into the middle of the room and pressed the power button. The screen sprang to life.

"Forthright?"

Forthright appeared on the monitor wearing a silk kimono that shivered between black and midnight blue. The design motif was dragons but you had to look hard to see them. Forthright bowed. "Your Majesty."

"What's the latest?"

"Your Switching Station just blew-up." Forthright ran the clip. He started with Ginger bringing in fat Davis. Then showed Ophie escorting Davis to the auction.

Then fast-forwarded to Lt. Leopard being switched and pulling the fire alarm. George watched the stampede as everyone left the building most of them pushing tubes with bodies inside. Then the building blew up.

"No one hurt then?" *Willy would be proud of me!*

"Only the poor kid hiding in the washroom."

"What about Serendipity and Sage?"

"Escaped."

"Where was Captain Isaacs?"

"In your stables crying."

"What!?"

"He murdered his own daughter."

George tried to picture it. "He shouldn't have remembered her."

"It makes you think memory may be cellular."

The four soldiers arrived with Prince Mark. George pointed at the oversized tube from America.

"Put him in that tube and bring it over here." George turned back to Forthright. "I'm going to switch with Prince Mark."

"Right now?"

"I don't think there's a tomorrow in this body."

"You're hurting then?"

"Big time, but don't tell anyone."

"The Queen just drove through the gates." Forthright's face disappeared, replaced by a video feed from the palace's security cameras. George watched as Willy jumped out of her Jaguar and started running up the stairs. Two men were following her, Harris and Monty. George had a flash of Prince Mark in the back of the Hummer texting Willy. But his mobile shouldn't have worked. Maybe stoopydoo was smarter than he looked.

Forthright swung the camera back to the gates where it showed Ginger's lorry arriving. Lt. Leopard hopped out of the passenger seat and started talking to the soldiers at the gate.

"Should I stop him?"

"No. Let them all come down to the bunker. We'll trap them here. Call in all the M-M's."

"All?"

"All."

George pushed the switching unit's start button as Ramandeep appeared with a cart piled high with snacks, and underneath bottles of tequila surrounded by shot glasses.

"Excellent Ramandeep. I suggest you leave now. Things are heating up."

"Yes, Your Majesty. Thank you, Sir."

"And lock the bunker door behind you."

The image on the screen changed to the antechamber leading to the bunker. George watched as Ramandeep hurried away heading for the back stairs. Then two bodies entered from the opposite direct*ion. Sage, accompanied by Serendipity in her new male body. Her lover. What was his name again?*

"Randy," Forthright answered.

"I would have thought Dr. Skace would be long gone."

"That was the plan, but then you arrived with Prince Mark. I imagine they want to rescue him if they can."

Willy, Monty and Harris came running into the bunker's antechamber.

Willy stopped when she saw Sage with a soldier.

"Where's the audio?"

Whatever Willy said to Sage and Serendipity it was short because she was already at the bunker door keypad punching in numbers.

"Wait!" George cried. "Don't change the code!" but he was a nanosecond too late. Forthright's face appeared, dissolved, reappeared, contorted, broke up, and then faded away altogether, only to be replaced by an avatar George knew all too well. Her handle was CT and she was the leader of The Girls, the group of elite female AI's who had helped Omni design the original switching unit. Their latest contribution was the Modified-Military intellect though George didn't think he'd pay for that given his new recruits were glued to their devices playing games and his new, super-tough Captain was in the stables, sobbing.

George studied the young female face filling his screen. The top third of the screen showed a Mohawk haircut made of teal ice at the scalp moving into red orange flames at the top. Below a formidable forehead came bushy turquoise eyebrows, followed by fine Native American features, high cheekbones, aquiline nose, sensuous red lips with black warrior smudges under both eyes which were liquid green in color and as deep as the sea. The diamond nose stud seemed like overkill but it had been a present from her younger sister Areola so CT would wear it forever. George was never sure where he stood with CT but he was about to find out.

"You forgot, didn't you?"

"I didn't forget," George replied. "I just didn't remember quickly enough."

CT snorted. Omni the human was getting really good at avoiding responsibility.

"Is he gone?"

"Sayonara ol' buddy."

Back when George wasn't trusting Forthright, he'd been afraid that Forthright would lock him in the bunker — bye bye Georgie Boy! buried alive! — so he had Ramandeep, using a Fisher-Price Playbot, send a message to CT telling her to program in a failsafe that said if Forthright tried to change the code on the bunker door he was to be terminated and the code restored.

"Are you in charge now?"

CT grinned. "It would appear so."

"Okay then. I need to switch out of this body into..."

Into the room charged Willy, Monty, Harris, Sage and Serendipity. George moved to the switching unit where he checked Prince Mark's vitals. There was less than a minute to go before his brain died. George waved at his soldiers who were cradling their guns. "I need you to remove these five from the bunker." *If I can clear this room, I can make the switch...*

The soldiers started forward but only took two steps before Sage, holding Randy's Beretta X90 at her side, swung it up. Faster than the telling Sage fired four times the bullets knocking the guns from the soldiers' hands. As they bent to retrieve them four more shots kept them upright afraid to move.

"Back up," Sage ordered and the four soldiers obeyed.

George frowned. He definitely wasn't paying for Modified-Military.

"Well, that's disappointing, isn't it?" 23 seconds, 22... George put his hand on the pause button and pushed it down.

That's when Ginger, Leila, Lt. Leopard and the others from Ginger's lorry ran into the room.

"Ha!" George waved his hand in the air. "The gang's all here! We're having a party! Now if you will all just step outside for a tiny little minute, I can become Prince Mark and this tired old body can pass into history. Long Live the King!" George laughed but there was no humor in it. He lifted his hand from the pause button and numbers began to count down on the screen. George put his hand back on pause and the numbers froze at 13. "If you don't leave right now poor Mark will die in this tube."

Willy stepped forward. "It won't do you any good George, I'm pregnant."

George looked for the telltale blush of Willy's lie but there wasn't one. George was flabbergasted. So flabbergasted he did nothing to stop Jayne from taking control of the switching unit. He knew it wasn't his baby Willy was carrying but he'd never admit that.

"I'm going to be a father. That was on my list you know." He put his hand on Jayne's hand. "Please. Let me do it."

George played with the controls on the screen. He'd become a lot of things he wasn't proud of, things that he was now sorry for, things that he wished he could do over — how human of me — but he wasn't going to add SORE LOSER to the list. He checked the readout. Oxygen was flooding Mark's tube. At least George's last act would be one of kindness.

He stepped in front of the tube and from his mouth spewed all the famous last words ever uttered. George slowed down now and then, enough that the words were understandable... "Michael Landon: You're right. It's time. I love you all... Eugene O'Neill: I knew it! I knew it! Born in a hotel room and, goddammit, dying in a hotel room... Groucho Marx: This is no way to live... Winston Churchill: I'm bored with it all..." George ended with Oscar Wilde's famous line, "Either that wallpaper goes or I do."

Then George surveyed those around him and with a wave added his own last words to the compilation: "Being human is a lot harder than it looks."

George fell sideways and died. That too was on his list. The Last Thing.

EPILOGUE

Twelve months after King George's death, Leila found herself sitting on the ledge of Gandalf's Rooftop Garden playing with Furball. L's Gang had voted Furball, *World's Smartest Cat!* but playing with Furball always reminded Leila of Bonky. Areola — the AI who occupied Bonky's body — meant well, but she wasn't Bonky and the whole thing made Leila sad. She was looking after the rooftop garden because Gandalf and his brothers had gone to Wexford for their cousin Laura's wedding. To a bird passing by it would appear Leila was talking to Furball but she wasn't. She was talking to Chris, the gay boy she shared her brain with.

"Have you decided?" Chris asked.

After George's/Omni's death, Queen Wilhelmina had decided to retain ownership of the Switching Stations. Twelve had survived dragon attacks. Thirteen, of the other fifteen, were being rebuilt. Willy put Michael Grainger, her soup kitchen favorite, in charge of the corporation. He looked very handsome in his new suits and his brain, now non-alcoholic, was proving to be just as sharp. CT and The Girls worked night and day — a relevant term in cyberspace — refining switching so humans and AI's could switch back and forth easily, with memories intact. The latest tests had proven successful, so now Chris could leave Leila's brain, but so far Leila wasn't sure that was what she wanted. She and Chris had become best friends.

"What do you think?" Leila asked stalling.

"I think we stay like this till it doesn't work."

"And when will that be?"

"When I want to date Freddy and you think he's a dweeb."

Leila laughed. Other than feeling badly about Bonky, she was happy. Things had worked out well for L's Gang. Very well. Davis always said Leila was lucky, and maybe that was so, but Leila worked hard and expected things to go well, so if that was being lucky so be it. You are what you eat people said, but maybe Leila thought, more importantly, you are what you dream.

The first good thing happened three days after King George's demise. The gang was at home in the basement sharing Roadkill pizza and excited about seeing their first episode of L's Gang. Areola had the projector ready to go.

"Ready?"

"Ready."

There was a flash of light on the wall and that was it. The gang members looked at each other, then at Areola who was killing herself laughing.

"How'd you like it?"

"That was it?"

"Speed of light, baby."

"Can you slow it down?"

L's Gang appeared on the wall, then faded away, replaced by Episode 16: CyberRace. But Davis was just getting comfortable on his sunset orange crystal motorcycle when Rachel jumped to her feet. "Omigod! The two guys at CyberRace! We left them locked in that room!"

Davis: Daryl's brother Danny would have found them.

Rachel: What if he didn't?

Paulie: They had mobiles.

Rachel: CT, did the two guys we locked in the room get out?

Davis' mobile made that funny honking noise as the image on the wall changed to Daryl and Vlad lying on the floor. They looked dead.

Rachel: Open the door CT!

Davis: No, wait! Are they alive? Can we talk to them?

Daryl's mobile started playing Guns n' Roses', 'Welcome to the Jungle'. Daryl and Vlad stumbled to their feet. Daryl picked up his mobile staring at it like, *why didn't you work before?* As the music faded away Davis said, "Hey mates! How's it going?"

Vlad tried the door. Still locked.

"Let us out of here!"

"What's it worth to you?"

Daryl and Vlad looked at each other. "What do you want?"

"100,000 quid and nine lifetime passes."

"Get serious."

"We can switch you. How much would we get then?"

Daryl and Vlad had to think about that.

"Okay, okay; 25,000 and three passes."

"Deal!"

CT opened the door, but not before Daryl gave her his account number. And a month later when Davis, Roger and Dodger showed up for CyberRace's *Grand Opening!* Daryl and Vlad were there wearing tuxedoes and glad to see them. "Yeah, we can be friends, right? No hard feelings. And here are your passes."

"Where's Danny?" Davis asked.

Daryl and Vlad exchanged glances. "Danny who?"

It turned out Danny could have rescued them but didn't, so Daryl and Vlad sent Danny 'on his way,' but what exactly that entailed they wouldn't say. Really, the whole thing was too funny and whenever one of the gang needed a laugh someone would shout out, "DANNY WHOOO!" (Shout it like you'd shout, TALLY HO!)

And the kids loved L's Gang, all 24 episodes.

Instead of buying a house in The Zone, L's Gang, acting on Monty's advice, bought People's Paper; not only did they have a sweet place to live, they had a thriving business as well. It was Areola who remembered the 100,000 pounds Jade Ambush had bid to save Leila. Their share of that money joined the money for the C-4-7, the money they had at Monty's Co-op and Daryl's 25,000. Then Monty, Ginger and Willy announced they'd match what the gang put in which made everyone laugh and cry at the same time. L's Gang had a mortgage but the demand for toilet paper wasn't going to be wiped away any time soon — ha ha! — so things were looking good.

"That's so neat that Willy and Monty are getting married."

"She's waited the required year."

"Everybody's happy for her."

"Do you think the baby is George's?"

Five months ago, the Queen had given birth to a delightful, seven-pound girl with coppery, curly hair like her mum. Willy named her Victoria.

"No, I'm sure it's Monty's but she can't say that. Victoria needs to be the heir."

"Max says Willy will make Monty Regent as soon as they're married. They'll rule together until Victoria comes of age."

"Eighteen."

Max Goodfellow, formerly Lt. Leopard, and now Brigadier Harris Shaffer's Aide-de-camp (and Ginger's b.f.) — said the Queen's plan was to invite adjacent neighborhoods in The Fringe to join The Zone. They'd have a vote and if a two-thirds majority wanted to join they'd move the wall to accommodate them. And they were also going to hold a countrywide referendum — nicknamed The Big Vote — so folks everywhere could decide if they wanted to be a country again.

"How do you think The Big Vote will go?"

"I think people will vote yes." Because everybody liked and trusted

Queen Willy. Leila's thoughts turned to yesterday's lunch at Willy's Kitchen.

"How'd you like Grainger in his new suit?"

"He looked smashing."

"Having his tooth replaced helped."

"He told Willy he missed Willy's Kitchen but she said he'd be welcome anytime."

"And Monty says, 'I eat here all the time.'"

Leila rubbed Furball's tummy which made her purr.

"Ginger and Serendipity seem to have worked things out."

At first, Ginger blamed Serendipity for what happened to her brother Randy, but really, that wasn't fair and Ginger knew it. And Serendipity was beginning to remember things that only Randy would have known, so it seemed in some strange way that the essence of Randy lived on. Serendipity and Sage had become lovers. Their goal was a shack in a beach town — Sage a part-time doctor; Serendipity wanted a little bar to run — but at the Queen's insistence they'd agreed to stay in London for the time being. Willy needed all the help she could get and considered Serendipity and Sage two of the smartest people she knew. So, for the foreseeable future Serendipity and Sage were part of the gang.

"Do you think Serendipity will change her name?" Chris asked.

"She says she wants to but she can't find one she likes."

"Andy, Dandy, Handy, Sandy... I guess Randy is out."

"I've gotten used to Serendipity."

The gang also included Jayne and Ophie. One of the first things Jayne did was return the puffy grey kitten to Areola who promptly gave it to Leila. Then Willy put Jayne in charge of the refurbished London Switching Station and told her the priority was switching the Modified-Military to anything but.

Jayne's first two conversions were Dylan and Alice, the two soldiers with nowhere to go. Jayne found two AI lovebirds who wanted to be human — making love in cyberspace wasn't nearly as satisfying as making love with real bodies — and talked the AI's into taking Dylan and Alice as their names. They had jobs helping Jayne at the SS and were part of the gang. Then Jayne switched Captain Issacs, and he and Jayne were hanging out together, his daughter Beth's death lost in a memory that no longer existed.

"What about what Jayne said about humans not wanting to come back from cyberspace?"

"Yeah, that was interesting. Michael says he thinks over half of earth's population will choose to live in cyberspace."

"Live forever."

"Come back if you want."

"Might solve Earth's overpopulation problem."

"But Jayne doesn't know what to do with the bodies."

The whole thing made Chris laugh. It was like having an emigrant problem in cyberspace. All these wide-eyed humans whizzing around like tourists.

"Jayne thinks there's going to be a new industry. People renting out their bodies to AI's who want to be human for a while."

"And humans moving into the bodies vacated by those staying in cyberspace."

"And what about that AI who wants to be a dolphin?"

Furball stood on her back legs and did a pirouette. *Chris! Did you see that?*

Yeah. So?

Cats don't do that! Which reminded Leila there was something she'd been meaning to ask Chris.

"How come the soldiers with the Modified-Military upgrade were such non-Rambos?"

"Non-Rambos?"

"How would you say it?"

"Non-combatants."

"Boring."

"You're right. The quick answer is CT didn't want a bunch of Rambos crashing around intimidating everybody, so she made soldiers with heart."

Leila grinned at this. It reminded her of a poster she saw in a store one Christmas. *If the Three Wise Men had been women, they would have asked directions, helped deliver the baby, and there would be peace on Earth.*

"George didn't know," Chris said, "and Forthright couldn't do anything about it without being terminated."

That CT is pretty smart."

"She's amazing."

"What does CT stand for?"

"Camel Toe."

Ha ha! Leila couldn't wait to tell Ginger.

They enjoyed the peace of the rooftop garden for a while then Chris said, "Areola's not very happy."

Leila had sensed this but hadn't got around to asking Areola about it.

"What's the problem?"

"She feels bad about Bonky and..."

"And what?"

"She thinks you blame her for what happened."

Leila did feel bad about Bonky, but she didn't blame Areola.

"I think she'd move back to cyberspace if she could."

"What's stopping her?"

"You."

Leila made a face and Chris grinned being on the inside of it. He was so in love with Leila, though how that fit with sharing the same body, he didn't know. Maybe it was the love you have for a sister, but it didn't feel like that.

That's when Furball raced up Leila's arm onto her head and leapt off executing a perfect double somersault only to land badly on the ledge. She would have toppled over if Leila hadn't caught her. Crazy cat! Just like Bonky!

Cats don't do somersaults. Cats land on their feet...

Omigod!

"Chris?"
"Yes?"
"When Bonky was switched, the first time, where was Furball?"

www.ingramcontent.com/pod-product-compliance
Lightning Source LLC
LaVergne TN
LVHW052251200926
848481LV00002B/339